How I Gave Up My Low Fat Diet
and Lost 40 Pounds !

How I Gave Up My Low Fat Diet and Lost 40 Pounds !

**Everybody's Guide
to Low Carbohydrate Dieting**

Dana Carpender

HOLD THE TOAST PRESS
Bloomington

Printed in the United States of America.

For information:
Hold the Toast Press
PO Box 6581
Bloomington, IN 47407

The author genuinely feels that the advice given in this book is safe and sound for most people, but there are exceptions to every rule. When dealing with health, it's important to be careful. The author is *not* a doctor *nor* a registered dietician, but rather a layperson with a longtime interest in nutrition, who has rediscovered a time-honored way of losing weight and improving health. If you have health problems, you *must* be under a doctor's supervision while shifting over to a low carbohydrate diet. This is especially true if you have any of the health problems associated with hyperinsulinemia. The author is *not* qualified to diagnose, prescribe, or treat any ailment, and this book is *not* intended to do so. It is for your information only.

ISBN 0-9668831-0-1

To Gaylord Hauser,
who started it all.

Contents

Contents

Foreword

I don't think there's any such thing as a coincidence. It's my belief that we get what we need when we need it and sometimes we just get what we deserve. I must have done something right because Dana Carpender came into my life and nothing has been the same since.

I must admit, I don't like to diet, especially if I have to measure, starve, eat things I don't like, or exercise. (I always say "Every time I feel like exercising, I lie down until the urge passes.") This has been the first diet I have actually enjoyed. I didn't — and still don't — measure, starve, eat things I don't like, or, most important to me, exercise.

One more point before I tell what happened to me: It doesn't feel like dieting because after all those years of living on that dangerous low fat "safe" diet, I always feel like I'm cheating, not dieting!!

It was *Guiding Light* that did it—that infamous afternoon soap opera. I met Dana on a discussion list for *Guiding Light* on the internet. We were all arguing about foods that are good and bad for us; meat in particular. I was saying how I tried to never eat meat because it was so dangerous healthwise, while everyone agreed except this maverick named Dana.

This crazy woman was trying to convince me to eat not only meat, but lots of eggs!

I have serious kidney disease. No protein allowed!!! Imagine my outrage after 8 years of starving and suffering on a low fat diet. I had worked all those years on a low fat diet to get my cholesterol down to 413 (from 990), my triglycerides at almost 1300 (from almost 1500), my blood pressure to 140/110, my creatinine (kidney function, normal at about 1) to 5, my BUN to 81, and my HDL to 24. What a reward for 8 years of low fat misery. I was a stroke waiting to happen until Dana completely changed my life.

To prove her wrong (My mission in life: To prove any woman wrong,) I told her I would go on this silly diet and as soon as I gained

5 pounds, I would be done with it. I needed an excuse to eat all that wonderful decadent stuff. Also, consider that my kidney disease causes outrageous cholesterol and triglyceride readings for which, my doctor informed me, there was nothing I could do — I was sure this craziness couldn't help. Dana gave me a long list of items to eat and proper vitamins as well, carefully working around the limitations of my disease.

As you recall, I don't measure what I eat, so I just ate from the list she provided me. I did not ask my doctor about this diet, which I know is a "no no", but he never would have condoned such a thing. My hindsight and bloodwork tell me I made the right decision. I started to eat all the things my doctor had told me NOT to eat. I really wasn't nervous because I was certain I would gain the 5 pounds in a day or two and the whole fiasco would be over.

NOT!!!!!

I lost a pound a day for 20 days. Dana labeled me "carbohydrate intolerant". (I thought I was only intolerant of people.) I had gotten down to 212 pounds from 250 on low fat over the 8 years, but I was stuck at that 212 and couldn't shake it no matter how many fruits and veggies I crammed down. I was ecstatic about the weight loss; getting down to 192 on Dana's method.

However, I was quite worried about my upcoming bloodwork in a couple days. Surely 20 days on a "fad diet" like this — eating 3 eggs a day, lots of meat, veggies, and piles of real butter and olive oil — couldn't alter my bloodwork that drastically — at least not for the better. NOT (again)!!!

Here are my results after this short period of time: My cholesterol was down almost 100 points to 337, triglycerides were down over 50% to 606, my blood pressure was normal for the first time since I was 18 years old, my creatinine, which was up to 6.5 at one time and had remained steady at a horrible 5 for 3 years, had actually gone down to an astonishing 4.4, my BUN was slightly up at 92, and my HDL was reaching almost normal range at 33. All of these figures got even better in the following three months, but this shows how fast your body changes when it receives the proper foods.

It's been 10 months since Dana saved me. (Am I a televangelist??) I've cheated some, eating that damn cancerous sugar on occasion, but holding my own pretty well. I love this way of eating because it's so easy to keep your weight stable. My cholesterol, considering my kidney disease and how it affects my bloodwork, is quite good in the 300 area. My triglycerides will rise a little if I cheat by eating sugar, but it's good to know they drop again quickly when I behave. They're still high, but good considering my kidney disease. My BUN is at its lowest in 8 years at 65. My blood pressure is normal to LOW.

My HDL is now in the normal range at 41. All this happened after thirty-something years of high blood pressure, two mild strokes by the age of 44, and hating diets, especially low fat. Go figure.

I used to take 3 Percocets and a sleeping pill every night just to get to sleep. My legs are really bad from the kidney disease, and I can't get to sleep. Now I'm down to 2 Percocets and 1/2 a sleeping pill, hoping to get down to 1 Percocet eventually. Between Dana's diet and my new-found magnet therapy, my leg pain is virtually gone. I stopped taking my blood pressure pill (again without telling my doctor) after 1 month on this diet, and also discontinued my strongest diuretic, continuing with just the weaker one. I have always abhorred drugs, and I'm now taking fewer drugs than I ever have since the onset of my kidney disease in 1990.

I've thanked Dana a thousand times since we met on the internet. Someday I'll thank her in person with a big hug instead of only a cyberhug. Most of the folks on our *Guiding Light* discussion list still think we're fanatics or lunatics eating all of this type of food. I have fond memories of thinking the same thing about Dana a year ago. Everyone I know who has done this diet correctly has had great success, even more for health reasons than weight loss. I read a book many years ago that stated that the largest percentage of illness is actually caused by what we eat, and now I believe it.

ROB DOUVRES
CAPE CORAL, FL.

(Author's note: Although I support Rob's right to take his own risks and make his own judgements regarding his health, I can't endorse the idea of folks with health problems not consulting their doctors before making major changes in their health regimen. Please keep in mind that Rob did get bloodwork done regularly, to alert him to any potential problems.)

Introduction

Hi. My name is Dana Carpender. I'm a real, live person — that's me on the inside of the cover! I'd like to tell you about a strange, unanticipated experience I had three years ago now — how I gave up my low fat diet and lost 40 pounds. But first, I'd like to share two thoughts:

 "If you always do what you've always done, you will always get what you've always got."

Definition of insanity: Doing the same thing over and over and over again, while hoping for different results

Before I tell you my story, here's a little quiz.

True or False

___ I have been pretty faithful about cutting fat and increasing complex carbohydrates.

___ I have had a struggle to lose weight on a low fat diet, or to maintain my weight loss.

___ I think I am addicted to food.

___ I work out mostly because if I didn't, I'd be *gaining* weight.

___ I am hungry all the time, and don't know why.

___ I am tired and cranky a lot, and don't know why.

___ I have been eating a low fat diet to lower my blood pressure, cholesterol and triglycerides — and it's not working.

___ I have bad energy slumps, particularly in the late afternoon.

If you answered "true" to one or more of these questions, you're not alone!! When I've asked these questions of groups of dieters, almost every hand in the room has gone up!

If you've been wondering what the heck is wrong with you, that your healthy weight loss diet just doesn't make you slim and healthy, or why you're hungry *all the time*, no matter *how* much you eat, take heart. IT'S NOT YOU!! It's the diet. There is a very large group of people for whom a low fat, high complex carbohydrate diet is exactly the WRONG approach to weight loss and health. And the more of those questions you answered "true", the more likely it is that *you* are one of those people.

That's the good news. Here's the better news!! I can teach you the *right* diet for people like us. I can teach you how to eat so that you lose weight. You'll eat real food, not strange, manufactured low fat stuff, or packaged diet club meals. You'll be able to eat in restaurants and fast food places. You'll have more energy than you ever dreamed possible. Your moods will improve till you wonder where all that cheerfulness is coming from! And maybe best of all, you won't be hungry all the time. *In fact, you'll be so un-hungry, you'll be amazed!!*

Sound good? It's better than just good. It's fantastic, incredible, unbelievable — and TRUE!! I've been living this way for three years now. Not only have I lost 40 lbs and kept it off, but I've watched my friends and family have incredible success with this way of eating. And through the magic of the Internet, I've found hundreds more folks for whom these dietary principles have made the difference between obesity and fatigue, and vibrant, energetic trimness!

So if you're ready to look and feel better than you ever have before, turn the page, and read on.

How I Gave Up My Low Fat Diet
and Lost 40 Pounds !

Chapter One
Here's What Happened to Me

In February '95, I was trying to lose weight for my wedding. Despite active work (I'm a massage therapist by trade) and a low fat, high complex carbohydrate diet, I had gotten up to 175 lbs. at 5'2". I signed up at the local municipal fitness center and started doing 4 to 5 step aerobics classes a week. I cut back even further on my fat, and substituted grains for meat a lot. (You know the drill — cutting up one low fat turkey smoked sausage in a huge casserole of potatoes, with lowfat cheese sauce made from cottage cheese and fat free cheese powder; eating pasta with fat free sauce for dinner three nights a week; using that slimy reconstituted butter powder on my veggies; buying lowfat *everything;* all that stuff.)

And I didn't lose an ounce. Oh, everything got firmer and higher, I looked a little better, and I felt a little better —I was fit, but fit and *fat.* I went to my wedding looking like a pretty little pale pink baby blimp, as you can see on the inside cover of this book. I bought new shorts to go on my honeymoon because all my old shorts were too small.

Well, by Labor Day, three months later, I had gained *another* ten or fifteen pounds. My *new* shorts were too small, and I was beginning to panic. Especially since my blood pressure was also up — borderline high for the first time in my life.

But I had been reading an old book on nutrition, one that I got at a used book sale. It was by a fella named Gaylord Hauser, one of the very first people to preach nutrition in this country — he worked with the old film studios, with stars like Greta Garbo, and with royalty. And back in 1952, Gaylord Hauser was saying something that was the exact opposite of what we have been told for the past 20 years: he said that obesity didn't have *anything* to do with overeating. He said that obesity was a *carbohydrate intolerance disease.*

I thought to myself, "Heck, nothing else is working! What do I have to lose?" I stopped eating high carbohydrate foods — that's starches and sugars — and *two days later* my shorts were loose. That was it!! I cut back even further on carbs, and started to read everything I could find on low carb dieting.

Well!! In two and a half weeks, I had lost ten pounds — eating eggs, meat, cheese, sour cream, real mayonnaise, and nuts.

Sounds insane, doesn't it?

But that wasn't all!! I also had discovered that *I felt hugely better on a low carbohydrate diet* — my energy level was higher, and much more constant. I felt oddly clearheaded, and more positive, more emotionally resilient. Little things just didn't bug me anymore, and even big things were easier to shake off.

Hunger Gone!

Best of all, I wasn't hungry all the time anymore!

I had *always* been hungry before — I would have that nice, "healthy" breakfast of whole grain cereal and skim milk, and by an hour and a half later, I could have eaten the *carpet,* I was so hungry! I'm not talking "head hungry" — I mean real, empty, growling stomach, getting tired hungry. I had wondered, sometimes, what was wrong with me, that I was hungry all the time. I had read — and maybe you have too — that if I ate a "healthy diet" — low in fat and high in carbohydrate — and "listened to my body", it would know how much food it needed. Unfortunately, it seemed to need enough for an entire army division!!

But on low carb, all of a sudden, I had a "normal" appetite. I could eat a cheese omelette for breakfast, and *not be hungry again until 2 in the afternoon.* It was astonishing!

I even *forgot to eat* once or twice! My husband is a skinny thing with a light appetite, and he sometimes forgets to eat. I could hardly believe that! I would say, "What, you forget to breathe, too?" But now, I would come home planning to cook supper, sit down to check my email, and look up two hours later, saying, "Oh, yeah, I was supposed to cook..." *For the first time in my life, I just wasn't emotionally involved with food.*

I'd even stop eating before I was done, sometimes!! That was astounding, too. I'm a charter member of the Clean Plate Club. If it's on that plate, it's MINE, and I'm gonna eat it. But all of a sudden, I'd be too full to finish sometimes, and push my plate away.

Obesity is a carbohydrate intolerance disease.

Well, I continued with the diet, and I continued to lose weight, and to feel better. *Eventually, I lost 40 lbs. — and lost most of that without exercise.* I'm not knocking exercise. I do work out, and think it's very important. You'll find a chapter on exercise later in the book. But I think it's also important to note that I did 4 to 5 step aerobics classes a week without losing an *OUNCE* on my low fat diet—but lost 35 lbs on low carb before I ever started working out again.

Am I a skinny girl now? No, I'm not. Last time I was tested, my bodyfat was at 26%, which is healthy, but not skinny-skinny. It is, however, considerably better than the 33% bodyfat which is average for American women my age. More important, the weight is staying off, and *that's* what success looks like in the world of weight loss. Over 95% of people who lose weight gain it all back within three years. I'd rather lose 40 lbs and keep it off, than lose 60 lbs and gain it back. And I bet you feel the same!

Just as important, *I've never felt better in my life!* I have more energy at 40 than I did at 15! Furthermore, my bloodwork — my cholesterol, blood pressure, all that jazz — is fantastic, despite the fact that heart disease runs in my family. (For those who want to know, at last testing, my cholesterol was 196, my triglycerides 80.

My HDL — good cholesterol — was a magnificent 69, and my cholesterol/HDL ratio — supposed to be the most important thing — was 2.8. Anything under 4, so I'm told, is excellent. The nurses were stopping me in the hall, wanting to know what my secret was!)

Of course, I've told a lot of friends and family about this approach to eating. When you start losing weight, people come out of the woodwork, wanting to know how you did it. (Naturally, they're hoping the answer will be "Why, I watched TV and ate potato chips, of course!" No such luck.) I told a lot of people about this before I wrote this book. And what happened?

My sister lost 30 lbs, and had to have all her clothes taken in. As a bonus, her asthma improved! My friend Leslie lost 20 pounds using just *some* of the low carb principles I taught her. One day at the drug store, I spotted a total stranger about to buy those highly advertised diet shakes, and was pushy enough to tell him my story. When I ran into him a year later, I hardly recognized him — he'd lost 70 pounds, and gone off his diabetes medication!!

I went on local cable access television, and gave a lecture that was the inspiration for this book. It became the most popular show in the history of the station, and I've gotten many phone calls from total strangers telling me that they saw the show, went low carb, lost weight and improved their health. Over and over, I've seen this work.

I'm totally sold on low carb dieting — and I'm convinced that, for many people, low fat/high carb is *worse than no diet at all.* In fact it's gotten to the point that when I see people in the grocery store with that cart full of low fat fake food, I want to run up to them and yell, "Don't do it, buddy! It's a lie, it's all a lie!" And that's why I've written this book. *Low carb has changed my life so much,* I just *have* to tell people about it.

Isn't This a Fad Diet??

"That's just a fad diet!" That's the accusation people throw at low carb dieting. But let me ask those of you who are my age — forty — or older, a question: Don't you remember that when we were kids, everyone *knew* that if you wanted to lose weight, you gave up potatoes and spaghetti?

When I discovered that low carb was working beautifully for

me, I read everything I could get my hands on about this subject: *Healthy for Life*, and *The Carbohydrate Addict's Diet*, both by Drs. Richard and Rachael Heller, researchers at Mt. Sinai Hospital; *The Zone*, by Barry Sears; *Protein Power*, by Drs. Michael and Mary Dan Eades, who have

...Low carbohydrate is anything BUT a fad diet!

treated thousands of people for obesity at their clinic in Little Rock; and the well-known *Dr. Atkins' New Diet Revolution*. I came to understand the biochemical principles that make this diet work.

Maybe more interesting, I found many *old* nutrition texts advocating low carb. For instance, *Calories Don't Count,* by Dr. Herman Taller, from 1962, was fascinating. Dr. Taller got interested in low carb when one of his colleagues at the hospital where he worked suggested he try drinking polyunsaturated oil to lower his cholesterol. He started dutifully gulping six ounces a day of vegetable oil. Not only did his cholesterol drop — so did his weight!! *And he'd added an extra 1600 calories a day of pure fat!* Where does *that* fit into a low fat diet?!

I found *Eat Fat and Grow Slim,* by Dr. Richard Mackarness, with a preface by the wife of polar explorer Vilhjalmur Stefansson. Back in the twenties, Stefansson saw the Eskimo eating nothing but meat and fat, and thriving on it. He decided to see if a "civilised" man could do the same. He lived on nothing but fresh meat and water for a year, while being monitored by physicians at Bellevue Hospital.

Not only did he not come down with scurvy or beri-beri, he thrived. He came out of the experiment several pounds lighter, and with lower cholesterol, which was the only measure of cardiovascular fitness they had back then. Later in life, in 1955, having developed a middle-aged paunch and suffering from a cerebral thrombosis, or blood clot, he went back on his Stone Age Diet, as he called it, with his wife joining him this time. The typical dinner in the Stefansson household, according to Mrs. Stefansson, was a steak and a cup of coffee, and occasionally a half a grapefruit for dessert. They both lost weight. According to his wife, Stefansson had been slightly irritable and depressed but became his old ebullient, optimistic self again — and as a little, added bonus, his arthritis cleared up!

I even found an old diet book when I went to Vermont to help my mother settle her Aunt Betty's estate. We were clearing out Aunt Betty's house when I found *Eat and Grow Thin* — a diet book from 1914, outlining — you guessed it — a low carbohydrate program.

In fact, I learned that the *very first* mass-market diet book in the English language was published in 1852, and it was a *low carbohydrate diet*. It was written by an Englishman named William Banting.

A low carbohydrate diet practically forces you to eat real food, with real nutritional value, rather than processed, chemical junk.

How fat was William Banting? (*"How fat was he?!"* I hear you cry.) He was so fat he had to walk down stairs backward, or he'd fall over. Doctors would tell him to eat less, and he'd try, but he'd be so awfully hungry that he just couldn't stick to it. (Sound familiar?) Then the doctors suggested exercise, so he went out and rowed on the Thames River every day — and it would make him so hungry, he'd eat more and not lose weight. (Do you know this story?)

Finally, Banting went to a doctor because he was going deaf. The doctor looked in Banting's ears, and discovered that Banting was going deaf because he had fat pressing on his eardrums! The doctor put Banting on a low carb diet, and it worked! Banting was so pleased that he wrote a volume called *Banting's Letter on Corpulence*, and spent the money to publish it himself. It was a big success, and for a while in London in Victorian times, "banting" was the popular term for "dieting". Banting lived into his eighties, never regaining the weight.

What all of this told me is that, historically speaking, low carbohydrate is anything *but* a fad diet.

In retrospect, I should have known this. When I first got interested in nutrition, twenty years ago, I read Adelle Davis, who stressed the importance of protein and essential fats, and said that overweight people should avoid most carbohydrates, especially white flour and sugar. I also read *Psychodietetics*, by Cheraskin and Ringsdorf, who linked mental instability to sugar and other refined carbohydrates.

I gave up white flour and sugar completely, felt hugely better, *and lost weight like crazy*. How I let myself be convinced a decade later that a big plate of white flour pasta is health food, I'll never know, except... It's so seductive, isn't it? I don't know about you, but I *wanted* to believe. It was like telling an alcoholic that it was healthy to have a six pack and a shot for dinner, or giving Dracula the key to the blood bank.

Now I know better. I know that a low carbohydrate diet is medically sound, and has withstood the test of time. And you'd have to pry my jaws open with a crowbar to get me to eat a high carb meal again.

Another thing that convinces me that a low carbohydrate diet isn't "fad dieting": It practically *forces* you to eat real food, with real nutritional value, rather than processed, chemical junk, or nutritionless, refined white flour products and sugary, ultra-processed cereals. Have you *looked* at the ingredients on some of those low fat products? They don't come from a farm, they come from a lab! How can *anything* that has to be made in a factory be essential — or even beneficial — to human nutrition? It just doesn't make sense.

Let me give you an example. Here is a list of the ingredients in Paul Newman's Own Salad Dressing, Original Recipe. This is a dressing you may have been avoiding; after all, it has 16 grams of fat in a serving. However, it only has *one* gram of carbohydrate. Here's what's in it:

Olive oil, vegetable oil (soybean and/or canola oil), water, red wine vinegar, onion, spices, salt, garlic, lemon juice, distilled vinegar.

Sounds like food to me! You could whip this up in your own kitchen, if you wanted to. Paul started out making it in his basement.

Now, for contrast, here is the list of the ingredients in one of the most popular fat-free Ranch Dressings on the market (which, by the way, has 11 grams of carbohydrate per serving):

Water, corn syrup, cultured lowfat buttermilk (cultured lowfat milk), vinegar, sugar, cellulose gel, potato maltodextrin, xanthan

*gum with potassium sorbate, calcium sodium EDTA and sorbic
acid as preservatives, propylene glycol alginate, phosphoric acid,
artificial color, natural flavor, monosodium glutamate, parsley,
green onions, DL tocopherol acetate, spice, polysorbate 60, yellow #5.*

What the heck is *that?* I'm not sure what propylene glycol alginate is, but it sounds suspiciously like anti-freeze to me! Are we really supposed to believe that spicy corn syrup with unpronounceable chemicals is a wiser choice than olive oil and vinegar? You tell me which sounds like some bizarre fad!

Here's another example. A famous company makes both regular grated parmesan cheese and fat-free fake parmesan cheese. Here's what's in the real stuff:

*Grated Parmesan cheese (part skim milk, cheese culture, salt,
enzymes), cellulose powder, potassium sorbate to protect flavor.*

Okay, I'd rather they left out the preservative, but this is basically real food. (If you're curious, cellulose powder is just fiber; it's used to prevent caking.) But dig what's in the fat-free stuff:

*Grated cheeses (parmesan and romano from cow's milk) (part skim
milk, cheese culture, salt, enzymes) starch, rice flour, enriched flour
(durum wheat flour, thiamine mononitrate, riboflavin, niacin, ferrous sulfate) water, malto-dextrin, cellulose powder, salt, and less
than 2% whey, buttermilk, potassium sorbate as a preservative,
glycerin, gum arabic, sodium phosphate, artificial color.*

In other words, they've diluted the real, nutritious cheese with a bunch of refined starch and chemicals. Again, which sounds more like a fad food to you?

On a low carb diet, we eat *real food*, the food that mankind has survived on for centuries: meat, poultry, fish, cheese, eggs, vegetables of almost every sort, nuts, seeds, olives, fresh natural oils and real butter. How anyone who has been eating low fat processed cold cereal and white flour bagels and low fat, sugar-filled cookies and strange, chemical salad dressings could think of these natural low carb foods as a nutritional step *down* is beyond me.

Chapter Two

So, What Do You Eat?

Well, what I *don't* eat is at least three quarters of what you find in your grocery store. I don't eat bread, pasta, potatoes, rice, crackers, cereal, chips, dried beans like kidneys or pintos, nothing thickened with flour or cornstarch, like canned cream soups or jarred gravies. I also eat almost no *sugar*, except for trace amounts in things like mayonnaise and worcestershire sauce. No candy, ice cream, cookies, cake, donuts, danish, very little ketchup, steak sauce or barbeque sauce (which have more sugar than ice cream!), etc. It may shock you to know that I also eat only a little fruit, and no fruit juice; they're high in natural sugars.

So What's Left to Eat!? Plenty!

Most days for breakfast, I have three fried eggs. For a change, I'll have a cheese omelette made with two or three eggs and jalapeno jack cheese — that's real cheese, not low fat cheese — with salsa on top. Sometimes I have eggs scrambled with peppers, onions and mushrooms, or 4 or 5 sausage patties, or a hamburger. If I'm eating out, hey, steak and eggs is always good! Hold the toast and hash browns, of course.

Lunches, if I'm eating at home, are usually tuna salad made with celery, peppers and onion, with mayonnaise — again, *real*

 **It's hilarious going into Burger King and ordering a Whopper, hold the bun. They look at you!**

mayonnaise, not low fat — or chicken salad with chopped pecans. Sometimes I'll make a protein shake, from a recipe I'll be sharing later on. If I'm out, I usually have a chicken caesar salad, hold the croutons. If I'm going Mexican, I'll have fajitas. I'll skip the tortillas, pile the guacamole, sour cream, and pico de gallo right on top, and eat it with a fork. At the gyros joint, I get the meat , onions, sauce — all the insides of a gyros, without the bread — on top of a Greek Salad. And extra olives. Fabulous!

Like everybody, I sometimes just catch some fast food. Most fast food joints have some kind of grilled chicken salad, and I get these a lot. Sometimes I'll get a burger and a salad instead. I'll put the hamburger patty, pickles, onions, all that stuff, on top of a garden salad, and eat them together. Pretty good! It's hilarious going into Burger King and ordering a Whopper, hold the bun. They *look* at you! You'd think I'd ordered roasted puppy on a stick or something. "Whaddaya mean, hold the bun?" What word didn't you *get*?

Since it's only my husband and me for dinner, we usually have a light meal — just a chop or a piece of chicken or a burger. Sometimes we have a salad or a vegetable, sometimes not. I make roasts fairly often — with just the two of us, they leave a lot of leftover meat to nibble at for days. Very convenient!

- -

It's pretty hard to feel sorry for yourself when you're eating this way!

- -

When I'm feeling creative and energetic, I make skillet cacciatore, with chicken and peppers and onions and tomato sauce and wine; or I make hamburger stroganoff, with lots of mushrooms and sour cream; or chicken paprikash, again, with lots of sour cream. I occasionally make cream soups — with real cream, not skim milk thickened with flour — or something really exotic, like Tandoori chicken. On the other hand, sometimes I get pretty down-home, and brown some pork sausage with onions, and melt cheese over the top.

For snacks, I often eat nuts. I like pecans fried in butter, with ginger and soy sauce! I also love pumpkin and sunflower seeds, and these are usually available at convenience stores and truck stops. And I've created a sugar-free chocolate mousse that is to *die* for!

Sound good? It's pretty hard to feel sorry for yourself when you're eating this way!

But I'm a Vegetarian!!

Don't panic. It is possible to be a low carb vegetarian. I know a few. But understand that rice and beans and whole grain bread and fruit are *not* your healthiest foods if you have a weight problem, or a family history of heart disease and diabetes. It is *not* true — as militant vegetarians assert — that mankind has subsisted for most of its history on grains and beans. Those things have only been a major part of the human diet since the Agricultural Revolution, about 10,000 years ago. Before that, for the vast majority of mankind's 2 million year history, grains and beans were in very limited supply, and our bodies did not evolve to utilize them in large quantity.

If you're an ovo-lacto vegetarian, meaning you eat eggs and dairy products, even a diet as low in carbohydrate as mine should be fairly simple. If you're a vegan, you'll be somewhat more limited — but tofu and tempeh are low carbohydrate, and there are more and more low carbohydrate meat substitutes on the market. For that matter, I'm pretty certain that if you lived largely on nuts, seeds — especially sprouted, raw nuts and seeds — and low carb vegetables, you'd do okay, so long as you took a good vitamin supplement.

Please understand, though, that in the context of limiting carbohydrate, I'm not at all certain that vegetarianism is a superior choice nutritionally. If it's right for you, that's great — but eating meat and eggs and cheese has gotten me very far indeed.

Chapter Three

Yikes!! Sounds High Calorie!

I know what you're thinking: That stuff is loaded with fat! And fat is loaded with calories!! How can I eat all that rich food and lose weight? And won't eating all that fat — all that *saturated* fat — make me a heart attack waiting to happen? *Just how the heck does this work, anyway?*

As a dieter, I'm sure you've heard that one pound of fat equals 3500 calories. You've been told that you have to cut 3500 calories from your weekly intake to lose one pound of fat. You've also been told that since fat has more calories per gram than anything else, if you cut the fat out of your diet, you'll lose weight, right? You've also been told that the opposite is true — that if you eat 3500 extra calories in a week, you'll gain a pound.

It sounds so easy, doesn't it?

A Calorie Is NOT a Calorie

There's only two problems with this. One, not all bodies are the same, and two, not all calories are the same.

"Oh, come on! A calorie is a calorie is a calorie!" That's what we've heard for years. And in one sense, that's true. A calorie is just a measure of energy — of fuel. Just like we buy fuel for our cars in gallons, we buy fuel for our bodies in calories. (By the way, that means that when ads say that their food is "loaded with energy", they mean "loaded with calories". Doesn't sound quite as good, does it? Any food which contains calories supplies energy.) And each calorie represents the same amount of energy, whether from fat, protein, or carbohydrate. And it is true that if you eat 3500 calories more than your body burns, you'll gain a pound of fat. And if you eat 3500 calories less than your body burns, you'll lose a pound of fat.

Foods have effects on the body separate from their calorie value.

What calorie theory has missed, however, is that *foods have effects on the body separate from their calorie value.* What kind of effects? Dig this:

Back in the '50s, two British doctors named Kekwick and Pawan did an experiment. They fed obese people a diet of 1000 calories a day — a very low calorie diet. The calories were the same; the *kind* of calories varied. And they found that on a thousand calories a day of carbohydrate, most subjects lost very little weight. But when subjects were fed a thousand calories a day of protein and fat, but *almost no carbohydrate*, they lost weight easily!!

So Kekwick and Pawan tried another experiment: They tried feeding their dieters 2000 calories a day (sounds more comfortable to me!), in a "balanced diet" — meaning carbohydrate, along with protein and fat. The dieters didn't lose any weight, which won't come as any surprise to those of you who have struggled to lose weight at 1200 calories a day, much less 2000.

But here's the exciting part: When Kekwick and Pawan knocked the carbohydrate out of the diet, and fed their subjects a diet of protein and *fat*, they started losing weight! In fact, most of them found that so long as they didn't eat carbohydrates, they could eat *2600 calories a day*, and still lose weight!! Something was affecting the number of calories they burned.

So much for a low fat diet.

By the way, Kekwick and Pawan aren't the only ones to have tested this. A fella named Dr. Frederick Benoit heard about their study, and decided to check it out. Working at Oakland Naval Hospital, he tested seven men who weighed between 230 and 290 pounds.

First, Dr. Benoit put the men on a total fast — what we might call the no-calorie diet. If calorie theory is correct, this should have caused the fat to come off faster than anything, right? Wrong. They did lose weight, an average of 21 pounds in 10 days. Sounds great! Except only 7.5 lbs, on average, was fat. The rest was water and *muscle*. Very bad news. They lost twice as much muscle as fat!!

Then Dr. Benoit fed his obese men 1000 calories a day — admittedly a very low calorie diet, but a thousand calories more than they had been getting. Those 1000 calories contained almost no carbohydrate, some protein, and a lot of *fat*. These guys were chowing down on bacon, cream cheese, heavy cream, stuff like that. Guess what happened?

In a ten day trial, they lost *twice* as much fat as they did eating *nothing at all!* An average of 14 lbs of fat each. And they lost almost no muscle — just a half a pound each.

Are you beginning to wonder why you've been told to avoid fat? I sure am.

You can't eat *unlimited* calories on a low carbohydrate diet. But you *can* eat enough calories so that you never have to be hungry again — and still lose weight.

Sound good?

Another Glitch in Caloric Theory

Then there's the other problem with calorie theory: it doesn't take individual differences in metabolism into account. Have you ever known someone who cannot gain weight no matter what they eat? I have a friend like this. His name is Tom. He's 6'6", and weighs about 160 lbs. He's muscular, but very, very thin. We used to date years ago, so I saw how he ate — we would go to an all-you-can-eat restaurant, and Tom would eat *five full plates* of food. When we got home, he'd eat a whole *pint* of Haagen-Daz. Just an hour later he'd be saying, "Do you think we should order a pizza?" Tom still eats

> **You can't eat unlimited calories on a low carbohydrate diet. But you can eat enough calories so that you never have to be hungry again — and still lose weight.**

this way. When we have him and his wife over, I have to cook for eight — and he's still just as skinny as can be, at age 36.

Ever known someone like this?

Yet studies have shown that under some conditions, there are people who can *gain* weight on 1000 calories a day! In fact, when I taught low carb dieting at my health club, one women said she had gained weight on *700 calories a day*, a starvation diet.

When people like Tom eat more than their usual intake of calories, medical studies have shown that their bodies simply crank up their metabolism and burn the extra calories off. The body adjusts the metabolism to the caloric intake. The person's temperature goes up very slightly, and they throw off the extra calories as heat — a process with the fancy name of "post-prandial thermogenesis".

But those of us who fatten easily don't do this. Instead of burning off those extra calories, we store them instead; it's been called the "thrifty gene". And for centuries and centuries, this thrifty gene was a very, very good thing to have. If the crops had failed, you and I would have survived, and Tom would have died a painful death from starvation. We — you and me, the fat folks — we have *superior* bodies! *That's why there's so many of us!*

I want you to think about that for a minute. If, like me, you've been overweight most of your life, if you grew up dreading school every day because of how the kids would make fun of you, if you've gone to the beach in a tee shirt and cutoffs because you'd rather *die* than be seen in a bathing suit, you probably think of yourself as having a flawed body. Like you got a factory second or something. It's not true!! *You have a superior body, a body that evolution favored!* Right now, I want you to stop thinking of yourself as third-rate goods. You got the good kind of body!! You just live in the wrong time and place.

It's only because we have the incredible luck of living in a time and a place where food is abundant year after year after year, all year long, that this genetic superiority is turned against us. Luckily, science is finally beginning to understand some of how those thrifty gene genetics work — and at the same time, learning why obesity is so very unhealthy, as well.

Chapter Four

The Problem with Carbs

Glucose, the sugar that your body burns as fuel, is a carbohydrate, and is essential for a few organs in the body; the rest can run on fat, or on an alternate fuel called *ketones*, produced when your body burns fat for fuel without any carbohydrate. This sounds as if you have to eat at least *some* carbohydrate, right? (And all of the programs I'll outline for you do contain *some* carbohydrate, mostly in the form of vegetables. What we're avoiding here is *concentrated* carbohydrate foods: starches and sugars.)

But no, even though some glucose is essential, carbohydrate foods are not, for a very simple reason: your body can turn protein, and to a much lesser degree, fat, into carbohydrate as it is needed. And this is, in many ways, a superior way to get glucose.

You've been told, no doubt, that you need carbs for energy. Yet after nearly twenty years of binging on pasta and bread and potatoes and fat-free cookies, fatigue is the single most common medical complaint in the country! Americans are just plain tired. The reason is simple, and lies in that old statement, that carbohydrates, and especially sugar, are "quick energy". Quick energy *sounds* good. But is it?

Let me ask you this: Would you burn straw in your woodstove to heat your house? Of course not. But straw is quick energy! And that's what's wrong with it, right? It burns *too* fast. If you wanted to burn straw for heat, you'd have to sit next to that woodstove and throw in another handful every three or four minutes. If you tried to put in a whole bale of straw, for lasting energy, it wouldn't work that way, would it? You'd burn the house down, because it still wouldn't burn gradually; it would all burn at once.

Here comes the million dollar question...
Why should a population that is sedentary and
obese get most of their food as pure fuel?

In the same way, your body doesn't have any way to use carbohydrates gradually — except to store them as fat.

Or think of it this way: Gasoline is quick energy. *Really* quick energy! So quick that if you were to drop a lit match into your gas tank, it would burn so fast you'd be extremely fortunate to survive. The fact that gasoline is such quick energy is why cars have carburetors or fuel injectors — to make sure only a tiny bit of gasoline gets lit at a time.

Your body doesn't have a carburetor. Your body doesn't have any way to feed the carbohydrate you eat into your bloodstream gradually. When you eat a breakfast of cereal, milk, juice, and sugar in your coffee — four sources of carbohydrate — it floods into your system fast. Very fast! Your body senses this as a threat, and takes action to fix it.

Fuel, by the way, is the *only* thing your body can use carbohydrates for. Protein can be used to make glucose for fuel, but it is also essential for body repair and maintenance, making enzymes, creation of antibodies to protect you from disease, all sorts of things. Fat can be used for fuel, but is also used for making hormones, cell walls, useful stuff like that.

So here comes the million dollar question: Why should a population that is sedentary and obese get most of their food as pure fuel? It makes no sense.

On a low carb diet, your body rapidly remembers how to use fat — including your stored fat! — and protein for fuel. And it makes fuel out of fat and protein at the rate it needs it, not too slow, not too fast. The result? Energy that is stable and constant, instead of the roller coaster ride from sugar-break to sugar-break.

Moderation?

"I believe in moderation in all things", people frequently tell me, implying, of course, that my avoidance of carbohydrate is immoderate, their intake of carbohydrate, including highly processed sugar and white flour, is moderate. I agree that moderation is a cardinal rule of health and happiness. One question, however, remains to be answered: What is "moderate"?

Suppose, for instance, an individual were to eat only half of the sugar that the average American does. Sounds pretty moderate, doesn't it? Just think, only half!

* *

What's moderate? If you were to drink one can of sugar-sweetened cola per day, and eat no other sugar at all, you would still be consuming well over twice the sugar that your Victorian Era ancestors did.

* *

Yet a person who ate only half the sugar of the average American would still be eating more than *ten times* the sugar that the average American ate in 1800, and more than four times the average American sugar intake in post-Civil War times. *So what's moderate?*

If you were to drink *one* can of sugar-sweetened cola per day, and eat *no other sugar at all,* no cookies, no candy, no ice cream, no cold cereal, no prepared foods with added corn syrup, you would still be consuming well over twice the sugar that your Victorian Era ancestors did. If you consumed a 1500 calorie-per-day diet — a not-uncommon level among women — that one can of cola would represent fully 10% of your calories — one tenth of your nutrients replaced with pure, valueless sugar. *So what's moderate?*

The explosion of American sugar consumption, from about 7 pounds per person per year in 1800, to an incredible 152 pounds per person per year currently (and somebody's eating more, folks, because I'm eating less!), represents an increase of over *2000%*, the single most drastic dietary change in the history of humankind. The second most drastic change was the Agricultural Revolution itself, when humankind went from eating very few grains and beans, to making them the staples of the diet. To simply cut back "a bit" on these substances, and then call one's consumption "moderate", makes a joke of the very concept of moderation.

In short, I *am* moderate. It is the standard American diet which is *desperately* immoderate.

Okay, Explain How This Works

So how the heck does this work? How can I eat fatty foods like meat and eggs and cheese and nuts, and not only lose weight, but improve my health?

We've been told all these years that we needed to lose weight to protect our health, because obesity would make us ill. It's no secret that fat people have more heart disease, high blood pressure, diabetes, and cancer than slim people. The assumption has been that obesity *caused* all these diseases.

Wrong!! The latest research is beginning to make it clear that the reason obesity is associated with high blood fats, high triglycerides, high blood pressure, adult onset diabetes, and even the female cancers is *not* because obesity *causes* those problems, but rather because all of those problems *along with obesity* are symptoms of the same underlying problem — *carbohydrate intolerance disorder,* also referred to as *hyperinsulinemia.* It all has to do with *insulin* — too much insulin.

What Does Insulin Do?

I'm sure you've all heard of insulin; it's that stuff diabetics have to inject. You may also know that those of us who are not diabetic produce insulin in our pancreas. But you probably don't really understand insulin's function in the body. It's really very simple — insulin's job is to take glucose — sugar — out of your bloodstream, and into your cells. Period. Full stop.

Having a lot of sugar in your blood is very bad for you, you see. If it happens too often, for too long, it's the disease we call *diabetes,* and it causes damage to blood vessels all over your body, and kills off pieces of you, bit by bit. It's not hard to understand why. Capillaries, your smallest blood vessels, are so very small that, in anatomy class, they showed us movies of individual red blood cells folding themselves in half and wiggling through, one at a time. Picture what would happen to a tube that small and fragile if you tried to force Karo syrup through it. *Now* you know why high levels of sugar in your blood will harm you!

Insulin is what makes your body store calories as fat.

So, when your body senses that your blood sugar level is high, it goes right into action, pumping out insulin to get that blood sugar back where it belongs. Insulin acts sort of like an usher or a door-man. It takes that sugar by the hand, and takes it to a special place on your cell, called an "insulin receptor". This is like a door for the sugar to go through. The insulin opens the door, and waves the sugar on through.

The first place the insulin takes the sugar is to your muscles. If you happen to be lifting weights or something, that's great!! But what percentage of the time do you lift weights? For most of us sofa spuds, the muscles just aren't demanding that sugar. "What am I supposed to do with this?" the muscles ask. Then the insulin takes the sugar to your liver, and asks if it would like to store it as "glycogen", a form of carbohydrate your body keeps in storage. But most of us have as much glycogen as our bodies can handle.

So, the muscles don't want the sugar. The liver doesn't want the sugar. What to do with it now? Easy. The insulin opens the doors on your fat cells, and waves that sugar in, and the sugar is converted to fat in the process. Then, to make sure the stuff doesn't escape, the insulin slams the door shut, and *holds* it shut.

Insulin Stores Fat

Do you get what I'm saying? *Insulin is what makes your body store calories as fat.* And sugar — carbohydrates — in your blood makes your body produce insulin.

Now, this has some interesting implications. A hundred thousand years ago, this ability of insulin to cause fat storage was a very good thing. As I mentioned earlier, before mankind invented agriculture about 10,000 years ago, we didn't have access to large quantities of concentrated carbohydrates at all — most carbohydrates in a prehistoric diet came from vegetables — but there was considerably more carbohydrate available in the summer and fall, when the fruit was ripe. We ate carbohydrate, stored fat, and then had that fat available to get us through the long cold winter.

But lack of food in the winter is not a big problem for most of us anymore — in fact, most of us do our best gaining from the end of November to the end of December, don't we? We eat large quantities of carbohydrates all year round, and store fat all year round, and we end up... well, round!

Here's the flip side of the fat-storage function of insulin: *With no insulin, you simply cannot store fat.* Period. Can't be done. Any juvenile onset diabetic knows this — one of the warning signs of juvenile onset diabetes is drastic weight loss. I knew a guy with this problem who told me that when his pancreas gave out, he lost 20 lbs in two days! *No fat storage without insulin.*

The Insulin Cycle

This gives us a powerful weapon in the fight against fat! If we can control insulin levels in our body, we can control fat storage. What causes insulin release?

Rising blood sugar levels. What was happening to me, and what may be happening to you, is this: I would eat a big serving of carbohydrate — that whole grain cereal, or some pasta, or juice, whatever — and my blood sugar level would rise very quickly in response. Never forget that *all* carbohydrates are actually a form of sugar — simple carbohydrates are the sweet sugars, like table sugar and the sugar in fruit; "complex carbohydrate", another name for starch, means "a whole bunch of sugars linked together" — but chemically, it's all types of sugar.

So I'd eat those carbs, and my blood sugar would go shooting up — remember, the body has no way of absorbing the stuff gradually. My pancreas, seeing all that sugar in my blood, would say, "Hey, we have all this sugar floating around! Time to put that stuff away!" and it would release a big dose of insulin. The glucose in my blood would be marched right off to be stored as fat, and my blood sugar would drop drastically. Two things happened at the same time: I had a bunch of new fat in my fat cells — gee, what fun! — and I had no calories in my blood to use as fuel, so I got hungry and tired. I would eat more carbs — after all, carbs are low fat, and good for you! — and it would happen all over again. It was a vicious cycle: eat carbs, store fat, get hungry, eat carbs, store fat, get hungry.

But it was even worse than that. You see, medical research indicates that the more you go through this cycle, the more insulin your body releases. It's almost as if your pancreas gets panicky — "What?! *More* sugar? I thought I just got rid of this stuff! I'd better make a whole LOT of insulin!" And your blood sugar comes *crashing* down.

Are you beginning to understand why you're tired and hungry a lot?

The Hunger Problem Gets Worse!

Ah, but there's more. You see, stable blood sugar is only one thing that makes you feel full and satisfied. Another thing that determines whether you feel full or hungry is a chemical with the tongue-twisting name *cholecistekinin*, which is why it's usually referred to as CCK. CCK is a chemical that is released by your brain in response to the right combination of food, and makes you feel satisfied. In laboratory experiments, rats who were injected with CCK would sit in the midst of food and starve themselves, because they simply weren't hungry.

And what combination of food causes your brain to release CCK? Certain amino acids, which are found in proteins, combined with *fat*. Without the fat and the protein — say, with a big plate full of pasta with fat-free sauce — you can eat and eat and *eat*, and *never* get filled up. Does this sound familiar?

Carbs Can't Fill You Up

This problem of crashing blood sugar, coupled with a lack of the foods needed to release CCK, is a *huge* weakness in low fat/high carb diet theory. After all, the whole point of a low fat diet was to lower your calorie intake. Since fat has 9 calories per gram, and protein and carbohydrates have only 4, the theory went, if you cut out the fat, you could eat more food for fewer calories. And since carbohydrates are bulkier than proteins, and since many of the best protein foods also include fat, it looked like if you replaced those protein/fat foods with carbohydrates, you could eat a huge pile of food and still lose weight.

 Obesity is up by a whopping 30%! It's because we're eating a diet that is biochemically destined to never fill us up.

The hitch is that Americans *have* dropped fat consumption a *lot* — 25% overall. Guess what? We're eating *more* calories! And obesity is up by a whopping 30%! It's because we're eating a diet that is biochemically destined to *never fill us up.*

Here Comes Addiction!!

And now you can understand why carbohydrates, especially when eaten without protein or fat, are addictive. *They actually make you hungry!!*

People talk about "food addiction"; it even has its own Twelve Step group, Overeaters Anonymous. But I don't know anyone who's addicted to food in general. I only know people who are addicted to carbohydrates.

Think about it. What do *you* binge on? What foods make *you* lose control? What foods do you *crave*?

Cookies? Sugar and starch!
Chips? Starch!
Ice cream? Sugar!
Bread? Starch!
Candy? Major sugar!

Do you like eggs? Do you enjoy a good steak? Does a fine cheese taste great? Of course! *Do you binge on them?* No. We enjoy these foods a great deal, but our hunger for them is finite. They fill us up. They satisfy us. We eat these foods *normally*.

They tell you, eat low fat, and control your portions. I tell you that you will never be able to control your portions for the rest of your life if you are HUNGRY ALL THE TIME!!

But eating carbohydrates is like eating hungry pills. All the Snackwells in the world won't fill you up. They make you hungrier and hungrier and hungrier, until you start to wonder if you're crazy.

Aren't you tired of being hungry all the time? They tell you, eat low fat, and control your portions.

I tell you that you will never be able to control your portions for the rest of your life if you are HUNGRY ALL THE TIME!! I cannot think of anything more unnatural, more cruel, than telling people that they must sit in the midst of more food than any society has ever had available in the *history of the world,* and be *hungry*. No wonder people gain back their weight.

But you don't have to be hungry. I'm almost *never* hungry anymore. Certainly no one has ever been more carbohydrate addicted than I was, but I don't sit around going, "Oh, I wish I could have a potato, I wish I could have cookies, I wish I could have pasta." I can remember that those things tasted good — but somehow, I just don't care much anymore. That awful, driving hunger is *gone*.

You'll be astounded how fast you can break the addiction cycle.

Promise!

How carbohydrate addicted have I been? You might be tempted to think that I never really cared much about this stuff in the first place. Don't you believe it!! When I was fourteen, I was stealing money from my parents to support my sugar addiction. I ate a half-pound Mr. Goodbar *and* a half-pound Hershey's with Almonds on the way home from school every day. I also ate about a pound of lemon drops or 5-6 rolls of Wild Cherry Lifesavers during classes — sugar in my mouth every moment, all day long. I *also* ate three to five desserts in the school cafeteria at lunch every day. All of this in addition to whatever sugar I got in my meals at home. I had one *mean* monkey on my back!

When I was fifteen, I would start my school day with three or four chocolate donuts from the student store, washed down with three or four cups of vending machine cocoa. Because I was "watching my weight", I would have a chocolate milkshake for lunch instead of real food. What I remember most vividly from that year is wandering around my high school, muttering, "I'm so tired! I'm soooo tired!" Dead on my feet at fifteen — from "energy food".

Insulin Doesn't Just Make You Fat and Tired!

But obesity's not the whole story. You see, medical research is beginning to link high levels of insulin with all sorts of other health problems — high cholesterol, high triglycerides, high blood pressure, adult onset diabetes, and the female cancers. There's even some evidence we'll be discussing later that high levels of insulin may increase pain and inflammation and weaken your immune system.

High Blood Pressure

For example, high levels of insulin in the blood will cause your kidneys to hold on to sodium. You've probably heard that sodium is what you're supposed to avoid if you have high blood pressure. But you may not have heard that for the *vast* majority of people, a low sodium diet doesn't improve their blood pressure at all. It turns out that for many people, the problem is not that they're getting too much sodium in their diet, but rather that because of the insulin in their blood, their kidneys are hanging on to too much sodium, and thus hanging on to too much water, with high blood pressure as a result. You can take diuretics —

water pills — or you can control your insulin levels, and lose the extra sodium, and the extra water with it.

You remember that I mentioned that on low fat/high carb my blood pressure was borderline high for the first time in my life? It normalized within a couple of weeks on this diet — probably because about the first five or ten pounds I lost were water. I didn't sleep much for the first few days — too busy going to the bathroom!

(By the way, some critics say you *only* lose *water* on low carb, to which my response is: *FIVE GALLONS*?! I've lost *FIVE GALLONS* of water?! I doubt it, but if I've lost that much water, I'm sure glad to be rid of it!)

Heart Disease

Then there's heart disease. If Americans know one thing, it's that fat and cholesterol will give you heart disease. Cholesterol is practically a poison, for heaven's sake!

No, it's not. Believe it or not, cholesterol is an essential part of your body!

First of all, your brain and your nerves have high levels of cholesterol. Sounds pretty important right there! Many of your hormones are made from cholesterol, including your sex hormones. It's cholesterol in your skin that turns to vitamin D in the sunlight. And cholesterol is essential for the walls of every cell in your body.

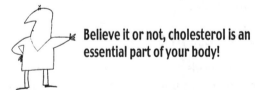

Believe it or not, cholesterol is an essential part of your body!

In fact, cholesterol is so important that if you stop eating it, your body makes more. More than two-thirds of the cholesterol in your body is made *by* your body, and if you stop eating cholesterol, your body simply increases production to make up the difference. If you eat more, your body makes less.

Unless something messes up the balance mechanism. What can do that? *Insulin!* Insulin actually makes it harder for your body to take cholesterol out of your bloodstream, and into the cells where

Cholesterol is so important that if you stop eating it, your body makes more!

your body uses it. Since your body only knows how much choles-terol it has in its cells, *not* how much it has in its bloodstream, your body thinks it's not getting enough. Your body then goes to work making cholesterol! This tendency of insulin to inhibit the retrieval of cholesterol from the blood is quite enough to cause dangerously high cholesterol all by itself.

If you lower your level of insulin, your body can get access to the cholesterol in your bloodstream. It calms down, stops making too much cholesterol, and starts using up the excess in your blood. The result? Your LDL, or "bad" cholesterol, drops! That is, if you're one of the many, many people for whom insulin was the whole prob-lem in the first place.

Which explains an article in *Southern Medical Journal* in Janu-ary 1988. Dr. H.L. Newbold was treating a group of people who had serious food allergies. He found that most of them could eat beef without trouble. So he told them to eat steaks with plenty of fat — and other meat if they could tolerate it — plus a few raw veggies and a little fruit. Guess what? The average patient's cholesterol dropped from 263 to 189! Further, their HDL (good cholesterol) was going up, while their bad LDL cholesterol was going down.

The problem is *not* cholesterol in your diet. Think about it: Beef is high in cholesterol, right? Cows are vegetarians! They eat grass, and on modern farms are fed a lot of grain — the same low fat, high carb grain you've been told to eat to be healthy. *So where does the choles-terol come from?* It comes from the cow's own body, which has been fooled by insulin into thinking the cow needs more cholesterol!

Certainly my cholesterol is *great* after three years of feasting on fat, while avoiding grains and other carbs. And I've seen the same thing happen to many other people. *However!!* This does not seem to work for everybody. There is a minority of people who, when they go on a low carb diet which includes lots of fatty red meat and egg yolks and other sources of saturated fat, have a sort of 50/50 reac-tion: Their triglycerides come down, and their good cholesterol (HDL) goes up, which is fine; but their bad cholesterol (LDL) and total cholesterol go up, as well, which is not so good.

No one is quite certain why this should be so; the simple, basic answer, no doubt, is that people are different, and there's more than one cause of cholesterol troubles. The Eades feel that some people are sensitive to a chemical called arachidonic acid, which often is

Oddly enough, there is very little evidence that eating cholesterol causes high cholesterol in any body.

found in tandem with cholesterol and saturated fat. Dr. Atkins feels that a minority of the population is sensitive to saturated fats (NOT to cholesterol in the diet — oddly enough, there is very little evidence that eating cholesterol causes high cholesterol in any body). Either way, the solution is the same.

If you have cholesterol trouble, get tested a few months after going on your low carb diet, and see where you stand. (This presupposes that you know where you stand *before* you go on the diet! If you don't, take care of that little matter right away. Otherwise, when you get tested after having been on the diet for a while, you'll have no idea whether those numbers — no matter what they are — represent an improvement, or a worsening, of your health.) Keep in mind that the numbers are not as important as the ratios; if your LDL and total cholesterol have gone up a little, but your HDL has gone up a *lot*, and your triglycerides have come down, you may actually be at lower risk, even though the numbers look worse at first glance. Also be aware that total cholesterol can actually be too *low*; anything under 170 or so starts to correlate with a higher risk of some diseases, including cancer. You're shooting for a total cholesterol number of between 170 and 220.

Be *very* aware that the most important thing is the ratios, *not* your total cholesterol number! My friend Mary, who typeset this book, and has been on a Basic Low Carb diet, called me in a panic one day because she'd just gotten her bloodwork, and her total cholesterol number had jumped quite a lot. (Her total cholesterol had always been in the range we now know to be too low, though no one had ever told her that.) However, when we looked at her ratios — total cholesterol/HDL, triglycerides/HDL, LDL/HDL — it turned out that she had a *remarkably* low risk of heart disease; her HDL (good cholesterol) was very high, and her triglycerides were very, very low. (Since we had no idea what her LDL/HDL breakdown or triglycerides had been when her total cholesterol was so low, we have no idea if she's healthier or not — but it would be hard to have better ratios than Mary has now.)

How do you work those ratios? Easy. Get a copy of your bloodwork (it must be "fasting bloodwork" to be accurate regarding triglycerides), and a simple pocket calculator. Divide your total cholesterol number by your HDL number; the result should be *4 or below.*

$$\frac{\text{total cholesterol number}}{\text{HDL}}$$

Then divide your LDL by your HDL; if you're a *man,* a result of *3.55* gives you average risk, anything below that is better. If you're a *woman, 3.22* gives you an average risk, anything below is better.

$$\frac{\text{LDL}}{\text{HDL}}$$

And for perhaps the most important ratio, divide your triglycerides by your HDL; *anything less than 2 is good.*

$$\frac{\text{triglycerides}}{\text{HDL}}$$

These three numbers should give you a clear idea of where you stand, in terms of risk of heart disease.

If it turns out that you are in the minority whose ratios worsen on a low carb diet with unrestricted fat intake, what do you do? Well, first of all, you *don't* go back to a low fat/high carb diet — you'll lose the beneficial HDL and triglyceride levels you've been achieving. Instead, you take care to improve the balance of *types* of fat in your diet. This means choosing lean meats, and trimming the fat, throwing away every other egg yolk (you could eat egg substitutes instead, but I think they taste nasty, I'm suspicious of the chemicals in them, and anyway, they cost an arm and a leg), perhaps choosing reduced fat cheeses and sour half and half instead of sour cream.

**Be very aware that the most important thing is
the ratios, not your total cholesterol number!**

Also make very, very sure you've eliminated "hydrogenated vegetable oils" — margarine and vegetable shortening — from your diet *completely*. This will include ruling out just about all commercially deep-fried foods; almost invariably these are fried in hydrogenated oils. But then most deep fried foods are breaded, so you shouldn't be eating them anyway! Regular-joe type peanut butter, like Skippy and Jif and Peter Pan, is loaded with hydrogenated oils. (Sugar, too!) Peanuts are okay for low carbers, in moderation, but if you want peanut butter, buy natural peanut butter, the kind with oil on top. (That's why the manufacturers hydrogenate the oil in most peanut butter, to keep it from rising to the top.) The unnatural saturated fats created by the hydrogenation process, called *trans* fats, are far more damaging than any naturally occurring saturated fat.

Many people find that a daily dose of soy foods has a very beneficial effect on cholesterol levels. You could start drinking a protein shake every day (recipe later) using a soy protein powder. There are also soy capsules on the market if you prefer. Or you could eat tofu, but most people I know don't want to eat tofu daily.

At the same time, increase your intake of fish — shoot for at least three fish meals a week; more won't hurt — and of healthy fats, like olive oil and olives, raw nuts and seeds. If you really dislike fish, you might consider taking EPA supplements, either from fish oil or from flax seed; these can have a very beneficial effect on cholesterol. Supplements of GLA (another healthy oil), from either evening primrose oil or borage oil, have also been shown to help lower cholesterol. Capsules of both these oils can be found at any health food store. Soluble fiber helps some people; you might take a fiber supplement — just be sure that it's sugar free. Niacin — vitamin B3 — has been clinically proven effective for lowering cholesterol, but needs to be handled with care; also be sure you're taking a good, broad-spectrum multiple vitamin and mineral supplement — more about both of these later.

All of this should do the trick!

Depression and Mental Illness

Have you noticed how many people seem to be depressed these days? It seems to me that there are a whole lot of folks these days who have no real definable problems, and yet are miserable and anxious a lot of the time. Sometimes I think everybody but me is on Prozac!

Now, I'm not going to tell you that a low carbohydrate diet will cure all mental illness. The brain is an incredibly complex thing, and there's no one answer to all mental problems. There are some very real chemical imbalances for which antidepressant drugs and other medications are nothing short of a miracle and a blessing. Furthermore, if you've had a lot of serious emotional trauma in your life, I'm not sure there's any biochemistry that will fix it, just like that.

On the other hand, *your brain is a part of your body*. It amazes me how many people don't seem to realize that! I mean, we all know that if we put alcohol in our mouths, it affects our brains; if we put a joint in our mouths, it affects our brains; if we put pills in our mouths it, affects our brains. But it doesn't seem to occur to us that the food we put in our mouths affects our brains!! *Yet our brains can only be as healthy as our bodies.* They are *just* as dependent on the food we eat as any other organ; maybe more so. Is it any wonder that a country that lives on sugar, white flour and chips is having trouble with mental illness right along with physical illness?

So where does carbohydrate intolerance fit into this picture? Unstable blood sugar, just *exactly* like the blood sugar swings I just described, is enough to cause mental illness *all on its own*. Here's a list of the most common mental symptoms of low blood sugar:

- Nervousness
- Irritability
- Exhaustion
- Faintness, dizziness, weak spells
- Depression
- Headaches
- Mental confusion
- Trouble concentrating
- Insomnia — especially going to sleep, then waking up after an hour or two and lying awake feeling anxious.
- Internal trembling — feeling shaky inside, while your hands are steady.
- Anxiousness — constant worry about nothing in particular.

Quite a list, huh? And one that would send a lot of people straight to the doctor, and then to the pharmacy. But all of these symptoms can be cleared up by a diet that stabilizes blood sugar *if* (and *only* if) *blood sugar swings are what is causing them in the first place.*

Unstable blood sugar is enough to cause mental illness all on its own.

With America chowing down on a diet practically *designed* to destabilize blood sugar, is it any surprise that we're seeing a huge increase in antidepressant prescriptions? *I would lay the bill for the antidepressant explosion of the '90s directly at the doorstep of the low fat theory of the '80s.*

Another interesting new tidbit is the research that is starting to connect cholesterol to mental health. There's a strong correlation between very low blood cholesterol levels — under 160 — and depression, violence, and suicide. This does *not* necessarily mean that low blood cholesterol causes mental illness; mental illness of some kinds may cause low cholesterol. Or some third factor may be causing both. The research is inconclusive. But there is evidence that cholesterol is involved in regulating your brain's level of *serotonin*, a chemical that makes us feel cheerful and calm, the very chemical that Prozac and the other new anti-depressants are designed to increase. Pass those eggs!

. . . .

I would lay the bill for the antidepressant explosion of the '90s directly at the doorstep of the low fat theory of the '80s.

. . . .

Here's another problem with the low fat/high carb diet as most Americans eat it: It robs the body of B vitamins. All carbohydrates require B vitamins to be processed in your body, but *only* whole grain, unrefined carbohydrates contain enough B vitamins for their own metabolization. If you eat a lot of white flour and sugary low fat stuff (or sugary high fat stuff, for that matter!), your body will take the B vitamins from the good stuff you eat to process the refined junk.

Why is this so important? Because *all* of the B vitamins include mental problems among their deficiency symptoms. If you get deficient enough, you'll quite literally go insane. It's unlikely to go that far, but lower level deficiencies can make you anxious, irritable, jittery, even paranoid. B deficiencies can also make you tired, which is pretty depressing in its own right.

A low carb diet stops this B vitamin drain on your body — and contains most of the B-rich foods, including meat (especially organ meats), eggs, nuts, seeds, and peanuts.

Is a low carbohydrate diet *guaranteed* to cure *all* depression and other mental ills? No, of course not. But it will help many, many people. And the wonderful thing is that it's both free and harmless to find out if it will help *you!* One of the most common remarks I hear from low carb dieters is how much more cheerful they feel — when most diets make you cranky!

In fact, I know of at least one person who had a very low carbohydrate diet prescribed by their psychiatrist as a treatment for depression. Closer to home, I have one member of my immediate family who got off of Prozac using a low carbohydrate diet and nutritional supplements, and feels better than he ever did on the drug. And a dear friend of mine — who, by the way, is not overweight by any stretch of the imagination — is an adult victim of child abuse, suffering from depression and Attention Deficit Disorder. Despite being very slim, he has found that keeping his blood sugar stable by avoiding large amounts of concentrated carbohydrate and eating plenty of protein is *instrumental* to maintaining balanced mental function. He feels better than he ever has. That's not too shabby for a program most people use to lose weight!

Kinda gives a new meaning to "A sound mind in a sound body", doesn't it?

Diabetes

After years and years of the insulin cycle, many people start to lose the ability to use insulin properly. With all that abuse, the places on the cells that use insulin, those insulin receptor sites, start to malfunction. It's like the hinges on the door start to wear out. This is called "insulin resistance." Your body churns out even MORE insulin to get the sugar out of your blood and into fat storage. If this continues, you start to have both high insulin levels and high sugar levels in your blood, and eventually we call it adult onset or Type II diabetes. Now, along with the damage caused by high levels of insulin, you also have the damage caused by high blood sugar levels. Very bad news indeed.

 One of the most common remarks I hear from low carb dieters is how much more cheerful they feel — when most diets make you cranky!

I've talked to a woman who actually gave herself adult onset diabetes by eating a low fat/high carb diet. (She didn't lose much weight, either!) So long as she sticks to her low carbohydrate diet, her blood sugar is normal, and she needs no medication. Pretty cool!

You should know that since America went low fat, Type II diabetes has skyrocketed. And the number of diabetics world-wide is predicted to double *again* between now and 2025. Some researchers think it's just because the population is getting older. But guess what? This disease, traditionally called "adult onset" diabetes, is now growing rapidly in American *children*. Think that might have to do with the fact that the average American kid gets *half* his calories from sugar, and a whole bunch more from white bread, canned pasta, and chips, hmmm?

You don't want diabetes. It's an incredibly ugly disease. It can give you heart disease, make you blind, make your fingers and toes die, one by one, cause impotence in men. If you suspect your blood sugar is unstable, take the warning, and do something about it *now*.

Cancer

Then there's cancer. Women, in particular, have been told to fear breast cancer from a diet high in fat. It is true that women who are obese have a higher risk of breast cancer than women who are not. Because of this, it has been assumed that a low fat diet will prevent breast cancer, just as it has been assumed that a low fat diet will cure obesity. Wrong!!

It will amaze and reassure you to hear about the Harvard Nurses Study. This was a HUGE study — 90,000 nurses were included, and they were studied for over five years, which is almost unprecedented in scope. The researchers divided the nurses into five groups by their fat intake. The group with the *lowest* fat intake had the *highest* rate of breast cancer! Haven't read about that lately, have you?

In February of 1998, the New England Journal of Medicine published an article in which the statistics from seven different studies of the effect of low fat diet on breast cancer were analyzed. Guess what? There was no evidence that a low fat diet decreased the risk of breast cancer. In fact, once again, the statistics indicated that a very low fat diet increased the risk of breast cancer.

It's also interesting to note that the first formula for predicting cancer risk in populations was presented in a medical paper in 1843, by a fellow named Stanislaw Tanchou — and it was based on grain consumption. The more grain a given population ate, overall, the more cases of cancer would be found. This is echoed by a 1996 study reported in the highly respected medical journal *The Lancet* that examined breast cancer rates in Italian women. The study showed a *decreased* risk of cancer associated with *increased* fat intakes (no doubt that healthy Italian olive oil), and an *increased* rate of cancer associated with an increased consumption of *carbohydrate,* especially starches.

There *have* been some studies that indicate that a high fat, high meat diet correlates mildly with colon cancer. I have some thoughts on that.

First of all, most studies don't separate different kinds of fat. There *are* kinds of fat that are dangerous! Ironically, the same polyunsaturated oils we've been told to eat in place of saturated fats *do* lower our risk of heart disease — but raise our risk of cancer. These oils break down very quickly when exposed to air (throw out that old bottle of corn oil right now!) or heat — it's much safer to fry things in butter or lard! Or, for that matter, to fry in monounsaturated oils, like olive oil, peanut, or canola. These are far more stable when heated than the polyunsaturates. (For that matter, fresh lard — NOT the very processed lard you buy at the grocery store — has more monounsaturates than saturates.) And what kind of foods do we usually fry in that polyunsaturated oil? Carbohydrates!! Potato chips, french fries, donuts, all that stuff.

Let's face it, the average American who eats a high fat diet is eating a *ton* of processed food, very little fiber, and almost *no* vegetables. *None* of the cancer studies have been done on people following a low carbohydrate diet — people who aren't eating white bread, sugar, cold cereal, french fries, chips, and all that other garbage. Think there might be a difference, hmmmmm?

And while we're on the subject, how many of you have been told that while the origin of most cancers remains a mystery, we do know for certain what food it is that cancers feed on: SUGAR. Would you like to starve any potential cancers in your body? Try a low carbohydrate diet. In fact, I've read about a few medical studies where ketogenic diets — the very lowest carbohydrate sort of diets — have been shown to slow and even reverse tumor growth, in animals and in pediatric cancer patients, by limiting the glucose available to feed the tumor.

How many of you have been told that while the origin of most cancers remains a mystery, we do know for certain what food it is that cancers feed on: SUGAR!

Now, I know some — perhaps most — of you are in severe shock right now. I had the same experience. I used to manage a health food store. Finding out that my body runs better on red meat than it did on brown rice was kind of like having the law of gravity revoked! For the first month or so, I kept expecting to keel over dead from the fat in my diet! But the weight kept coming off, and I kept feeling better and better — and eventually, I just stopped worrying. And now I have the bloodwork to *prove* that my diet is healthy!!

I've looked at this pretty carefully, and not just for my own health's sake. I took Argumentation and Debate at Indiana University a few years back. (I decided I needed to be more outspoken and opinionated!) When I got to my Scientific Argument assignment, I decided to do low carbohydrate dieting. I was required, for the assignment, to argue both sides of the question, so I spent *hours* online, looking through Medline — an online database of medical journal articles. I was looking for some evidence in favor of all the carbohydrate they've been pushing at us — current recommendations are now to eat 6 to 11 servings a *day* of grains, for heaven's sake!

So I searched under everything I could think of — high carbohydrate and heart disease, high carbohydrate and triglycerides, high carbohydrate and cholesterol, high carbohydrate and diabetes — I read abstracts until my brain hurt, and I found *NOTHING* that indicated that a high carbohydrate diet was good for helping heart disease, cholesterol, triglycerides, etc.

I found several studies that showed that a high carb diet seemed to correlate with high triglycerides — in particular, fructose (fruit sugar) has been found to raise triglycerides, even in kids. Guess what they sweeten soda pop with these days? High fructose corn syrup. And most parents consider fruit juice — *loaded* with fructose — to be the "healthy" alternative to pop or Kool-aid, never considering that their children get the sugar in up to a dozen pieces of fruit in just one big glass of juice.

I found one study where they put the subjects on a low fat/high carb diet with restricted calories, and had half of the group run, half not. Only the ones who ran improved their blood fats — so I guess it wasn't the low fat/high carb diet, was it?

I found the studies I mentioned earlier, where children with cancers were put on a very, very low carbohydrate, high fat diet. The growth of their cancers slowed or stopped. In animal tests, animals with cancers actually had the tumors shrink on a very low carb, high fat diet! Plus, this sort of diet avoided the horrible wasting which often comes with cancer.

In another study, published in the *Journal of the American Medical Association*, a high carbohydrate diet used in treating adult onset diabetics was found to raise triglycerides and "bad cholesterol", the VLDL , and make their sugar control even worse. A diet high in monounsaturated *fats* seemed to *improve* these things.

So didn't I find anything that showed that low fat/high carb worked? Well, sort of. One study in *The Lancet* covered one 68 year old man with high cholesterol and a family history of heart disease. They put him on a low fat/high carb diet, and gave him medication as well. At the end of a year, they tested him, and he was *worse*. They adjusted his medication, and cut his fat back to 10% of calories —

It will surprise you to know that despite the highly touted "Food Pyramid", the absolute human requirement for carbohydrate is zero!

surely a very unpleasant diet. At the next testing, they found what they termed a "mild improvement". Whoopee. I don't consider that a ringing endorsement of a low fat/ high carbohydrate diet.

In fact, it will surprise you to know that despite the highly touted "Food Pyramid", the absolute human requirement for carbohydrate is *zero*, but there are fats the body cannot do without. So the question remains: Why are the government and the medical establishment pushing carbohydrate?

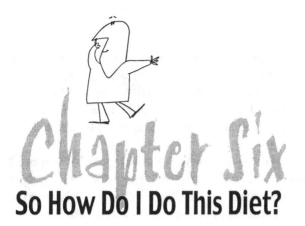

Chapter Six

So How Do I Do This Diet?

There's more than one way to limit carbohydrate in your diet. As you've gathered, I've read a big stack of books and articles on this subject, tried several approaches, and talked to a lot of people about what they've tried. And no one approach seems to be best for everybody.

So what I'd like to do is explain a few different approaches you can take to cutting the carbohydrates from your diet, and the fat from your body. I want to give you enough information that you can come up with what works best for *you*. We all know that the hardest thing about losing weight is keeping it off. The reason, of course, is that people "go on a diet" — and then, when they've lost the weight, they go *off* the diet, and go back to eating the same old way that got them in trouble in the first place.

The good news is that you're going to feel so great, and be able to eat so much wonderful food, that you'll consider that a very small sacrifice indeed!

I'm not going to lie to you. To keep the weight off, you're going to have to change the way you eat *forever*. You're never going to be able to have cereal for breakfast every morning, and potatoes with dinner every night, and eat cake every time someone at the office has a birthday, and keep the weight off. The good news is that you're going to feel so great, and be able to eat so much wonderful food, that you'll consider that a very small sacrifice indeed!

Motivation

So let's talk motivation for a minute. I am *painfully* aware that most people would quite literally rather *die* than change the way they eat. In fact, they do it every day. Of all the dangerous things you may be exposed to today — environmental pollutants, drunk drivers, second-hand smoke, etc. — the one *most* likely to kill you is what's on your dinner plate.

So why don't people change how they eat? Or rather, why don't people *permanently* change how they eat? Huge numbers of people change the way they eat temporarily, but eventually drift back to the same old diet that made them sick in the first place. Why?

Well, some people go into dieting with the idea that this is a temporary thing. As I just mentioned, they're going to go *on* a diet, and then they're going to go *off* the diet. A woman I spoke with who had lost and regained her weight many, many times admitted to me that she always goes on a diet believing that she's going to lose the weight fast-fast-fast — and then she'll be able to go back to eating whatever she wants, whenever she wants, and miraculously not gain the weight back. Of course, she knows this is nonsensical, but the dream persists nonetheless.

Of all the dangerous things you may be exposed to today, the one most likely to kill you is what's on your dinner plate!

By the way, it is perfectly honorable to decide that you'd rather be fat than limit what you eat. It's *your* body and *your* life, and if eating carbs is more appealing to you than the weight loss and other health benefits to be had by giving them up, that's *your* decision, and no one has the right to question it. There are far more important things in life than being slim. But it's very, very important to understand that certain things are mutually exclusive in this world; as the old saying goes, you can have *anything* you want, but you can't have *everything* you want. You simply have to *choose*. There's no way you can eat a poor diet — lots of sugary, starchy, refined and processed junk — *and* look and feel as good as possible, too. If you spend much time wishing you could have both, you'll make yourself miserable, as this woman was.

As the old saying goes, you can have anything you want, but you can't have everything you want.

What I *really* don't want to hear coming out of your mouth is the word "can't", as in "I can't give up sugar!" or "I can't stop eating bread!" Do you have a couple of big guys in dark glasses who come to your house, hold you down, pinch your nose to force you to open your mouth, and shove the junk down your throat? Didn't think so. You *can*. And if you'll do it for just a few weeks, it will become far, far easier than you can possibly realize right now, due to changes in your biochemistry.

What "can't" really means, of course, is "I don't want to." And depending on your life, your body, your emotions, that may be a valid statement. On the other hand, it may be a cop out. Because if you were really comfortable with that decision, you wouldn't try to disown the responsibility for it by using the word "can't."

So the next time you catch yourself using the word "can't" this way — for instance, "I can't resist the donuts in the break room" — try taking responsibility for that decision instead. Say to yourself — aloud if you possibly can — "Eating donuts is more important to me than my physical and mental health." "I would rather eat donuts than lose the next ten pounds." "Five minutes of eating donuts is worth three or four hours of feeling lousy, and a five pound water-weight gain." If you can say these things aloud, and *mean* them, feel comfortable about them, then go ahead and knock yourself out. But don't go giving your power away so that you can lie to yourself about what you're doing.

A very common reason people don't stick with changes in eating habits is *sheer hunger*. This, of course, is the big stumbling block of calorie-controlled diets. Very, very few people have what it takes to sit around and be hungry for the rest of their lives. Fortunately, this is *not* a problem on a low carb diet. Once you choose the approach

> As a child, I'd head back to the cookie table at the Girl Scout meeting before I'd finished the cookies I had, because I was afraid they'd all be gone when I wanted more. Guess what? It's thirty years later, and they're still making Oreos!

which is right for your body and lifestyle, you need never go hungry to be healthy and maintain your weight loss!

A third challenge to healthy eating is *boredom*. People just get tired of eating the same thing over and over again. We've been indoctrinated by advertising to think of food as entertainment. I was appalled at an ad for fruit juice blends that featured a cute kid saying, "You know what happens when you drink the same thing all the time? Your tongue gets kinda bored." I wanted to smack him upside the head and holler, "You spoiled brat! Get down on your *knees* and thank *God* that you have good food to eat and clean water to drink!" Tongue gets kinda bored, indeed!

The purpose of food is nutrition, not entertainment! If you've been using food as a diversion, *do* something! Read a book, surf the Internet, go for a walk, take a class, anything from massage to ballroom dancing to physics. Take up needlework (hard to eat while knitting!), volunteer at your church, the animal shelter, the library, a political campaign. Look, I can't tell you what things you'll enjoy doing. But neither can junk food! Address the real problem. Distracting yourself with cookies or chips never improved anything; it makes you feel a tiny bit better in the short run, and far, far worse in the long run.

That being said, eating *should* be pleasurable and varied. Unfortunately, many people are now what I call "willfully helpless" about food. They don't cook, they don't know *how* to cook, they don't *want* to know how to cook. They're used to getting variety in their diet by using highly processed prepared foods — whack-'em-on-the-counter biscuits, Hamburger Helper, stuffing mix, boxed potato dishes, etc., etc., etc. — all of which offer very little in the way of nutrition or satiation, and all of which are simply *loaded* with carbohydrates of the

> It is my observation that people choose their food far more by emotion than by any other method. If it isn't what we grew up on, it's hard to think of it as real food, normal food. Further, it's hard to think of what mama served us as dangerous, because we know mama served us that food with love, and that must mean it's alright.

cheapest, most damaging kinds, not to mention all sorts of other interesting chemicals. When these things are removed from their diet, they perceive their diet as having little taste excitement (not that *I* would call that stuff exciting!), and grow bored and rebellious. The funny thing is, they were probably eating the same carb-y stuff over and over again — so why wasn't *that* defined as boring?

I know of two solutions to the boredom problem. The expensive solution is to eat out a lot, exploring local restaurants for fabulous low carb dishes — lobster one night, Greek lamb kebabs the next, Tandoori chicken after that. Hey, if you've got the budget, go for it!

The other solution is to *cook*. And to get caught up in exploring all of the really fabulous foods a low carb diet has to offer! That is why as soon as I finish writing this book, I'm starting on the companion volume, which will help you get over the "What the Heck Do I Eat Blues" really quickly. It's not going to be just a recipe book, although it will have recipes in it. It's going to help teach you to go through standard cookbooks, spotting the recipes that are fine for the low carb dieter, and the recipes that can easily be adjusted for us, as well. We'll talk about processed foods, fast food, quick meals, menu planning, all that stuff.

In the meanwhile, there are a few low carb cookbooks on the market; I've listed them in the back of this book. I've also included the Internet address for an online low carb recipe archive.

So you won't have boredom as an excuse anymore, will you?

Then there's *emotion*. It is my observation that people choose their food far more by emotion than by any other method. If it isn't what we grew up on, it's hard to think of it as real food, normal food. Further, it's hard to think of what mama served us as dangerous, because we know mama served us that food with love, and that *must* mean it's alright.

Some of this problem of emotional eating is solved on a low carb diet; for most of us, meat and other low carb foods are familiar and "friendly". Eating them without a potato or some macaroni on the side is a little odd at first, but the food we *can* eat is reassuringly "normal".

Here's another way emotion can mess you up: You think you *should* crave sugar and junk, even when you don't! After all, you always have. It's part of your self-image, and that kind of thing is hard to let go of. I talked with a woman named Cindy who tried a very low carb diet, and it worked like a charm. She felt great, lost weight, wasn't hungry, and was *very* surprised to find that she didn't crave sweets. But Cindy thought she *ought* to crave sweets — that's who she *was*, what she was all about. She ate the sweets even though she didn't really *want* them! They didn't even taste very good — but they upset her blood sugar, and made her hungry and tired again. A few times of doing this, and Cindy up and quit her diet — and when I spoke with her, she was just starting all over again.

I had some trouble with this self-image thing, too. When I went low carb, I discovered that food still tasted good, I still enjoyed eating,

> **If you're genuinely scared that giving up carbohydrate addiction will mean the end of intense emotion in your life, I gently suggest that a little counseling may be in order.**

but the huge emotional pull was gone. It wasn't a *passion* anymore. I felt emotionally detached from food for the first time in my life.

On the one hand, this was good; it made eating moderately, to satisfy the needs of my body, much easier. On the other hand, I had always been obsessed with food! If I wasn't obsessed with food anymore, who was I? And where would I find that passion in my life? It was a little scary.

Then I got mad. Why should I have to settle for the "passion" of a physical addiction? What a cheap substitute for real passion! I have a *great* marriage — that sure brings a lot of passion to my life. But I developed two new passions, too — becoming as good a low carb cook as I had been a low fat/high carb cook, and telling others about

---

how low carb dieting had changed my life. This book is part of the new passion that entered my life when I abandoned the "passion" of physically craving carbohydrates.

To think of food which will make you profoundly ill as a reward is one of the most dangerous things you can do!

If, indeed, you have been using food addiction as an easy substitute for finding real passion, real emotion, in your life, it's time to do something else. I can't tell you what to be passionate *about* (although I highly recommend sex!), I just know that food addiction is a cheap and dangerous substitute for real emotion. If you're genuinely scared that giving up carbohydrate addiction will mean the end of intense emotion in your life, I gently suggest that a little counseling may be in order. It's time to find out what you've been hiding from.

Then there's our tendency to use food as a reward. You know, "I've worked so hard all week, I *deserve* a hot fudge sundae" (or a deep dish pizza, or a candy bar, whatever). Try this sentence on for size: "I've worked so hard all week, I *deserve* to take drugs." Different impact emotionally — but not that big a difference physically, as we've seen. To think of food which will make you profoundly ill as a *reward* is one of the most dangerous things you can do!

But you do deserve rewards! So right here, right now, think of some other ways you can reward yourself. How about splurging on some low carb treat that you adore? A whole lobster, perhaps, or an expensive gourmet cheese. My low carb cyberpal Kathy bought herself a 25 pound sack of macadamia nuts!! I think she spent the kids' college fund!

But rewards don't have to be food. How about treating yourself to a pedicure every Friday on the way home from work? You could get a massage, buy yourself some fresh flowers, take a long, hot bath with your favorite scented oil and a trashy novel. Refuse to answer the door if the kids knock! When's the last time you had a new shade of lipstick? Guys, how about that magazine subscription you've been wanting? Or a full hour on the phone, long distance, talking to an old high school buddy you haven't seen in *way* too long? If you're doing this diet as a couple, I'll bet you can come up with some great rewards you can give each other!

Of course, the big reward for successful dieters is *clothes!* Don't wait until you've reached your goal weight. As soon as your clothes are loose on you, buy at least one new outfit you really, really like. Yes, you're going to shrink out of it, but in the meanwhile, it'll make you happy, and keep you on track. Anyway, what better use for the money you're not spending on junk food anymore?

You're not depriving yourself of anything – you're indulging yourself in feeling fantastic!

These are the sorts of rewards that won't bite you back. Give this some real thought, and know that you *are* worth it!

Another way that emotion ruins diets is the ol' "I feel unhappy, so I'll cheer myself up by eating X" routine. Most of us think of carbohydrate foods — and sweets in particular — as "the good stuff", a reward. If we're unhappy or hurt, we use these foods for solace. If we're "denied" these foods, we feel hurt and rebellious — like Mommy is punishing us.

But everything is a matter of perspective. We all make decisions from a sense of perceived benefit, versus perceived loss. It's all a matter of what's really important to you. People think I have *killer* willpower because I can watch other people eat donuts or chocolate cake without blinking — or, more importantly, joining in. What they don't realize is that I'm not *resisting* those things at all — I genuinely *don't want* them anymore. (They also don't realize that I'm not quite so strong with potato chips!) Why don't I want them anymore? How did a girl who *stole* to support her sugar habit as a child get to this point?

My perceived benefit and perceived loss changed. First of all, now that I've been low carb for so long, most sweet things just don't taste as good as they used to. In fact, most of them taste way, way too sweet — downright nasty! So the perceived benefit of eating the junk food — the taste — has lessened a lot, and the perceived loss of passing it up is almost nothing.

Anyway, if I pass up donuts, and someday I really regret it, guess

I feel good. I mean, really good!

what? They'll still be making them. Unless the world falls apart, any junk food I pass up today, I can find again tomorrow. (This was a very important realization for me, by the way. As a child, I'd head back to the cookie table at the Girl Scout meeting before I'd finished the cookies I had, because I was afraid they'd all be gone when I wanted more. Guess what? It's thirty years later, and they're *still* making Oreos!)

Then there's the other side of the benefit/loss equation: The benefit and loss of *not* eating carb-y garbage. The loss side of not eating the carbs used to be withdrawal — all the uncomfortable symptoms that came with falling blood sugar. That's certainly not a problem anymore! There's no physical addiction to fight anymore; it's *gone*.

And the *benefit* of not eating the carbs is tremendous! My weight loss? Well, sure. But that's not even most of it.

I feel good. I mean, *really* good. Here I am, forty years old, and I have far more energy than I did at fifteen! I'm cheerful the *vast* majority of the time! My mind is clearer than it used to be. I wake up bright-eyed and pleasant. I'm not hungry and tired and cranky all the time. Now *there's* a benefit!

You see, on calorie-controlled diets, you eat about like you always have, only *less*. You don't feel much better; in fact, you usually feel *worse* — hungry, irritable, tired, deprived. After all, your blood sugar is dropping, and you're not pushing it back up again! You're on an energy roller coaster, getting shakier by the day.

Not so on your low carbohydrate diet! You feel better and better, more and more energetic, less and less hungry — while eating food that tastes really great! You're not *depriving* yourself of anything — you're *indulging* yourself in feeling fantastic! And who wants to mess that up?!

When my friends tell me that life is too short to "deny" myself sugary junk, I tell them that life is too short to live it feeling lousy all the time! (It's also too short to live it without men flirting with me!)

Okay, end of pep talk! You're ready to decide the best approach to low carbohydrate dieting for *your* body and *your* lifestyle. Let's go!

What Approach Is For Me?

First of all, you need to try to figure out just how carbohydrate intolerant you are. The more intolerant you are, the more drastic the change in your diet will need to be. Make sense? So how do you tell?

Well, here's a list of indicators, things that have been linked to carb intolerance. How many of them apply to you?

- I have had a weight problem since I was quite young.
- I have bad energy slumps, especially in the late afternoon.
- I get tired and/or shaky when I get hungry.
- I'm depressed and irritable for no reason.
- I binge badly or frequently on carbohydrate foods.
- I carry most of my weight on my abdomen.
- I have high blood pressure.
- I have high triglycerides.
- I have high cholesterol.
- I have adult onset diabetes.
- I have heart disease.
- I have had a female cancer (breast, cervical, ovarian, uterine)
- I have had a stroke.
- I am an alcoholic.
- Obesity runs in my family
- High blood pressure runs in my family.
- High triglycerides run in my family.
- High cholesterol runs in my family.
- Adult onset diabetes runs in my family.
- Heart disease runs in my family.
- Female cancers run in my family. (breast, cervical, ovarian, uterine)
- Stroke runs in my family.
- Alcoholism runs in my family.

If the answer is "yes" to more than two or three of these, you're likely to be pretty intolerant. The more yes answers, the more intolerant you're likely to be. And the more people in your family have these problems, the more intolerant you're likely to be. (I had at least *ten* yes answers before I went low carb! Obviously, I haven't changed my family health history, but I don't have those energy slumps and depressed spells anymore!) Keep this in mind when choosing an approach.

The second thing you need to consider when deciding on an approach to cutting carbs is just how much weight you really need to lose to be happy. I've lost 40 lbs, and as I said before, that makes me "normal" weight, but does *not* make me skinny. I'd have to become a fair amount more restrictive with my diet to lose another, say, 20 pounds. For instance, I have a couple of light beers or glasses of dry wine every evening. If I gave up alcohol, I'm sure I'd lose more. It's not worth it to me. I'm happy where I am.

Let us not forget that today's standards for female thinness are not normal, either medically or historically. Marilyn Monroe, considered by many the most beautiful woman in the world less than fifty years ago, was, by all accounts, a size 16.

So ask yourself: Will I be happy if I go from being a size 20 to a size 14, plus improve my health and energy? (Or from a 14 to a 10. Whatever.) Or will I only be happy if I get down to a size 7? If you want to really get seriously thin, you're going to have to be more restrictive — and *stay* more restrictive — than if you just want to reach a healthy, attractive size.

Let us not forget that today's standards for female thinness are *not* normal, either medically or historically. Marilyn Monroe, considered by many the most beautiful woman in the world less than fifty years ago, was, by all accounts, a size 16. In the 1950s, a size 12 was considered "perfect". Now that's where "plus sizes" start. Even department-store mannequins have grown smaller and smaller! For that matter, men, if you look at pictures of what Hollywood considered strong and muscular men 50 years ago, they look much more real than today's "buff" hunks. I would encourage you to aim at being healthy and attractive, not at looking like one of Calvin Klein's junkie-models, or a cut-up bodybuilder. Obsession isn't any healthier than hyperinsulinemia!

(This seems like as good a place as any to put in a word to those of you — you know who you are —who are obsessive about your weight. I'm not certain, but I really don't think that a low carb diet is suited to becoming unhealthily thin. You're much more likely to reach a normal weight, with none of the health problems that accompany obesity. But I will say this — if you're going to become really nutso about thinness, this is about the healthiest way to do it.)

The third thing you'll need to take into account is whether you're a man or a woman. Unfair as it seems to us ladies, men do lose weight more easily than women do. Often they do just fine with some of the less restrictive approaches, while we women are stuck with the more restrictive approaches. Just biology, I'm afraid — as we'll discuss later, estrogen encourages both fat formation and water retention.

And the fourth thing to consider is how active you are. If you're going to work out four or five times a week, or if you have a heavily physical job, you may be able to tolerate a little more carb — but just a *little*, mind you. Remember, even 5 step aerobics classes a week and a physical job didn't help *me* lose weight when I was loading up on carbs.

Still, exercise does improve carbohydrate tolerance a bit. I suspect that this is the reason that the Chinese do pretty well on a low fat/high carb diet: They have no cars, and so they walk or bicycle everywhere they go. Makes a difference. (That being said, the Chinese today have far *more* heart disease than Americans did a hundred and fifty years ago — when people were eating plenty of meat and eggs and lard and butter, but only 1/10 of the sugar we do now!)

So, if you're going to work out heavily, you may be able to tolerate one of the less stringent low carb diets. Your scale, your energy level, and the fit of your clothes will tell the tale.

Two Kinds of Change

Okay, you know you have to change *something* to lose weight, right? I mean, the one thing we know for sure *doesn't* work is whatever you've been doing — or you wouldn't be reading this!

Remember that earlier I said you can have *anything* you want, you just can't have *everything* you want? Well, that's very true of low carbohydrate dieting. On some carb-restricted diets, you never have to give up any favorite food — but you have to control your portions two meals a day, and you can't eat whenever you feel like it. Conversely, with some other plans, you have to give up a fairly wide variety of foods entirely — but you may eat as much as you like, whenever you like.

. . . .

You know you have to change something to lose weight, right? I mean, the one thing we know for sure doesn't work is whatever you've been doing.

. . . .

There are two things — two "vectors" — you can change if you want to lose weight. You can change the *quantity* of what you eat — like on a calorie controlled diet. Or you can change the *quality* of what you eat — which foods you choose. *The more you're willing to change one, the less you have to change the other.*

For instance, if you were to eat nothing but 200 calories a day of Moonpies, you'd probably lose weight. You'd feel lousy, and destroy your health, and be hungry all the time, but you'd lose weight. That would be a change strictly in quantity. (Well, for me it would be a change in quality, too! But if you've been eating mostly carbs, it wouldn't be much of a change.)

My guess is you don't want to drastically restrict the quantity of what you eat. Most of us have tried that. It hasn't worked very well, and it's made us miserably hungry. We've ended up gaining the weight back. So just changing quantity isn't for us.

On the far end, there are many people — I'm one of them — who, so long as they eat very few carbohydrates, can eat pretty much as much as they want and lose weight. That's a change strictly in *quality* — and it's a lot more successful for most people.

In between, there are some compromises — hybrid diets where you limit quantity some, and also keep a close eye on quality. I'll describe a few of these for you, too.

Be aware, however, that the more of those questions above you answered "yes", the more you're going to have to limit your carbs to be successful. These things are *not* graven in stone; I know

> There are two things — two "vectors" — you can change if you want to lose weight. You can change the quantity of what you eat. Or you can change the quality of what you eat — which foods you choose. The more you're willing to change one, the less you have to change the other.

people who have to stay under 10 grams of carbohydrate a day to lose weight, and others who can lose easily on as many as a hundred. (For comparison, the average American eats about 300 – 400 grams of carbohydrate a day.) And there are a few folks who will have to count both carbohydrates *and* calories.

So if you were slim all through your childhood, only started putting on a little weight after the kids came, only have 30 pounds to lose, and your only health problem is borderline-high blood pressure, you're probably not going to have to be as strict as someone who's been heavy since they were 8, has 90 pounds to lose, and has a family history of heart disease and diabetes, along with sky-high cholesterol and really bad energy swings. Make sense?

I'm going to describe several approaches to carbohydrate restriction in your diet — first, I'll tell you about basic low carb dieting, as popularized by Dr. Robert Atkins of *Dr. Atkins' New Diet Revolution* and Drs. Michael and Mary Dan Eades, authors of *Protein Power*. This is what I do, what works for me. If you answered yes to more than a few of the questions above, this may well be your best bet.

Then I'll explain a couple of diets that are similar to this — the cyclic ketogenic diet, and the Paleolithic diet. Both of these have useful things to teach us about maximizing our success on a low carb diet.

Next, I'll tell you about an approach that might be termed the "mini-binge" approach — a form of carb-restricted diet where you still get to eat carbs once a day, but have to control your portions somewhat. This approach was invented by Drs. Richard and Rachael Heller, of Mount Sinai Hospital, and is described in their books *The Carbohydrate Addict's Diet* and *Healthy for Life*. For reasons I'll get into when I explain this approach, I *hated* this diet! But I know many people for whom it's been a godsend. Who knows? You might be one of them.

Then I'll tell you a little about the best-selling book *The Zone,* by Barry Sears, Ph.D. This book is very technical, and Sears' approach seems best suited to those who have only a few pounds to lose, but some of the concepts are useful to us all.

Finally, I'll tell you about a diet I've devised myself — not for me, but for some friends of mine who, for one reason or another, I didn't want to put on a strict low carb diet. It has been very successful for several of them, and I think you should know about it. It combines some carb restriction, some portion restriction, and a useful concept called "the glycemic index" — don't panic. I'll explain when we get there.

And finally, for those of you who prefer the "meal replacement" approach, I'll teach you how to make a highly nutritious, high protein, low calorie, sugar-free shake, without spending an arm and a leg.

Once you understand all these different approaches, and understand the principles involved, you'll be able to customize a program for your body, your lifestyle, and your preferences. And that's a very nice place to be!

Chapter Seven
Protein Is the Key

On all of these diets — heck, on *any* diet — the most important thing you can eat is *protein*. In fact, that's what the word "protein" means — "first in importance." Your body absolutely has to have a certain amount of protein every day, just to replace the cells that die. And if you get less protein than you need, *your metabolism drops.* Don't want that!!

Further, protein will fill you up and stabilize your blood sugar more than any other kind of food. That's why eating eggs for breakfast will keep you full and energetic till lunchtime — or even beyond — but cereal will leave you hungry by 10:00. (That's why we have coffee breaks, you know — so people who had carbohydrates for breakfast can get another fix and get their blood sugar back up. It really ought to be called a blood sugar break.)

The Opposite of Insulin!

Here's one more reason that protein is our friend. Remember all that stuff I said about insulin? Well, your body makes a hormone that is the *exact opposite* of insulin!! While insulin ushers sugar into your fat cells to be stored as fat, and then slams and locks the door, this opposite hormone opens the door and lets the fat back out to be burned for fuel!! This opposite hormone is called *glucagon*.

Eating enough protein is very, very important!

When you eat carbohydrate, your body *only* makes insulin. And if you're carbohydrate intolerant, it makes way too much insulin. But if you eat protein, your body makes only a *little* insulin — and, at the same time, it makes glucagon! All of a sudden, your fat *storage* and fat *burning* hormones are in balance!

So you see, eating enough protein is very, very important.

(By the way, the other thing that makes your body produce glucagon is our old pal *exercise*. You knew it was good for you, right?)

Before I go any farther, let me talk a little about protein foods. I learned when I was in the health food industry that a lot of people didn't know what foods had protein in them, and I want to be sure you *do* know. The best protein foods are meat, poultry, fish, eggs, cheese, soybeans and some foods made from them, like tofu and tempeh, protein powder, and brewer's yeast or nutritional yeast. (This last item is *not* the same as baking yeast!! Don't go eating baking yeast; it's alive and can grow inside you. Nutritional yeast is dead, and loaded with protein, vitamins, and minerals.)

It is possible to get protein from other foods. For instance, you can get protein from rice and beans, or macaroni and cheese, or peanut butter and bread. However, these foods have a *lot* of carbohydrate in them too — so if you're carbohydrate intolerant, these are *not* good sources of protein for you.

How Much Protein Should I Eat?

Both *The Zone* and *Protein Power* use some rather complicated formulas for calculating your exact protein requirement. Personally, their formulas didn't work for me. They're supposed to let you calculate your body composition — how much fat vs how much lean — but I got a *wildly* different result with these formulas (20 percentage points different!!!) than I did when I had my body fat professionally tested at the YMCA a month or two later. I attribute this to being built funny — you're supposed to measure your waist at the level of your navel, and your hips at their widest point, and take a ratio. Unfortunately, my navel is not at my waist, but at the level of the widest part of my hips, which threw the calculation *way* off.

To tell you the truth, I don't think it's essential to be so precise. So instead of making you do a bunch of math, I'll give you the down-and-dirty formula that's been kicking around the health food industry for years. *Take your ideal, healthy weight (not a model-skinny, anorexic weight) in pounds, divide it in half, and that's the number of grams of protein you should get in a day.* So if your healthy weight would be 130 lbs, your minimum protein requirement every day would be 65 grams. This is reasonably close to the government standard of 0.8 grams of protein for every kilogram of active body weight, and a whole lot easier to figure.

Be aware, too, that some researchers feel that your protein intake should be based on your actual weight, not your ideal, healthy weight. If you're very heavy, there's some reason to feel you'll need more protein than average, at least to start.

In general, figure that the vast majority are going to need at least 60 grams of protein a day, and very few are going to need more

 Take your ideal, healthy weight in pounds, divide it in half, and that's the number of grams of protein you should get in a day.

than 150 grams a day. If you stay in this range, you should do fine. In fact, I think it's best to eat a bit more than your minimum requirement. As you may recall, your body does indeed need some glucose, and on a low carb diet will derive some of that glucose from protein, which means you may need a bit more than the minimum.

Some bad things have been said about excess protein recently. You should know that my *very* conservative nutrition text, where I got that government figure for protein intake, says that it's okay to eat up to *double* your minimum protein requirement for the day. That's a *huge* amount! So don't worry. As for the old wheeze about protein

....

The vast majority are going to need at least 75 grams of protein a day, and very few are going to need more than 150 grams a day.

....

being hard on the kidneys, there have been a couple of peer-reviewed medical studies in respected journals recently that lay this to rest pretty effectively. One compared kidney function in people who had eaten a high protein diet for years to kidney function in long-time vegetarians living on a low protein diet. No difference in kidney function was found. Another studied kidney function in bodybuilders who were eating tremendous quantities of protein, and concluded that their kidney function was a bit *better* than average.

So how much protein is in stuff? Eggs have 6 or 7 grams apiece, and meat has about 7 grams per ounce — so, for instance, a quarter pound hamburger has about 21 grams. (You'd think it would be 28 grams, but what fast food joints advertise as Quarter Pounders are weighed *before* cooking, and then shrink. That 7 grams per ounce figure is cooked weight.) Cheese also has 7 grams an ounce — an ounce of most cheeses is a cube an inch square. So we're looking at maybe two or three eggs for breakfast, and a 4 oz serving of meat, fish or poultry for lunch and dinner as a reasonable protein requirement for most of you. (Neat trick: Figure the size of a minumum serving of meat by looking at the size of your palm. Your minimum serving should be about the same size as your palm, both in diameter, and in thickness. Your very own built-in gauge!)

On most of these programs you can eat more protein than this if you want (I do) — but you should do your best not to eat *less*.

Spread It Out

It's best not to eat all your protein at one or two meals. Instead, spread it out in at least three meals a day, and maybe even a couple of snacks, unless you're on a program that doesn't allow eating between meals. If you eat way too much protein at one shot — over 30 grams or so — there's a tendency for your body to turn it into *sugar*, and here comes insulin again!

It's a good idea always to eat a substantial portion of your protein at breakfast. This will help you control your blood sugar, your hunger, and your energy all day long. In fact, it makes far more sense to eat your biggest dose of protein in the morning, rather than in the evening, unless you're going out dancing after dinner. Watching TV and running the dishwasher just don't take that much fuel!

So, protein at every meal, but the biggest dose at breakfast — at least 14 grams (two eggs worth!).

Okay! On to the diets.

Basic Low Carbohydrate Diet

First, the basic low carbohydrate diet, as exemplified by Atkins and *Protein Power*. (This is also very close to what was advocated by Dr. Herman Taller in *Calories Don't Count,* and by Dr. Richard MacKarness in *Eat Fat and Grow Slim.*) This is the type of diet I eat, the diet that works for me, and that I feel best on. For *many* of you, this will be the diet of choice.

All of these programs were developed by medical doctors. "Atkins" is short for *Dr. Atkins' New Diet Revolution.* Robert Atkins was originally trained as a cardiologist, but became famous as an advocate of low carbohydrate dieting back in the seventies. He is an industry unto himself — along with a radio call-in show and a line of nutritional supplements, he runs the Atkins Center in New York, where he uses what he terms "complementary medicine" — the combination of standard medicine with diet, supplementation, and alternative medical disciplines — to treat a wide variety of illnesses. Atkins feels very strongly that unstable blood sugar and hyperinsulinemia (high levels of insulin in the blood) are aggravating factors in a whole host of diseases. Obviously, I agree with him — but should note here that much of the medical industry does not.

Protein Power, on the other hand, was published in 1996 by Drs. Michael and Mary Dan Eades, who run a weight loss clinic in Little Rock, Arkansas. They, too, have had great success treating thousands of people for obesity with a low carbohydrate diet — and have found that a whole host of other ills, from heart disease and high blood pressure to rashes, gastro-esophageal reflux, and asthma — clear up when they get people's carbohydrate metabolism under control.

The Atkins and *Protein Power* programs are essentially similar, which is why I'm lumping them together. The focus differs some, and the Eades' research is more recent, with some information unavailable when Atkins wrote his book, but living on the diet is pretty much the same. They are examples of what I would call the Basic Low Carbohydrate Diet.

What Are These Diets Like?

On both these plans you base your diet on the protein and fat foods — meat, poultry, fish, eggs, some cheese, along with fats and oils, sour cream, mayonnaise, butter. Your carbs are very strictly limited; so much so that a few ample servings of vegetables, and a few nuts and seeds will just about use up your carb ration for the day.

As I said, the focus of the two plans is different. The Eades' highlight is making certain you consume an adequate amount of protein throughout the day, for the reasons that I explained in the last chapter. So the Eades want you to build your diet around the protein foods, with the high fiber, low carb veggies and maybe a smidge of low carb fruit, or a slice or two of low carbohydrate, high fiber bread filling in around it.

A Ketogenic Diet

Atkins wants you to eat just about the same way. But the Atkins diet is very specifically designed to be what is called a *ketogenic diet.* "What the heck is a ketogenic diet?" I hear you cry. A diet designed to make ketones in your body, of course. Well, what the heck are ketones? Ketones are *partially burned fat molecules,* and are the waste product of fat burning *in the absence of carbohydrate.*

You see, if you go on a strict low carb program such as Atkins or *Protein Power* — the Eades mention that their diet will cause ketosis, they just don't focus on it — your body runs out of glucose to use for fuel pretty rapidly. It then burns your *glycogen* (carbohydrate stored in your muscles and liver) for two or three days. Once that's gone, your body has *no choice* but to switch over to *burning fat for fuel* — both the fat in your diet, and the fat stored in your body. That fat burning creates ketones as a by product, and you spill those ketones in your urine and in your breath. You're in ketosis! (Actually, ketones are formed if you burn fat while on a diet WITH carbs, too — but they then burn up, so you don't go into ketosis.)

Ketosis is pretty interesting. First of all, ketosis has a *strong* appetite suppressant effect — you tend to be far, far less hungry than on a carb-containing diet, even less hungry than you might be on the less strict, hybrid carbohydrate-controlled diets. Some people have to *force* themselves to eat to get all their protein. (When was the last time you had to force yourself to eat!?)

Secondly, Dr. Atkins claims that fat burning in the absence of carbohydrates is a very inefficient way for your body to produce energy. "Inefficient" sounds bad, until you realize that it means that your body has to burn *more* calories — more *fat* calories — to do *anything* while you are in ketosis than it would on any other kind of diet. (Remember the stuff about Drs. Kekwick and Pawan?) He calls this "the metabolic advantage." In short, ketosis lets you crank up your metabolism the way a thin person's body does! This metabolic advantage, combined with the appetite suppressant effect, means that most people would have a hard time eating enough to gain weight on a ketogenic diet.

(Let me mention here that this metabolic advantage is controversial. Many researchers claim that it doesn't exist; that the only reason people lose weight on a low carb diet is because they are less hungry, and therefore eat fewer calories. Maybe; I haven't gone into a lab and tested it clinically. But I'm quite certain that I did *not* eat a low calorie diet while losing my weight, what with eating meat and eggs and mayonnaise and butter and fried nuts. Did I somehow eat slightly fewer calories? I suppose it's possible, though instinctively I doubt it.

 **If the only things that a Basic Low Carbohydrate Diet did for me were to make me less hungry so I automatically ate less and lost weight; while also improving my health, my mood, and my energy level, that seems quite enough for me!**

But you know what? *I don't care.* If the only things that a Basic Low Carbohydrate Diet did for me were to make me less hungry so I automatically ate less and lost weight; while also improving my health, my mood, and my energy level, that seems quite enough for me!)

There's another benefit to ketosis, one that means a very great deal to me. Ketosis seems to affect brain function — it makes many people happy. No kidding! It's very common for people to have a mild sense of euphoria when they're in ketosis, and I have even known of at least one case where a ketogenic diet was prescribed by a psychiatrist to treat chronic depression!

It takes a few days of strict low carb to go into ketosis. How do you know when it's happening? Personally, I don't think it's that important to know — if you're losing weight and you feel good, that's what counts, right?

But you can find out easily, by testing your urine, and many people find it's a good "reinforcer". You can buy ketone testing strips for about ten bucks at any pharmacy. (If you'd like to have twice as many for the same price, you can cut them lengthwise down the middle to make two strips. Make sure your hands are clean and very dry, and don't handle the test square if you can avoid it.)

You simply pass the test strip through your urine stream, wait for fifteen seconds, and then compare the color of the test square to the chart on the jar. If the color changes even a little toward pinky-purple, you're in ketosis. Again, I don't consider testing a big deal, but a lot of people find it motivating. (Another way you may know that you're in ketosis is that ketosis can cause bad breath. The more water you drink, the more ketones will be able to escape in your urine, and the less likely you are to have bad breath.)

By the way, don't get alarmed at the stuff on the jar about calling physicians and such. Ketone test strips are not made for us low carb dieters; they are actually manufactured for insulin-dependent (juvenile onset) diabetics, who have to watch for a condition called *ketoacidosis*. Remember I told you that diabetics can lose weight very rapidly because they have no insulin? Well, ketoacidosis is when they're burning fat very fast, *and* their blood sugar is going way up, and their blood is becoming too acidic, as well. If you don't have juvenile onset diabetes, your body will limit your ketone production. If you *do* have juvenile onset diabetes, you've got problems I can't help you with! (But be aware that back before there was artificial insulin, low carbohydrate diets were about the only way juvenile onset diabetics stayed alive for a while.)

Some people have to force themselves to eat to get all their protein. (When was the last time you had to force yourself to eat!?)

Ketosis induced by a low carbohydrate diet, on the other hand, is *not* dangerous, and may actually be beneficial. I believe that its appetite suppressant effect was designed by nature to help us get through the long periods of fasting that were common for centuries before — and even after — humankind invented farming. It has a "muscle-sparing" effect — lets you burn fat without losing any muscle mass, which would have been vital to prehistoric man. If you have a functioning pancreas, you can't go into runaway ketosis like a diabetic would; if you're making more ketones than your body is happy about, it will convert some protein into glucose, release a little insulin, and bring your level of ketones down a bit. So don't sweat it.

Dr. Lubert Stryer, Professor of Biochemistry at Stanford, says in the medical-school textbook he wrote that the heart and kidneys prefer ketones over glucose as fuel. So does the brain. I've heard and read that the brain "requires glucose" — if that's the case, my brain was dead *years* ago! Actually, I felt wonderfully sharp and clear-headed in ketosis. And ketogenic diets have been used for decades to treat seizures — it's hard to understand how a diet used to treat brain dysfunction could be *bad* for the brain.

I have, once or twice, been in ketosis so deeply that it was a bit uncomfortable; almost speedy. If you feel giddy, or speedy, or can't sleep for a few days, test for ketones. If you're in very deep ketosis, add five or ten grams a day of carbohydrate back to your diet, and the problem should vanish.

So How Do I 'Do' This Kind of Diet?

On both programs, they want you to go through a very strict first phase, to shift your metabolism as quickly as possible from burning glucose — carbs — to burning fat. On Atkins' two-week Induction Plan, you eat all the no-carb food — proteins and fats — you want, but only about two cups of low carb salad vegetables a day, for a carb intake of about 20 grams a day. This is designed to get you into ketosis quickly.

The Eades allow you 30 grams a day, again, with all the no-carb protein and fat foods you wish. They want you to stay at this level until your blood pressure, triglycerides, and cholesterol are normal and stable for at least four weeks — but they don't emphasize getting into ketosis, or testing for it, although most people *will* be in ketosis at this low level of carbohydrate intake.

After the initial ultra low carbohydrate phase, both diets allow you to add slightly more carbohydrate to your diet — but notice I said "slightly"! The Eades allow you to go to Phase II Intervention, which gives you 55 grams of carbohydrate a day. They want you to stay at 55 grams a day until you reach your goal weight.

**I've heard and read that the brain "requires glucose"
— if that's the case, my brain was dead years ago!**

Atkins, on the other hand, wants you to add carbs back to your diet very cautiously, because he wants you to stay in ketosis, with its appetite suppressant effect and metabolic advantage. You are to add just five grams a day of extra carb — from 20 grams a day to 25 — and stay at that level for a week or so, then creep up another five grams, and so on. You are looking for the level of carbohydrate intake where you are in a slight-to-moderate state of ketosis. You stay at that level for your ongoing weight loss, until you reach your goal weight.

**Fiber is technically a kind of carbohydrate.
However, it's a carbohydrate so big that our bodies can't
digest it, and we can't absorb it.**

On both programs, once you reach goal weight, you again cautiously inch up your carb intake a few grams a day, until you find a level where you neither gain nor lose — *and stay at that level for life.*

There is one really significant difference between the two diets, and one smaller difference:

Subtract Fiber from Carbohydrates

The big difference is this: in *Protein Power* the Eades explain the concept of the *Effective Carbohydrate Count.* They realized that when a total carbohydrate count is given for a food, it includes in it any fiber that the food might contain. Fiber, you see, is technically a kind of carbohydrate. However, it's a carbohydrate so big that our bodies can't digest it, and we can't absorb it — that's why we can't live on grass like cows do, and why fiber passes through us, keeping our bowels going.

The Eades realized that it makes sense to *only* count the carbohydrate that is "metabolically active" — that is, the carb that's going to push up your blood sugar and release insulin. So they want you to subtract the grams of fiber from the total number of grams of carbohydrate to get the Effective Carbohydrate Count — the amount of carbohydrate that can actually hurt you.

This can give you a *lot* more food in your diet! For instance, the total carb count for broccoli is about 4 grams for just a half a cup. But if you subtract out the fiber, you can have a *whole* cup — *twice* as much — for the *same* amount of carb! Green beans have 4 grams total carbohydrate in a half a cup — but one of those grams is fiber, so you can have 25% more, for the same cost in carbs. Not too shabby!!

Furthermore, there are even a few grain products that will fit into the Basic Low Carb Diet this way — I occasionally eat Wasa Fiber Rye crackers. They have 6 grams of carbohydrate per cracker, but 4 grams of that is fiber, leaving a mere two grams of usable carbohydrate per cracker, and they're nice big crackers, too! A couple of these add a nice crunch to a meal of tuna salad. There are other fiber-enriched grain products that will work, too — I'm thinking of ordering some oat bran tortillas, and the Eades recommend fiber-enriched "lite bread".

(Here's a plug for their book: one of the best reasons for going out and buying *Protein Power* — it's available in paperback — is that the Eades have an extensive table of fruits and vegetables with the fiber grams already subtracted out for you, which is very useful. But it's not too tough to look at a nutrition label, or a nutrition counter book; read the number of grams of carbs, and the number of grams of fiber, and subtract!)

I feel that this subtracting of grams of fiber from total grams of carbohydrate is the *only* way to go. For that matter, Dr. Atkins is now recommending this approach to his followers, although it isn't in his book. I recommend that you get in the habit of subtracting fiber grams from carbohydrate grams, no matter what program you choose to follow.

Caffeine, Or No?

The lesser difference is that Dr. Atkins wants you to give up caffeine, while the Eades say that there's no reason most people need to do this. It seems that some people react to caffeine with an insulin release, and some people don't. If you find that you're hungry shortly after drinking a caffeinated beverage, you might want to try giving it up. (On the other hand, if that caffeinated beverage was a diet pop, you might want to read the section on diet drinks in Chapter 15.)

I didn't give up caffeine. But I did find, very rapidly, that I couldn't tolerate anywhere *near* as much caffeine as I had. My guess is that the carbohydrates were such a powerful sedative for me that the caffeine I drank just about kept me even. Once I stopped eating the carbs, the caffeine was too much. My heart would race! I still drink a lot of tea, but most of it is half-caf — brewed in a big pot with one regular tea bag, one decaf bag. This seems to work just fine. You could use this approach to coffee, too, or alternate one diet cola with caffeine with one of the decaf kind.

How Do I Suggest You Do This Kind of Diet?

I have to admit that I never went through the very low carb initial phase both these books recommend. By the time I read Atkins' I had been eating low carb and losing weight for at least a week, and I was in ketosis when I tested, so I just didn't bother.

I counted carbs for the first few weeks, until I was pretty clear on which foods I could eat freely, and which I had to be cautious with. I don't count much anymore, haven't in ages. Truth to tell, I don't want to spend my life weighing and measuring and counting things, and I'll bet you don't either. I would recommend that you measure and count for a week or two to start, though, just so you're very clear on exactly how much carb you're getting.

I simply eat my protein, at least three times a day, more for snacks if I want. I avoid all concentrated carbohydrate foods — breads and pasta and cereal and potatoes and sugary stuff — and eat moderately of those which have some low levels of carbs — primarily veggies, cheese, cured meats, dry wine, and some nuts and seeds. If my weight starts to creep up, I cut back on the cheese and the nuts and seeds — and make sure I'm not using a really big wine glass!

. . . .

I don't want to spend my life weighing and measuring and counting things, and I'll bet you don't either.

. . . .

This should work just fine for most of you. Focus your meals on the no- or very low carb foods — meat, poultry, fish, eggs, or soy-based meat substitutes. You may have cheese, but both Atkins and the Eades feel you shouldn't eat more than a few ounces of cheese a day — cheese is both very calorically dense, and contains a few carbs. You may have these very low carb foods broiled, baked, fried, roasted, boiled, however you like — *so long as you add no breading, flour, sugary sauces, or the like.* Eat these foods freely, as much as you like, whenever you like. If you're hungry, *eat!* Just eat the stuff with no carbs in it.

You may also have fats freely — butter, oil, mayonnaise, sour cream and whipping cream. (Sour cream and whipping cream do

> **If you're hungry, eat! Just eat the stuff with no carbs in it.**

contain a few carbs, and you do have to count these toward your total.) You may eat the fat that comes with your meat if you like — you can have chicken skin again, *as long as it isn't breaded, or covered with sugary barbeque sauce.* The Eades feel that you should get more vegetable oils than meat fats, Atkins doesn't care. Either way it shouldn't make a difference to your weight loss.

To this add some low carbohydrate veggies, and other low carb items — a little sugar free tomato sauce, some cantaloupe or strawberries, a high fiber cracker or two, "borderline" vegetables, like onions and garlic, a tablespoon of sugar-free natural peanut butter — or my favorite, a glass or two of dry wine, or a light beer — to round out your menu. I rarely eat anything that has more than 10 or 12 grams in a serving.

Oddly enough, although cheese, heavy cream, and sour cream are allowed on a Basic Low Carb Diet, milk is not, for the most part. We think of milk as a protein food, but it actually has more carb than protein — 12 grams of carb and 8 grams of protein in an 8 oz glass. Plain yogurt is the same — you're better off using sour cream! (Fruit flavored yogurt has sugar, of course.) Once you're on maintenance you may be able to afford a glass of milk a day, if you love it.

Until then, I would *strongly* recommend that you get the majority of your few grams of carbohydrates from vegetables — you *know* that the vitamins and fiber are good for you, but also they will give you *far* more food by volume, and far more flavor and variety than any other carbs will. Sauteed mushrooms and onions over a steak can go a *long* way to making up for no baked potato! Tomato sauce, peppers, onions, mushrooms and wine make "Chicken *Again* " into Chicken Cacciatore. In fact, mushrooms, onions, garlic, and peppers are my four favorite veggies to cook with, though I have to go easy on the onions, since they are a "borderline" vegetable. Nutritious, though!

On the other hand, if you simply despise vegetables of all kinds, you can still do this diet, by eating mostly just protein and fats. You'll just have less variety than other folks. And you might want to take a sugar-free fiber supplement, if you know what I.mean.

Most of you will lose weight easily and have no hunger on the plan I just outlined, but a few of you may have a very stubborn metabolism. If you've eaten mostly meat, eggs and a few veggies for a week and still aren't losing, it's time to buy a food count book (actually, I recommend that for everyone!) and start counting your carbs. Cut back to between 10 and 20 grams a day, and that should do the trick.

There are a very few people for whom even this is not enough. Sad to say, those people may have to count calories as well as carbs. It's not common, but I've heard of it. The good news here is you should be able to eat more calories than you would on a calorie-controlled diet that included carbohydrates. Be aware that there is a point of diminishing return with calorie restriction — it is possible to cut back so far on calories that your metabolism slows down in an attempt to keep you from starving. The most level-headed suggestion I've read for figuring out how many calories you need is to take your weight and multiply by 12. That means that for my 145-150 lbs (I know I keep giving a range instead of a single weight; that's because it fluctuates from hour to hour, much less from day to day), I need in the neighborhood of 1800 calories. Make sure you get all your protein! Even counting calories, you shouldn't have much problem with hunger or energy loss. A real improvement, that!

Eat Your Fat!

Don't try to do low carb *and* low fat!! Not only will this *not* make you lose weight faster, but it's *dangerous*. Old time hunters knew that if they only ate very lean game, with no fat and no plant

Don't try to do low carb and low fat!! Not only will this not make you lose weight faster, but it's dangerous.

You may eat as much as you want, whenever you want, so long as you stick to the no-carb foods.

foods, they would come down with something called "Rabbit Fever" — they'd get sick from eating a diet of straight protein. *At the very least, 30% of your calories must come from fat.* I get *far* more of my calories from fat, and it seems to only do me good. So don't try to speed things up by eating only skinned chicken breasts and lettuce. You won't like the results. Anyway, there's some evidence that one of the effects of a low fat diet is to make your body try to hold onto as much fat as possible — after all, it isn't getting any new fat, so it can't afford to lose the old fat.

Remember, the reason you bought this book is because *low fat dieting didn't work for you!* Okay?

The Upside

Okay, what are the pros and cons of a Basic Low Carbohydrate Diet? This is how I choose to live, so there must be some benefits over the less stringent carbohydrate-controlled diets.

Well, first of all, most people will lose faster on this program than on the other diets, especially at first. As I mentioned, I lost 10 lbs in the first two and a half weeks. Sure helped me stay on track! Loss does slow after a bit, but is still usually more rapid than on the plans that keep a few carbs.

Also, there is *no risk of hunger* on this diet. The hybrid diets use insulin control to reduce your hunger a bit, so you can limit your portions without too much pain. But I don't like to limit my portions! (Truth to tell, I eat like a horse. No joke. When I make tuna salad for lunch, I eat a whole can's worth of tuna, with a huge pile of veggies and a couple of tablespoons of mayonnaise!) Because a ketogenic diet teaches your body to use calories inefficiently, you can eat more calories on this program than you can on the hybrid diets, and still lose. You may eat *as much* as you want, *whenever* you want, so long as you stick to the no-carb foods.

But since it also greatly suppresses hunger, most of you won't *want* to eat many more calories! While this is not a calorie restricted diet, most people do *not* end up eating a lot more calories than they did, simply because their hunger is dramatically less. On every other diet I've been on, I had to torture myself by sitting around, feeling hungry, waiting for the next meal. *I LOVE NOT BEING HUNGRY!!*

Even more, I love the way I *feel* on this program — I feel far better on it than I did on the hybrid diets I tried. I'm much more energetic, and my energy level is very consistent. Because my body isn't running on glucose, I don't have any "low blood sugar moments". When I've burned the calories from my last meal, I switch right over to burning stored fat without a hitch — no drop in energy! I'm happier, too.

Also, I'm much clearer mentally, which I like. Maybe best of all, I feel emotionally detached from food. It still tastes *great* when I do eat — but it has no real power over me anymore. It's not the focus of my life. And *that*, my friend, is a real blessing.

This is a *very* big issue for me. I am definitely a severe carbohydrate addict — one serving sets me off, craving more and more. And despite the fact that one of the hybrid diets is a Mini-Binge program named *The Carbohydrate Addict's Diet, this* addict feels that the best way to treat her addiction is to avoid the drug altogether.

When I tried the Mini-Binge approach — described later — after having been on a Basic Low Carb Diet for a couple of months, it startled me to discover just how drugged and drunk I felt after I ate the carbs that the program allowed. I decided that for me, a daily dose of my drug of choice was *not* the best way to treat the problem. I prefer, for the very most part, to abstain.

The Downside

First and foremost, of course, is that a Basic Low Carbohydrate Diet requires you to limit the *variety* of your diet quite severely. This isn't like a calorie-controlled diet, where you can make little bargains, like skipping 300 calories of chicken in favor of 300 calories of chocolate cake. There really is *no* room for indulging in high carb foods *at all* — one handful of M&Ms out of a gumball machine will screw up your weight loss for *days*. (Well, okay. We all indulge once in a while. We'll talk about that later.) You have to content yourself with the fact that you may eat as much as you like of the really *wonderful* foods that *are* allowed on this diet.

Carbohydrate Withdrawal

Also, some people have a hard time the first week or two on the program — they feel tired and headachy for a few days or even a week or two while their body is making the switch from a glucose burning metabolism to a fat burning metabolism. Or sometimes they'll feel great for the first two or three days, and then they "bonk" for a couple of days — feel so tired they can barely stand it. It's then that they're certain that they've made a terrible mistake!

But they haven't! It's really just a kind of withdrawal. Let me explain.

Enzymes ????

Enzymes are responsible for this — enzymes are what make all the chemical reactions in your body happen. In fact, the difference between living and dead tissue could arguably be defined as the presence or absence of an organized system of enzymes.

For *years* your body has been making mostly the enzymes needed to burn carbohydrate for fuel. Since your body will *always* burn carbohydrate in preference to fat — yet *another* reason eating carbs prevents fat loss — and since most of us have been in the habit of eating some carbohydrate every hour or two, your body gets used to making the enzymes it needs to burn that carbohydrate — *but it stops making the enzymes it needs to burn fat!*

It can take your body a few days to realize that there's been a change in plan and start producing fat-burning enzymes instead of carb-burning enzymes. For a day or two, your body just doesn't know how to make energy! And you bonk.

Take heart! The best treatment is to wait it out — it doesn't last — and to take aspirin, acetaminophen, or ibuprofen if you get a head-ache. Also, many people find that drinking a great deal of water — a gallon a day isn't too much — helps this as well. I try to remember to drink a full glass of water every time I urinate, just on principle. You will lose water VERY quickly on this diet, because your kidneys, free of excess insulin at last, will dump all that extra sodium, and with it your excess water. So keep up with your body by drinking more.

The bottom line is that the vast majority of bodies *will* figure out what's going on. When you come out the other side, your body will have figured out how to burn fat for fuel — and you'll have a limitless supply of energy! After all, even slim people carry around enough fat to get them through several days. You're going to be as-tounded at just how much energy you'll have!

On the other hand, I have known a few people who just didn't seem to reach this stage. If you give the Basic Low Carb diet a genuine, serious try for, say, three weeks, and still feel kinda foggy and logy, that's a good clue to try one of the hybrid programs. That's why I'm giving you more than one way of eating — because bodies are different!

Potassium Loss?

Another problem that affects some people is a temporary loss of potassium with the water you're losing. This happens because the same insulin reaction that makes your body hold onto sodium makes it elimi-nate potassium. As a result, you're likely to be a little short to begin with. Then you lower your insulin levels, lose the excess sodium, and drop a few pounds of water — and with it, even more of your potassium. (Once you've dropped the excess water, things will stabilize again.) If you've gone through the withdrawal phase, gotten your energy back, and then a week or two later, you lose your energy again, and feel kind of achy, weak, or crampy, potassium loss — called "hypokalemia" — is likely to be your problem. And if this happens to you, get more potassium *right away.* Your heart needs potassium to run properly!! *Don't mess around.*

 Hypokalemia ? ? ? ?

Load up on some of the wonderful low carb, high potassium foods. In fact, I recommend *highly* that you do this from the very beginning, whether you have symptoms of potassium loss or not. The recommended allowance of potassium is 900 mg per day.

Advertising has given Americans the unfortunate notion that they have to eat bananas to get potassium. Truth to tell, bananas are only so-so in the potassium department — 390 mg — and are *loaded* with carbs — *28 grams* in one banana! But one 3 1/2 ounce pork chop has the same amount of potassium as a banana, and *no* carbs at all! In fact, fresh meat is a pretty good source of potassium in general, and fresh fish is even better.

Best, though, are the low carb veggies and fruits. Broccoli has 405 mg of potassium in a cup, and only 4 grams of usable carb. Green, leafy vegetables are a *great* source of potassium — except for iceberg lettuce, which is pretty short on nutrients all around. Eat romaine, or other leaf lettuces instead. Avocados, a *wonderful* low carb food, have about 8 grams of usable carbohydrate in a whole avocado, and a whopping *1200 mg* of potassium!! Low carb fruits, like cantaloupe and berries, are good, and nuts are a good potassium source, too, especially raw almonds.

Clearly, you can get plenty of potassium on a low carb diet! But if you're the kind of person who just won't eat vegetables, you might want to take supplements to be on the safe side. You can take potassium tablets, if you like. If you buy the commonly available 99 mg tablets, you'll need to take 2 or 3 tablets a day. You can also buy some Morton's Lite Salt, which contains potassium, and use it in cooking or at the table. It doesn't taste just like regular salt, but it's not bad, and in things (rather than sprinkled on things) you'd never know the difference.

CAUTION: There are some blood pressure medications which are "potassium sparing", meaning that they keep your body from disposing of excess potassium normally. The most common of these is Vasotec, but if you're on *any* blood pressure medication, you should check with your doctor to find out if it is potassium-sparing. If it is, do NOT take potassium supplements!! Also, diabetes can sometimes interfere with potassium excretion. If you are diabetic, you too should not take potassium supplements.

Potassium is one of those very critical nutrients — too little can kill you, and so can too much. Therefore, if there's reason to believe that your body won't be able to maintain the balance itself, use caution. Eat your vegetables and fresh meats, but check with your doctor about supplements. That being said, the majority of the popula-

> **More people die of the effects of carbohydrate intolerance — heart disease, stroke, diabetes, cancer — than die of anything else!! Your carbohydrate intolerance is just as deadly as the severest allergy.**

tion doesn't have these problems, potassium supplements tend to be low dosage, and problems are rare. I just don't want that rare problem to happen to you.

Dinner Parties, and Cooking for Others

Another *big* drawback of this diet comes when you're out of control of your food. If you go to a dinner party, and there's nothing to eat but lasagna and garlic bread, it can get pretty rough. I know I can rarely eat much of the parish lunch at my church — often I just have salad and some olives, and that's *it*. (I eat breakfast before I go!) Every now and then, too, you'll run across a restaurant where *everything* is breaded, or has a starchy, sugary sauce on it — Chinese restaurants can be like this.

In these situations, you just do the best you can. Pick off the breading (I've been known to eat only the insides of fried ravioli and fried mozzarella at an Italian place. I ended up with a pile of shells, like I'd been eating clams. I've also been known to peel apart the layers of lasagna to eat the cheese and meat, and I've peeled the toppings off of pizza, leaving the crust!), eat the salad, order the best choice on the menu, whatever you can do. It's only one meal. If you're really close friends with the person giving the dinner party, you might ask if they could provide a piece of chicken or a chop or something. You could also volunteer to bring something along.

If you're going into a situation where you have no idea what you'll be served, it's a very good idea to eat before you go, or to carry something you can eat — some of those individually wrapped string cheeses, some nuts, whatever — along with you. I was at lunch at a convention last summer, watching everybody else eat vegetarian lasagna, while I was eating soy jerky. Not a gourmet lunch, but it got me through. (I could have had beef jerky if there'd been any; soy jerky was what was at hand. Not bad, actually!)

If you're embarrassed about asking for food exactly the way you want it at a restaurant, or about letting your friends know about your food restrictions before a dinner party, let me ask you this: If you had a deadly allergy, one that would cause you to go into anaphylactic shock and *die* at the mere *taste* of the wrong food, would you hesitate to bring it up to a waiter or a friend? Of course not, and no one would expect you to.

Well, more people die of the effects of carbohydrate intolerance — heart disease, stroke, diabetes, cancer — than die of anything else!! *Your carbohydrate intolerance is just as deadly as the severest allergy.* It just takes longer, that's all. Take care of yourself.

Of course, you'll want to be polite about this. There's a big difference between "I can't eat that! What are you going to feed *me*?" and "I don't want to be a problem, and I know you have a lot to do — but this is a serious health issue for me. But I'm *dying* to see you! Why don't you let me bring a piece of chicken along, and I'll eat the salad and the veggies with everyone else." Anyone who really likes you will have no problem with this. And if they *don't* really like you, what do you care what they think?!

Cooking for the Family

If you're cooking for the family, you'll either have to change your menus, or cook separately for yourself. This can take some adjustment, and that's why my next book will cover recipes, grocery shopping and menu planning. It's not as hard as you think to cook for you both; it just takes a little adjustment.

But before you serve the kids the spaghetti and cold cereal and white-flour rolls and desserts you don't eat anymore, I want you to think long and hard about this: Diabetes, heart disease, cancer, and

Your children got half of their genes from you. There's every reason to suspect that starchy, sugary garbage is no better for them than it is for you.

many other carbohydrate intolerance-related diseases are rising *rapidly* in *children.* Your children got half of their genes from *you.* There's *every* reason to suspect that starchy, sugary garbage is no better for them than it is for you. Furthermore, they're still growing, and need every nutritional advantage they can get. Just because they like and ask for garbage food is *not* a good reason to let them fill up on un-food that does nothing to help them grow strong and well. After all, if they liked and asked for whiskey or cigarettes, you wouldn't give them *that,* would you? Guess what? Carbohydrate intolerance has been strongly linked to alcohol and drug problems.

Furthermore, Weston Price, D.D.S., in his landmark work *Nutrition and Physical Degeneration,* demonstrated very clearly that "primitive" people who ate no sugar, white flour, or other refined foods had virtually *no* dental decay or crooked teeth. He documented clearly, in photo after photo after photo, the straight, strong, healthy teeth of the people who ate a native diet free of the garbage foods of civilization, and the crooked, rotted teeth and ill-formed facial bones of the children after just one generation of eating white bread and sugar. Dental work and orthodontia are expensive, painful, and for the very most part, completely unnecessary *given a healthy diet.* How much money do you want to pay to dentists to avoid having to say "no" to your children?

Also, sugar has been shown to disable the immune system for hours after it is eaten. The white blood cells, whose job is to go around and eat any germs that might be in the body, become far less active for 4 or 5 hours when sugar is eaten. Sugar also reduces the production of antibodies, which are essential to immunity. If you're being careful to wash your children's hands with anti-bacterial soap, but letting them have sugar several times a day, you're *way* off the track to preventing disease. Be warned.

End of lecture.

Game Rules for a Basic Low Carb Diet

1) Eat when you are actually hungry, and then eat enough to satiate your hunger, but not much more.

2) Eat all you wish of fresh meat, poultry, fish, and eggs. (By "fresh meat" I mean meat that has not been processed or flavored in any way.) Eat all you wish of cured meats (ham, bacon, sausages, cold cuts, etc) only if they have 1 gram of carbohydrate or less per serving. Fresh (uncured) meats are nutritionally superior. Use moderate quantities of cheese, and cured meats with 1 or 2 grams of carb per serving.

3) Use butter, oils, mayonnaise freely. Sour cream and heavy cream have about 1 gram of carbohydrate per ounce (2 tablespoons) — you can use them freely unless you're not losing. DO NOT USE MARGARINE, VEGETABLE SHORTENING, OR ANY OTHER HYDROGENATED OIL.

4) Eat at least two 1 cup servings a day of low carbohydrate vegetables — these include:

Alfalfa sprouts
Artichokes
Arugula
Asparagus
Bamboo shoots
Beans (green, snap or wax)
Bean sprouts
Broccoli
Cabbage
Cauliflower
Celery
Chicory
Cucumbers
Dill pickles (NO sweet pickles)
Eggplant
Endive
Fennel

Greens (collard, turnip, beet, mustard)
Kale
Kohlrabi
Lettuce (all kinds)
Mushrooms
Okra
Olives
Parsley
Peppers
Radishes
Scallions
Spinach
Summer Squash (zucchini, crookneck, etc.)
Turnips
Watercress

Onions, garlic, tomatoes, rutabaga, all are borderline vegetables, and may be eaten moderately — for example, half a small onion, or one or two cloves of garlic at a meal. **Avoid** carrots, lima beans, peas, corn, potatoes (white and sweet), winter squash (acorn, butternut, hubbard).

You may substitute a half-cup of berries (strawberries, blueberries, raspberries, blackberries) or a two-inch wedge of melon for a serving of veggies. These are the lowest carb fruits.

5) Nuts and seeds may be eaten moderately — stay below a half a cup a day, less if you're having trouble with losing. Avoid chestnuts — high carb. In a can of mixed nuts, the cashews and peanuts are higher carb than the other nuts — cashews are high enough that they should be considered an occasional treat, not a staple. Sunflower and pumpkin seeds, bought in the shell, are terrific munchy food, because having to shell each one slows you down!

6) You may have sugar free gelatin as desired — and you may top it with real whipped cream, artificially sweetened. (I find that just a little vanilla, no sweetener, is right for me.)

7) Beverages may include diet soda, sparkling water (watch out for colorless sodas, like Clearly Canadian — these are *loaded* with sugar!), sugar-free fruit-flavored drinks such as Crystal Light, tea — black tea, both regular and decaf, green tea or herb tea, — coffee, and of course, water. About 40% of dieters find that diet beverages inhibit fat burning. This problem has been blamed on both aspartame (Nutrasweet) and citric acid, a common ingredient of beverages. If you are drinking many artificially sweetened beverages and not losing, this may be your problem. Drop them and see if you start losing.

8) Drink plenty of WATER. A gallon a day is not excessive.

9) DO NOT EAT SWEETS (anything with sugar, honey, fructose, malt syrup, concentrated fruit juice etc., etc., etc.). Products with trace amounts — so little that it shows up on the nutrition label as 1 gram of carbohydrate or less — are okay in moderation. This would be things like commercial mayonnaise, worcestershire sauce, etc. Be aware that sugar lurks *everywhere*!

10) DO NOT EAT GRAIN PRODUCTS (bread, muffins, biscuits, bagels, pasta, cereal, etc.), CHIPS (fried pork rinds are okay! No carbs), or POTATOES. The exceptions to this rule are a few breads and crackers with so much fiber added that when you subtract it out, the carb count is negligible. Wasa Fiber Rye Crackers, for instance, have 2 g of usable carb per cracker, (All the other Wasa crackers have far more, so READ THE LABEL.) There are some "lite" breads which have enough added fiber that you can have a slice now and again if you like, as well. How do you know which? READ THE LABEL!

11) GET A FOOD COUNT BOOK, one that gives both carbohydrate counts and fiber counts. If it's not on the above list, and doesn't have a nutrition label, *look it up*. Remember that if you add 5 or 10 grams of carbohydrate from one source, you'll need to cut that number of grams somewhere else. Aim for less than 50 grams of carbohydrate a day, after you subtract out the fiber. Keep close track of your carbohydrates for a few weeks; after that you should be able to "eyeball" it — but if you plateau, you'd best start counting again!

12) Take a high potency, full-spectrum multiple vitamin daily. This should be a more-than-one-tablet-a-day product (you'll probably have to go to a health food store), and should give you a minimum of 1000 mg of calcium and 500 mg of magnesium a day. Minerals should be "chelated". It should also include at least 200 mcg of chromium, preferably in GTF, polynicotinate, or picolinate form. Vanadium is also a beneficial thing to have, if you find a multi that includes it. Another thing to watch for is a B complex that includes "folate", "choline" and "inositol" . These are not the only things your multi should include — it should, of course, have vitamin A, the Bs, C, etc. — but if you look for these things, the rest of what you need should be in there.

Typical Daily Menu for a Basic Low Carb Diet

Breakfast:
- Two eggs, scrambled in butter, with mushrooms, onions and green peppers
- Pork sausage patty
- Coffee, tea, or other carb-free beverage. You many have heavy cream and sweetener in your coffee or tea if desired.

Snack:
- Handful of pecans

Lunch:
- Tuna Salad, with celery, red onion, and mayonnaise, served on a bed of lettuce and avocado slices
- Two Wasa Fiber Rye Crackers, with butter if desired
- Diet cola, sparkling water or iced tea with lemon and artificial sweetener, if desired.

Snack:
- Slice of ham and a slice of cheese, with mustard and mayonnaise in between

Dinner:
- Steak, basted with olive oil and garlic, and broiled, topped with butter and bleu cheese blended together, and sauteed mushrooms
- Caesar salad, no croutons
- Glass of cabernet or merlot or other dry wine
- Fresh strawberries with real whipped cream (with artificial sweetener and vanilla).

Typical Low Calorie Daily Menu for a Basic Low Carb Diet

Breakfast:
- Two eggs, cooked any style, but without added fat
- One Turkey Sausage Link
- 1/2 cup sliced fresh strawberries
- Coffee, tea, or other carb- and calorie-free beverage

Lunch:
- Chicken Caesar Salad, made with 4 ounces grilled skinless chicken breast, 3 cups romaine lettuce, 1 tablespoon caesar salad dressing, and 1 tablespoon grated parmesan cheese

Dinner:
- 6 ounce sirloin steak, broiled, all visible fat trimmed
- 1/2 cup sliced mushrooms and 1/2 cup sliced onions, sauteed in 2 teaspoons olive oil
- 1 cup broccoli, with 1 teaspoon butter, and a lemon wedge
- 1/4 cantaloupe

Snacks, spread through day:
- 3 slices deli boiled ham, with 1 teaspoon Dijonnaise

OR
- 1/2 cup pumpkin seeds in the shell

This menu comes to about 1200 calories for the day. It contains plenty of protein for the vast majority of people, certainly enough that — combined with the moderate amount of fat it supplies — hunger should not be a problem. It contains *far* more than the recommended 5 servings a day of fruits and vegetables. And it's low enough in carbs for all but the most severely carbohydrate intolerant. It is a bit low in fiber; but remember that most carb foods — white flour pasta, bagels, etc. — don't offer fiber anyway. You could supplement with psyllium or another fiber supplement, or you could add some more low carb vegetables for a few more calories — how about some asparagus or an artichoke with your dinner, along with the broccoli?

Don't try to make this menu even lower calorie by leaving out the olive oil, the butter, the salad dressing, etc. These are healthy, natural fats, and your body needs them. Too, you shouldn't try to drop even a smidge below 1200 calories per day, and 1500-1800 calories per day is more reasonable, even for people who need to restrict calories. Remember that I don't count my calories at all, and most people won't need to. I just wanted to demonstrate to you how much good, real food you could eat, even if you are one of the unlucky few who need to restrict both carbs and calories.

Chapter Nine
Variations of the Basic Low Carb Diet

The Cyclic Ketogenic Diet

Boy, isn't *that* a mouthful! What's a cyclic ketogenic diet? It's a diet where you deliberately go out of ketosis from time to time by eating carbs.

You see, bodies have an almost endless ability to adapt, and that includes adapting to a ketogenic diet. It seems that you lose the metabolic advantage that you had originally, and it becomes harder to burn fat and go into ketosis, and weight loss can level off. There's speculation that your body becomes better and better at converting protein to glucose, but no one is entirely sure.

Some people feel that the solution to this is the *Cyclic Ketogenic Diet*. What this means is you eat a very, very low carb diet — that Induction thing I was talking about, maybe 20 to 30 grams of carbohydrate a day — five or six days a week. Then on the weekend, you eat carbs. Bunches of carbs. *Mostly* carbs! Come Monday, it's back on your very low carb diet again.

This approach was developed by bodybuilders, and has been spreading through the weight-lifting community under the names "Body Opus" and "The Anabolic Diet". The point was to burn fat while on the low carb part of the diet, and then, on the weekends, deliberately use insulin as an anabolic (muscle-building) hormone.

Bodies have an almost endless ability to adapt!

Muscle building?! I can hear you now. After all those bad things I said about insulin, what do I *mean*, muscle building?

Remember I said that when insulin took the sugar out of your bloodstream, the first place it took it was your muscles? Well, *if* when you produce that insulin you're lifting weights like a *madman*, that's a *good* thing. Gives your muscles lots of energy to grow! But you *have* to be working out *very heavily, right then*, or you just make fat.

Still, even if you're not a bodybuilder, and you're just going for a walk or cleaning the garage on the weekend, it's okay to put on a pound or two of fat — *IF* (big IF!) you then lose four or five pounds during the week, when you go back into ketosis. Many people find this approach works very well.

Too, it gives you a vacation from your low carb diet every week or two. (Many people, especially those who are not bodybuilders, only "carb up" every other weekend. Also, if you're not exercising *very* heavily during your carb-up, it's recommended that it last no longer than 12 to 24 hours.) That can be something to look forward to.

Or not. I've been to the point where it's very hard for me to get into ketosis for a long, long time now, and my weight has plateaued — I'm not regaining at all, but I don't lose any longer, either. I've considered the Cyclic Ketogenic Diet approach to break the dead-lock, and I may do it someday. But believe it or not, I really, really *don't* want to eat those carbs!!

First of all, there would be an instant gain of 5 pounds of water. That comes off very quickly, so it's no big deal, but it's annoying for my clothes to be tight for a few days.

More importantly, I feel *so* much better without the carbs in my diet that I am very, very reluctant to "carb up" for the weekend, or even one day. I have the awful suspicion I'd feel tired and cranky and sluggish, which is *not* how I want to spend a weekend. If you'd told me before I went low carb that I'd ever dread the idea of eating carbs, I would have laughed. Now I can hardly bring myself to eat them when I have an excuse!

Still, I thought you needed to know about the Cyclic Ketogenic Diet. So many people find it an effective strategy that I may just grit my teeth and try it, someday soon. Just remember that during the ketogenic portion, you need to stick to a *super* low carb diet. And if you find yourself having difficulty stopping the carb-up when it's time, this is *not* the approach for you!

Paleolithic Nutrition

Another fascinating variant on the low carb diet is the "Paleolithic" Diet — the idea that we should try to come as close as we can to the diet our caveman ancestors ate, on the theory that *that's* the diet our bodies evolved for. Proponents of the Paleolithic Diet point out that agriculture only started about 10,000 years ago, and that most scientists agree that 10,000 years is nowhere *near* enough time for evolution to occur — for the human body to become accustomed to eating lots of grains and beans. They also point out that paleoanthropology (the study of very old bones and living sites and such) shows that whenever people went from hunting and gathering — and eating mostly meat, and veggies, and nuts, and some fruit in season — to farming, and eating mostly grains, the results were *not* good. Invariably, the bones of the hunter/gatherers show that they were

Scientists agree that 10,000 years is nowhere near enough time for the human body to become accustomed to eating lots of grains and beans.

tall, with strong bones and good teeth, and the bones of the farmers show that they were shorter, with weaker bones and rotten teeth.

It's also interesting that an Austrian doctor named Wolfgang Lutz has done research showing clearly that "diseases of civilization" — heart disease and cancer — are in inverse relationship to how long a given population has been eating grains. In other words, the longer a group has been eating grains, the less of these diseases they have — because there's been more generations for evolution to

Audette theorizes that obesity, and most of the "diseases of civilization", are immune system reactions to eating food that is not suited to the human body.

work, to weed out the people who can't tolerate these unnatural foods. I have also seen articles linking grain intake, and especially gluten (a protein found in wheat and rye), to several autoimmune disorders, including crohn's disease and multiple sclerosis.

If you'd like a full rundown of the Paleolithic Diet, I highly recommend the book *Neanderthin*, by Ray Audette. *Very* interesting. Audette, who cured his own diabetes and rheumatoid arthritis with a Paleolithic Diet, theorizes that obesity, and most of the "diseases of civilization", are immune system reactions to eating food that is not suited to the human body. I know of many people who, having plateaued on a Basic Low Carb Diet, shifted over to Neanderthin or another Paleo-program and started losing again.

Once again, the centerpieces of a Paleolithic Diet are meat and eggs. However, some things that are allowed on your Basic Low Carb Diet are *not* allowed on a Paleo Diet, because they wouldn't have been available to cavemen. Ray Audette gives a simple guideline: If you couldn't gather it with a sharp stick and a rock, and eat it raw, it's not on the diet.

Note: You don't *have* to eat stuff raw, although with many things — like nuts and veggies — it's a good idea. You're just supposed to avoid anything you *couldn't* eat raw, if you had to. Our recent problems with contaminated meat from poorly-run packing houses have made us think of meat as a "must cook", but of course people ate steak tartare and sashimi for centuries. Uncontaminated eggs are also perfectly edible raw. (Again, I have to repeat: I am NOT suggesting you should eat your eggs raw; salmonella is a real problem with today's factory farming.) You shouldn't eat anything that *has* to be cooked or processed in any way to be edible.

For instance, beans and grains *have* to be cooked, so they're not allowed on a Paleo Diet — not even the low carb/high fiber crackers I eat on my Basic Low Carb Diet. Soy is a bean, and has to be cooked, so tofu, tempeh, and soy sauce are out, and you need to

If you couldn't gather it with a sharp stick and a rock, and eat it raw, it's not on the diet.

watch for "soy protein" and other soy derivatives on labels. They're very commonly used! (As you may have guessed from this, it's impossible to be a Paleolithic Vegetarian. Cavemen ate meat, no way around it.) Peanuts are a legume, too, and so are forbidden, along with cashews, although all other nuts are allowed. Potatoes aren't good for you if eaten raw in any quantity, so they're out, as are yams, beets, sweet potatoes, tapioca, etc.

Dairy products are also banned on a Paleo Diet, because cavemen didn't keep herd animals. These are perhaps the hardest for most people to give up. No cream in your coffee — but then, as I'll explain in a moment, you can't have coffee either — sour cream on your fajitas, cheese on your burger, or butter on your veggies. And of course sugar, in all its myriad forms — corn syrup, dextrose, lactose, malt syrup, etc. — is OUT. Audette will allow you a *drop or two* of honey in tea, and it seems to me real maple syrup could be used the same way — but who ever uses maple syrup except to slather over their (forbidden) pancakes or waffles? I'd avoid all sugar — even though a Paleo Diet also bans artificial sweeteners. (Don't think they had pink *or* blue packets in the caves, do you?)

Maybe the most brutal, coffee, as mentioned, is not allowed on a Paleo Diet. Tea — both regular and herbal — is. It's not the caffeine, it's the fact that coffee beans have to be roasted to be edible. If you're a caffeine junkie — I'm one of you! — you'll have to drink tea, hot or iced.

Alcohol is not permitted on a Paleo Diet, nor is vinegar (which means, among other things, making your own mayo and salad dressings with lemon juice only, no vinegar). It is assumed that cavemen didn't know how to ferment things. On the other hand, I've read articles about bears eating berries that had fermented on the bush, and getting swacked — I'd be willing to bet the cavemen made the same discovery. But I'd also bet they didn't make such a discovery every day! I'd say if you were doing a Paleo Diet, you could probably cheat *once in a while* with a glass of wine or hard cider without too much trouble. Beer and liquor, being grain products, would be out of the question. (By the way, Audette recommends "ingesting herbs" if you want to be intoxicated. Far be it from me to criticize, just watch out for the cops!)

Again, the centerpiece of the diet is protein — meat, poultry, fish, seafood, game if you can get it —nuts and seeds, preferably eaten raw, and vegetables. On a Paleo Diet you may eat any veggies you can eat raw — so potatoes are out, but carrots, banned from the Basic Low Carb Diet due to sugar content, are allowed. Audette outlaws green beans, since they're legumes, but I know Paleo dieters who eat them, since they can, indeed, be eaten raw.

In reality, there's some evidence that cavepeople ate a fairly high carbohydrate diet — but that almost *all* of those carbohydrates came from vegetables, which have a much more moderate effect on blood sugar and insulin levels. Remember, too, that those cave folks got a lot more exercise than we do! They had to run around picking all those

 It's impossible to be a Paleolithic Vegetarian. Cavemen ate meat, no way around it.

leaves and veggies and berries, and chasing their meat. They could afford a few more carbs than sedentary modern Americans.

A Paleo Diet is more liberal about fruit than a Basic Low Carbohydrate Diet. After all, the cavemen had access to fruit. However, I have two thoughts about this. One, that cavemen, unless they lived in the tropics, did not have access to fruit year 'round. And secondly, I wonder if they juiced their fruit — Audette allows unprocessed fruit juices on his Neanderthin program, but personally, I'd avoid them. Audette does warn against eating excessive fruit — and especially dried fruit and juice — if you want to lose weight, rather than just improve your health.

Still, you can have a bit more fruit on a Paleo Diet than you can on the Basic Low Carb Diet; if you're very fond of fruit, this is a plus. I've been known to drop dairy and soy and cashews for a few weeks in the summer, in exchange for eating some plums, nectarines, and cherries, which I love. I know a lot of fruit fans; if you're one of them, it might be worth giving up cheese and butter and soy and such to have a couple of fruits a day.

So your basic Paleo Diet would be meat, poultry, fish, seafood, and eggs, nuts and seeds, veggies and fruit. Tea — regular or herbal — fresh fruit juice (with caution) and water would be your beverages. Since the main point of the diet is *not* carb restriction (although it certainly has that effect) , but rather the avoidance of the theorized immune system reaction that proponents claim happens in response to the forbidden modern foods, it's very important to read labels even *more* carefully than on the Basic Low Carb Diet — you have to watch out for soy protein, casein or other milk products, MSG, any artificial additives at all. (As an example, most inexpensive canned tuna includes such additives. Cheap tuna is a staple of my low carb diet, but it wouldn't do for a Paleo Diet. I'd have to spend the money on expensive spring-water packed tuna instead.)

I have not spent very much time on a Paleo Diet myself, although I find the concept fascinating. I've done well enough with my Basic Low Carb Diet that additional restriction is not really alluring. *HOWEVER!*

If I were a person with multiple food sensitivities, or who had a great deal of trouble with the other low carb diet plans, I would try this. Also if I had respiratory problems, since most asthmatics and such should avoid dairy anyway, or if I had an autoimmune disease like rheumatoid arthritis or lupus or multiple sclerosis, I'd try it. The Paleo Diet has also been very effective for breaking plateaus for many dieters I know of every low carb stripe.

If you want to give the Paleo Diet a serious try — if the premise of the diet makes sense to you (as it does to me) — I would recommend that you buy Ray Audette's book. It's very interesting! I had to have it special-ordered by my local big-chain bookstore, and no doubt you could do the same. Or you could write to: Paleolithic Press, 6009 Laurel Oaks, Dallas TX, 75248.

The Mini-Binge or Carbohydrate Addict's Diet

Now, for a different approach entirely!!!

Drs. Richard and Rachael Heller are professors at New York's Mount Sinai Medical School, where they also run a weight loss program. They each discovered separately — before they met and married — that their problems with obesity and ill health were related to the carbohydrate in their diets. Rachael Heller had weighed 200 lbs by the age of twelve, and over 300 lbs. by her twenties. She had always struggled with severe cravings for food, and an inability to ever feel satisfied. Richard had fallen into poor dietary habits as a result of keeping up with a killer schedule — and came close to a heart attack. They both found that limiting their carbohydrates was an effective way to lose weight, improve their health, and, in Rachael's case, eliminate the incessant cravings for food that had plagued her all her life.

After having treated many people successfully for obesity with this plan, and writing the book *The Carbohydrate Addict's Diet*, they started to receive letters from their patients and their patients' doctors, saying, "My cholesterol is down", "My triglycerides are down", "My blood pressure is down", "I don't need my insulin anymore". They then researched the health effects of limiting blood insulin levels, and

By eating only low carb foods at two of your meals, you give your pancreas a rest, and allow it to act more normally when you do eat carbohydrates.

wrote *Healthy for Life*. The *Healthy for Life* plan is similar to *The Carbohydrate Addict's* plan, but focuses on obtaining the health benefits of low blood insulin levels, rather than specifically on weight loss.

Healthy for Life outlines a plan of progressive options, phasing you into a diet which eventually is substantially the same as *The Carbohydrate Addict's* plan. *Healthy for Life* also requires you to choose Exercise and Stress Reducing options. I have often recommended *Healthy for Life* to those whose concerns are primarily health-, rather than weight-, related. I also recommend it for those whose doctors or families are alarmed at their new approach to eating.

Since you bought this book largely because you want to lose weight, I think that *The Carbohydrate Addicts' Diet* is the more appropriate Mini-Binge Diet to describe. Here's the deal:

Remember our two "vectors", quality and quantity? Well, *The Carbohydrate Addict's Diet* is a hybrid — both qualitative *and* quantitative. The idea is to control your insulin levels — and therefore your hunger and your cravings — enough that you can eat smaller amounts without much unpleasantness — and you know what I mean by unpleasantness!

The rules of the plan are simple. You eat two *very* low carbohydrate meals a day — most people choose breakfast and lunch for their low carb meals. These meals must be of "average size", which the Hellers define as 4–6 oz of meat, or 2 eggs, or 2–3 oz of cheese, *plus* 1–2 cups of low carb vegetables or salad.

You are allowed *NO SNACKS* between meals at all. *Nothing* but carb-free beverages goes into your mouth between mealtimes. Not even a sugar-free breath mint.

You see now why I call this a hybrid diet. Between limited portions two meals a day, and no snacks, you are surely limiting calories on this diet as much as you are limiting carbs. But there's an upside to this! Read on.

The Hellers feel that those who have *hyperinsulinemia* (remember, that's a fancy word for carbohydrate intolerance that means "high levels of insulin") can calm down their pancreas' reaction to carbohydrate foods by eating them *only once a day.* (You may notice that this is the exact *opposite* of the "eat high carb/low fat mini meals" idea that has gotten a lot of press in the past few years.) By eating *only* low carb foods at two of your meals, you give your pancreas a rest, and allow it to act more normally when you do eat carbohydrates.

So do you get to eat carbohydrates? *Yes.* Your third meal of the day is your *Reward Meal.*

For your Reward Meal, you are allowed to eat a "balanced meal." You may eat *whatever you want,* in *whatever amounts you want!* Pretty exciting!!

However, the Reward Meal has a *strict* time limit of *exactly* one hour. Now, this time limit isn't just because there's a limit to how much you can eat in an hour, no matter how big a shovel you use — there's a physiological reason behind it.

You see, the Hellers' research also shows that when you eat carbohydrate foods, insulin release happens in two phases. When you start eating, your pancreas releases a dose of insulin almost immediately, to deal with the incoming food — and the size of this

- -

**For your Reward Meal, you are allowed to eat a "balanced meal".
You may eat whatever you want, in whatever amounts you want!
Pretty exciting!!**

- -

dose of insulin is related *not* to how much carb you're eating right now, but to the level of carbohydrate in *previous meals.* They believe that your body tries to predict from your last few meals how much carb you'll eat in *this* meal. This is why you *must* keep the carb content of your two non-Reward meals very low — to trick your body into a smaller insulin release.

The second phase of insulin release happens about 75 to 90 minutes after you start eating. Your pancreas checks back to see if you need some more insulin, or if it's already made enough. If you've stopped eating long enough ago that your body has had a chance to notice that you're done, your pancreas will be able to gauge just how much insulin you need. If you're still eating, it tends to get panicky again, dump out a *lot* of insulin, and drive you back into the "eat carbs, get hungry" cycle. This means that it is *VERY IMPORTANT* to stay within the one hour time limit for the reward meal.

Note: The most common form of cheating on *The Carbohydrate Addict's Diet* is extending the hour for the Reward Meal. *DON'T DO IT!!* It is *not* an arbitrary limit, remember; it is based on physiology, and going past the hour is a great way to end up hungry and craving again.

Also, you must keep your Reward Meal *balanced.* In the book, the Hellers state that the Reward Meal must be "balanced and sensible" — in other words, no dinners of nothing but Oreos and Mocha Almond Fudge — but they do say to eat whatever you want, in unlimited portions.

However, I have had a letter from the Hellers — very kind of them!! — stating the great importance of *balancing* the Reward Meal. They say that you should have a large salad, and then divide your plate mentally into thirds — one third should be protein, one third vegetables, and one third carbohydrates — whether a potato, or rice, or dessert, a drink, or whatever. (By the way, alcohol may *only* be consumed during your Reward Meal.) If you want to add more carbs, that's okay — *but you must also add more protein and veggies.* If you

The most common form of cheating on The Carbohydrate Addict's Diet is extending the hour for the Reward Meal. DON'T DO IT!!

can't fit down the extra low carb foods, you can't have more carbs. (Do I sound like mom? "If you can't finish your meatloaf, you must not be hungry for dessert!" Mom was pretty smart.)

Oh, and please note: You must choose which meal is to be your Reward Meal, and, for the most part, stick with it. Most people choose dinner, but I've known a lot of people who have found it worked better for them when their Reward Meal was lunch. Choose what fits your lifestyle — if you're feeding a family, it will probably be dinner. You may change which meal is your Reward Meal once in a while for a special event — say, a Holiday Brunch — but for the most part, you must keep your Reward Meal constant.

How Fast Will I Lose?

The Basic Low Carb Diet tends to cause a very fast initial weight loss. I lost 10 pounds in the first two weeks, and this is not uncommon. This initial weight loss tends to be mostly water. But even after the water is gone, many people lose fat at a remarkably fast pace on the very low carb plan.

On the other hand, the Hellers feel strongly that you should *not* lose weight too fast — that you should, in fact, lose no more than 1 percent of your body weight per week — for instance, if you weigh 185-190 lbs, like I did, you should be losing no more than 1 1/2 to 2 lbs a week. They have four plans for adjusting the diet to your own metabolism.

If you eat the basic plan — two low carb meals and a Reward Meal — for one week, and you find you're losing just about at the right speed, stick with it. If you are losing too fast, you add one low carbohydrate snack — about half the size of a low carb meal — each day. You may eat the snack whenever you wish. You also add the low carb snack if you get to your goal weight and are still losing.

If you try the basic plan for a week, and are not losing fast enough — or are not losing at all — you are to add a two-cup salad of low carb vegetables to be eaten *first* in your Reward Meal. Clearly, the point of the salad is to take the edge off your hunger before you get to the high carb foods.

If even *that* doesn't start your weight loss, the Hellers recommend skipping one of your two low carb meals *and* eating a salad first for your Reward Meal. Personally, I would suggest that if you have to cut back this far to lose on this plan, you would probably be better off on the Basic Low Carbohydrate Diet I outlined earlier, or perhaps on a Paleo Diet.

The Upside

So, does this plan sound pretty good so far? It certainly has its advantages!

Obviously, the biggest plus of *The Carbohydrate Addict's Diet* Mini-Binge approach is that you don't have to give up any particular food. If you have a very strong, negative, emotional reaction to giving up some particular carbohydrate food — bread or pasta or brownies, whatever — this program is *very* helpful. You can have *anything* you want, you just have to have it within the hour of your Reward Meal. There's a powerful psychological comfort in knowing that you're never more than 23 hours away from eating whatever you want!

Also, the Mini-Binge program makes eating out, or with other people, a whole lot easier. And it's a good strategy for family holiday meals. In either case, so long as you stick to your hour time limit, you're fine. (Slow service in restaurants, or lingering over courses at dinner parties, can be a real problem here.) Even though, for the most part, I am not on this diet, I sometime use it for one day on holidays as damage control, going back to my usual very low carb diet the next day.

If you cook for a family, the Mini-Binge approach expands your range of options of what to cook for the family, without forcing you to cook a separate meal for yourself. It can make menu planning *much* easier.

> **There's a powerful psychological comfort in knowing that you're never more than 23 hours away from eating whatever you want!**

If you're a vegetarian, *The Carbohydrate Addict's Diet* increases your range of options greatly — you can still have grains and beans one meal a day. (Although you'd still need to eat a concentrated protein — tofu, tempeh, eggs or cheese — even at your Reward Meal.)

Too, the Hellers do allow for some low fat products — those which still have a pretty low carb count — even at low carb meals, and feel that vegetable oils are preferable to animal fats. They also call for large quantities of low carbohydrate vegetables. Also, the Reward Meal allows for the consumption of the complex carbohydrates the media has been pushing. I'm convinced that for the vast majority of us, fat is not the enemy, and I'm quite certain carbs are *not* essential, but these aspects make *The Carbohydrate Addict's Diet* a lot more comfortable for those of you who are still suffering from severe fat phobia, and have not yet made the low carb "paradigm shift."

The Downside

What are the drawbacks of the Mini-Binge approach? There must be some, because I tried it for about three and a half months, and went back to the very low carb plan I started with.

First of all, for my body it wasn't low carb enough. I lost weight on this plan at first, but plateaued pretty quickly. I wasn't happy with the weight I was stuck at!

Also, I was often hungry, especially by the time dinner — my Reward Meal — rolled around. I was often *so* hungry that I started my hour by scarfing down several cookies! This is *not* the best way to begin what's supposed to be a balanced meal. And I found that for me, the hour time limit felt like a challenge! I would keep looking at the clock, and then jumping up to grab more food to fit down my throat by the end of the hour. "Gee, fifteen minutes to go! Better go eat some more, in case I'm hungry by bedtime."

The hour time limit felt like a challenge!

I think the thing that really made me decide that *The Carbohydrate Addict's Diet* was not for me, however, was how it made me *feel*. As I mentioned earlier, I found that after having been on a very low carb diet for a while, eating a big dose of carbs all at one go made me feel drunk or drugged. I really missed the energy I had found on the very low carb plan. I finally gave up the Mini-Binge approach when I fell asleep in front of company! Embarrassing!

Another big drawback to *The Carbohydrate Addict's Diet* is the "no snacks" provision — you are very strictly limited to eating *only* at meals. In some ways, this is good — we tend to be a society that is always consuming *something*. Being forced to think, "I am eating

If you're a person who's iffy about greenery, The Carbohydrate Addict's Diet is not for you.

now" and "I am *not* eating now", rather than just nibbling unconsciously, can be a useful spiritual and emotional discipline.

But cooking becomes a challenge when you're not even supposed to *taste* food outside of your mealtimes — which means no tasting while cooking. I am a person who has always cooked by instinct rather than by recipe, so not being able to taste as I cooked was frustrating. I finally learned to adjust the seasoning right before serving food; tasting it started the clock ticking for my hour.

The "food at meals only" restriction also makes occasions where everyone is munching for several hours at a go a real challenge. You can have one hour of unrestricted eating at one of these events, but if the buffet is spread for hours, it can be hard on the ol' will power. I prefer to be able to eat whenever I like, as much as I like, so long as I eat only low carb foods.

Another possible problem is that *The Carbohydrate Addict's Diet* calls for a *lot* of veggies, two cups at each of your low carb meals, and *both* a salad and a low carb cooked vegetable at your Reward Meal. This is part of why the plan works — they depend on all those vegetables to fill you up, and lower the calorie count of this hybrid plan. Without them, it would seem very skimpy indeed.

Now, I like vegetables just fine— but I'm well aware that *huge* numbers of Americans never touch a vegetable unless it's a potato, or the lettuce and tomato on their burger. If you're a person who's iffy about greenery, *The Carbohydrate Addict's Diet* is *not* for you.

So now you know why I didn't like *The Carbohydrate Addict's Diet,* even if it does allow you to eat anything once a day!

Yet I know many people for whom *The Carbohydrate Addict's Diet* has been a godsend, and who have been very, very successful at losing weight and maintaining a weight loss on it. For many of you, it will turn out to be the diet of choice, the one that lets you control your appetite and lose weight permanently. For others, the fit will not be quite right, and you'll do better on a Basic Low Carb Diet like me, or on another of the hybrid plans I'll be telling you about.

Mini-Bingo Game Rules

1) *For two meals a day,* you must have a moderate portion of a protein food with no more than a gram of carb in it. Protein portions at these meals should be 4-6 oz of meat, poultry or fish, or two eggs, or 2-3 oz of meat plus an egg or 2 oz cheese. Along with the protein, you should have 2 cups of very low carb vegetables (listed below.) If you can't stand vegetables at breakfast, you may skip veggies then, but you *must* have them with lunch and dinner. At these two low carb meals, you *must not eat* any foods but the protein and vegetables, plus very low carb fats and condiments (sugar-free salad dressing, mayo, sour cream, mustard, etc.)

LOW CARB FOODS
— if it's not on this list, don't eat it at a Low Carb Meal.

- All fresh meat, fish and poultry
- Many cured meats, such as ham, sausage or bacon — some have sugar, so READ THE LABELS
- Many luncheon meats — some have sugar or other fillers, so READ THE LABELS
- Many canned meats and fishes. READ THE LABELS
- Eggs
- Most cheeses — some have more carbs than others, especially the low fat kinds, so READ THE LABELS
- Fats and Oils, including all vegetable oils, butter, animal fats and mayonnaise. Avoid Miracle Whip.
- Some bottled salad dressings — many are LOADED with sugar, especially the low- and no- fat kinds. READ THE LABELS
- Sour cream

LOWEST CARB VEGGIES INCLUDE:

Alfalfa sprouts
Arugula
Asparagus
Bamboo shoots
Beans (green, snap or wax)
Bean sprouts
Cabbage
Cauliflower
Celery
Chicory
Cucumbers
Dill pickles (NO sweet pickles)
Eggplant
Endive
Fennel
Greens (collard, turnip, beet, mustard)
Kale
Kohlrabi
Lettuce (all kinds)
Mushrooms
Okra
Olives
Parsley
Peppers
Radishes
Scallions
Spinach
Summer squash (zucchini, crookneck, etc.)
Turnips
Watercress

Onions and tomatoes are borderline — you are allowed up to two tablespoons chopped onion and/or one half a tomato at a low carb meal. Although the Hellers don't say so, I would say garlic falls into this category as well — only 1 clove at a low carb meal.

You may have sugar-free gelatin with REAL whipped cream (whip it yourself with sugar substitute) at a low carb meal.

You may have up to two ounces (4 tablespoons) a day of milk, cream, or half and half in coffee at low carb meals.

READ LABELS on condiments — many are loaded with sugar; ketchup, barbeque sauce, and relish especially. Herbs, vinegar, mustard (except honey mustard), salt, pepper, soy sauce, hot sauce, and some horseradishes are generally "safe". You may have small quantities of lemon and lime juice.

BEVERAGES:
- Diet soda, Crystal Light, other calorie-free beverages
- Sparkling water — be careful to choose those with NO SUGAR OR CORN SYRUP
- Club soda
- Tea
- Coffee

All other foods MUST BE SAVED FOR YOUR REWARD MEAL

2) No eating between meals. Period. Full stop. No breath mints. Nada. Calorie-free beverages *only*.

3) One meal a day will be your Reward Meal. The Reward Meal must last for NO MORE THAN ONE HOUR, by the clock. Less is okay, but if you stop after 40 minutes, you can't have another 20 minutes later on. At the Reward Meal, you may eat any food you like. ANY food. However, you must eat roughly equal portions of protein, salad, low carb cooked veggies, and carbohydrate foods (starches and sweets.)

4) Alcohol must only be consumed during the Reward Meal.

5) If, after a few weeks, you are losing very quickly, you may add a low carb snack (half the size of a low carb meal) if desired.

6) If, after a few weeks, you are not losing as well as you'd like, you should eat a large salad FIRST at your Reward Meal.

Typical Daily Menu on a Mini-Binge Diet

Breakfast:

- Cheese omelette, made with 2 eggs and 1 ounce of cheddar cheese, cooked in butter if desired
- Coffee, tea, or other carb-free beverage, with a little cream and artificial sweetener if desired. Remember, you are limited to 2 ounces of cream or milk per day in coffee at Low Carb meals.

NO SNACKS!

Lunch:

- Quarter pound hamburger patty served on a large garden salad, with Ranch dressing
- Sugar-free gelatin with whipped heavy cream (artificially sweetened)
- Iced tea, sparkling water, diet soda, or other carb-free beverage

NO SNACKS!

Dinner: (Must be completed within one hour!)

- Salad of mixed greens, peppers, cucumbers, scallions, tomatoes and cauliflower, with dijon vinaigrette dressing
- Grilled salmon steak
- Steamed broccoli with lemon butter
- Fettucini Alfredo
- Glass of dry wine
- Scoop of ice cream

When your hour is up, you're done for the day!! No more food till breakfast.

The Zone — Hormonal Magic?

Perhaps the diet book that has made the biggest splash in the past few years is Barry Sears' *The Zone.* Sears, while advocating a diet lower in carbohydrate than the average American diet, and *much* lower than the low fat/high carb diets that people like Pritikin and Ornish advise, still recommends more carbohydrate than the *Atkins* or *Protein Power* diets allow — and, of course, correspondingly smaller percentages of fat and protein. He counsels us to construct our meals with a careful proportion of 30% protein, 30% fat, and 40% carbohydrate, commonly referred to as a 30-30-40 ratio.

Sears is a pharmacist, and he urges his readers to look at food as a precision drug-delivery system, where that "perfect" ratio of fat/protein/carbohydrate is eaten no more than five hours apart. This is to keep an optimal hormone balance at all times. Supposedly, this should allow the dieter to enter the ultimate state of well-being Sears calls the *Zone* — a place where thought is clear, energy is high, and hunger is non-existent. Sears *seriously* disses lower carb diets, especially ketogenic diets. (Despite this, he is good friends with Drs. Michael and Mary Dan Eades, of *Protein Power* fame.)

Only one little problem — I tried Sears' plan and, contrary to his assertion, I was hungry a *lot.* In fact, I was hungry *all the time!* And as I mentioned, I *hate* to be hungry. Several other people I know tried it too, and all of the folks who had been on a basic, very low

> Sears formulated his plan while working with serious athletes. How many serious athletes are profoundly carbohydrate intolerant? Most of us who have significant carbohydrate intolerance problems have always been too fat and tired to concern ourselves with serious sports.

carbohydrate diet for weight loss found that they were *very hungry* on the *Zone* plan, no matter how carefully they constructed their meals to Sears' standard.

On the other hand, on my very low carb, ketogenic-style diet, my thought is clear, energy high, and hunger non-existent — the very things Sears promises for the *Zone*.

The problem, I think, is that Sears formulated his plan while working with serious athletes. *How many serious athletes are profoundly carbohydrate intolerant?* Most of us who have significant carbohydrate intolerance problems have *always* been too fat and tired to concern ourselves with serious sports. So Sears developed his diet around people who had an okay metabolism to begin with. Indeed, the people I know who have done very well with this diet are men who have always been athletic, never had a serious weight problem, and only had a few pounds to lose in the first place.

Another drawback is that the foundation of the *Zone* is one of those tedious, careful calculations of body fat and lean muscle mass I mentioned, from which you determine your protein requirements — and it allows more protein the more you exercise. So serious athletes get to eat some decent sized meals, but those of us who are only moderately active get a smidge of cottage cheese, or a couple of ounces of chicken. Not *my* idea of a meal! This limitation has led critics to charge, not without reason, that weight loss on the *Zone* diet occurs largely because of serious caloric restriction, rather than because of any magical formula.

Interestingly, when I emailed *The Zone* web site, they sent me a letter and some info, including an update to the plan. The update said that if you were hungry after a *Zone* meal, it had too much carb, and not enough fat, for your body. Guess what my very low carb diet has? Much less carb, much more fat!

Further, since the publication of the *Zone*, Sears has upped his bottom limit on protein, so that even non-exercisers get a little more food. Apparently he got a lot of complaints about hunger!

If you are very athletic, and if you've only gained a little weight since hitting middle age, or since you went on a low fat, high carbohydrate diet, the *Zone* just might be for you. If you fall into those categories, and would like to try it, I recommend that you buy the book, or its sequel, *Mastering the Zone*, since it's a pretty complex approach, and one that I'm not going to try to describe in detail.

So What's the Point!?

So why did I even bring it up?

Because in *The Zone*, Sears has introduced to the non-scientific community a fascinating and very useful subject: *eicosanoid theory.*

Eicosa-*whut?*

Eicosanoid — eye-coe-sa-noid — theory. I'll try to keep it simple.

When I first started low-carbing, I joined an online low carb diet support group, or list. And on the list, people kept posting messages to the group that said things like: "I didn't have PMS this month. Is this the diet?" "My asthma is better. Is this the diet?" "My rash cleared up. Is this the diet?" "My arthritis doesn't hurt anymore. Is this the diet?" When, a few months later, *The Zone* and *Protein Power* (which also mentions this stuff) came out, it became clear that it *was* the diet — and that we had stumbled on to something *much* bigger than just weight loss.

What the Heck Are Eicosanoids?

The eicosanoids are a group of hormones. They were only discovered recently, in the eighties, because unlike the hormones we're all familiar with — estrogen and testosterone and insulin and such — eicosanoids are *intracellular.* What that means is that they're made, used, and destroyed all within the same cell, all in a split second. Since they never leave the cell, they don't enter the bloodstream, so they don't show up in blood tests, which made them mighty hard to find!

However, now that we've discovered them, we're rapidly learning that they control just about everything in your whole body, so it's important to take at least a glance at them. So here's a very basic explanation.

There are good eicosanoids and bad eicosanoids — this is simplistic; you actually need some of both, but you definitely want more of some than of others. They're sometimes called "series one" and "series two" eicosanoids, but "good" and "bad" will do. Here's a short list of things these eicosanoids control:

- Good eicosanoids open up your blood vessels, improving circulation and lowering blood pressure.

- Good eicosanoids strengthen your immune system.

- Good eicosanoids decrease inflammation and pain.

- Good eicosanoids increase oxygen flow.

- Good eicosanoids increase endurance.

- Good eicosanoids act as a blood thinner, preventing clots.

- Good eicosanoids dilate airways making it easier to breath.

- Good eicosanoids decrease "cellular proliferation" — the uncontrolled growth of cells.

- Bad eicosanoids narrow your blood vessels, lowering circulation and raising blood pressure.

- Bad eicosanoids weaken your immune system.

- Bad eicosanoids increase inflammation and pain.

- Bad eicosanoids decrease oxygen flow.

- Bad eicosanoids decrease endurance.

- Bad eicosanoids cause your blood to become sludgy, increasing the risk of clotting.

- Bad eicosanoids constrict airways, and can even cause asthma.

- Bad eicosanoids increase cellular proliferation, and can lead to cancer.

Guess what? It all comes back to insulin and glucagon!

That's a heck of a list, I'm sure you'll agree! It's clear that we want to have lots of good eicosanoids, and only limited amounts of bad eicosanoids.

Certain things that had puzzled medical science for years have been explained by this eicosanoid theory. For instance, we've known for quite a while that aspirin, along with lowering pain and inflammation, also thins blood, and prevents colon cancer. No one understood why aspirin did all these things — *until* we learned that what aspirin does is knock out one group of eicosanoids, called prostaglandins, for about four hours.

For that matter, scientists have puzzled for a while over the "processional effects" of exercise — along with strengthening the heart, exercise can do everything from lowering blood pressure to thinning blood to lessening the pain of arthritis. Turns out, as I'll explain shortly, exercise causes your body to produce good eicosanoids. Mystery solved!

Now, Sears and the Eades go into stuff like enzymes named "delta 6 desaturase" and such, but if you're like me, that's a bit too much. So let's cut to the chase. What can you do to skew your eicosanoid balance in your favor?

Guess what? It all comes back to *insulin* and *glucagon!*

You see, it turns out that the most powerful effect on eicosanoid production comes from the balance of insulin, which we've been talking about all along, and the opposite hormone we talked about, glucagon. You remember that insulin is the hormone that stores fat, and is produced when we eat carbohydrate; and glucagon is the hormone that releases fat to be burned, and is produced when we eat protein, or when we exercise.

Apparently, the most important thing you can do to skew your body toward making *more* good eicosanoids and *fewer* bad ones is to keep your insulin levels *low* and your glucagon levels *high* —

---

exactly what a low carb diet does! This explains why so many nagging little problems clear up on a diet that controls insulin levels. Exercise can only enhance that effect, by increasing your levels of glucagon. (By the way, exercise can make you burn fat at a higher rate even when you're not actually exercising — partly by increasing muscle mass, which needs more fuel than most tissues, but also by teaching your body to create glucagon, which it needs to burn fat. Just another reason to do what you already know you should.)

* *

One of the very real risks of a low fat/high carb diet is that by limiting protein intake, and raising blood insulin levels, it almost guarantees the formation of the bad eicosanoids. Ready to go low carb yet?

* *

Of course, since protein causes your body to produce glucagon, another thing you can do to enhance your good eicosanoid production is to make sure you get enough protein — again, if you follow one of these diets, you will almost certainly do that. One of the very real risks of a low fat/high carb diet is that by limiting protein intake, and raising blood insulin levels, it almost *guarantees* the formation of the bad eicosanoids. Ready to go low carb yet?

It *is* possible to raise bad eicosanoids by getting *way* too much protein — if you really overdo it, your body can turn some of the excess into carbohydrate — but unless you're really going nuts, eating a dozen eggs a day, or a couple of pounds of steak for dinner, I wouldn't sweat it.

Now, there are some things you can avoid, as well, to help this process along. We've talked a fair amount about fat, and how in the context of a low carbohydrate diet, fat isn't especially fattening or dangerous. However, I'm now going to tell you that not all fats are created equal as far as eicosanoid production goes — some fats are definitely healthier than others. None of them is as bad for you as sugar — almost *nothing* is as bad for you as sugar! — but some are better than others.

First and foremost, you want to avoid what are called *"trans fatty acids"*. I won't go into a big explanation, but you need to know that trans fatty acids are found in *"partially hydrogenated vegetable* oils". What these are, are liquid vegetable oils that have artificially been made into solid fats — primarily vegetable shortenings like Crisco, and margarine. I know that margarine has been touted as superior to butter for your health, but it just ain't so. Butter is a naturally saturated fat; margarine is an artificially saturated fat — guess which your body is better equipped to deal with?

On any low carb diet, you'll avoid most sources of hydrogenated fats — they're widely used in the food processing industry in everything from crackers to popcorn to cookies to bread. Since you'll limit or eliminate these foods, depending on which program you're following, your intake of hydrogenated fats will be sharply curtailed. Use butter in place of margarine when you fry your eggs, or melted on your vegetables. And if you choose one of the plans that allows some carbs, read the labels on any baked goods you buy, and avoid any that list "partially hydrogenated vegetable oil" — and there will be a *lot* of them! (In fact, finding commercial baked goods without partially hydrogenated vegetable oil can be a real challenge. Health food stores should have a few, at least.)

I know that margarine has been touted as superior to butter for your health, but it just ain't so. Butter is a naturally saturated fat; margarine is an artificially saturated fat – guess which your body is better equipped to deal with?

Have you heard that fish is good for you? Sure you have. Well, it's true, and the fatty fishes are even better for you than the low fat fishes — because fish oil has a *very* beneficial effect on eicosanoid production. If you like salmon, mackerel, sardines, tuna, or herring, these are *magnificent* sources of fish oils known as EPAs which increase good eicosanoid formation.

If you don't like fish — I really only like tuna — you can get EPA capsules at the health food store. They are highly recommended for people who have heart disease. Also, because of the eicosanoid effect, they are being recommended more and more for people with arthritis — a friend of mine with rheumatoid arthritis has started taking fish oil capsules and has had a *dramatic* reduction in pain and stiffness.

There are also fatty acids called GLAs which can improve good eicosanoid production. GLAs are found at high levels in breast milk, although not in most common foods — there's a trace in oatmeal, but not enough to make it worth the carbs, if you ask me. You can, however, buy supplements of GLA- containing oils — either evening primrose oil or borage oil. GLA supplements have a potent enough effect that they are used by many nutritionists to treat PMS, eczema, allergy, arthritis, immune disorders, high blood pressure and cholesterol, alcoholism, MS, lupus, scleroderma, and other diseases. *This* is the power of controlling eicosanoids.

Also, do you remember back in Chapter 5 when I mentioned that one suspected culprit in some cases of high cholesterol was something called "arachidonic acid?"

I said that most people would be able to eat beef and eggs with no problem, but that some people may be sensitive to a chemical called arachidonic acid, and would need to limit those foods, or they'd have high cholesterol. Sears feels that the reason some people have a bad blood cholesterol reaction to red meat and eggs may have to do with their sensitivity to arachidonic acid, rather than the actual fat and cholesterol in those foods.

Are you sensitive?

Possible symptoms of AA sensitivity include the following:

- chronic fatigue
- poor or restless sleep
- difficulty waking up, grogginess
- brittle hair and nails
- constipation
- dry, flaky skin
- proneness to rashes

As I mentioned earlier, if you should get your cholesterol checked and find that, unlike most people's, it's gone *up*, instead of *down*, on a low carb diet, there's a chance that the problem is sensitivity to arachidonic acid.

If you think this is your problem, you'll want to eat more poultry and fish. You can also buy lean meats, and cut off all visible fat.

For most people, just eliminating high carb foods from the diet will cause a big improvement in eicosanoid balance.

Again, it's those low protein and fat/high carbohydrate grains they feed meat animals that makes them high in cholesterol, and causes them to produce bad eicosanoids, too — and increases their AA levels. Game, by the way, not having been fed all that grain, is low in AA. Another thing you can do is to marinate steaks and roasts for a few hours before cooking in red wine and olive oil, with maybe a little garlic. The alcohol dissolves some of the AA, which is replaced by the healthier olive oil. Tastes great, too.

If you suspect you are AA sensitive, you'll want to go back to throwing away some egg yolks — they're high in AA. You could use egg substitutes, if you prefer, but they always tasted really fake to me, and I don't trust the chemicals in them. It seems simpler to just throw away every other yolk when you're making scrambled eggs.

HOWEVER! Remember that the *most* important thing you can do to regulate eicosanoid production is to *limit insulin*. For most people, just eliminating high carb foods from the diet will cause a *big* improvement in eicosanoid balance. The vast majority of you will *not* need to get radical about cutting out meat fat or throwing away egg yolks. Again, I usually eat three eggs a day, and my cholesterol couldn't be better. Pay attention to your own body.

In *The Zone*, Sears wants people to treat food as a drug, painstakingly administered to get into the optimal eicosanoid balance. He disapproves of using fish oil and GLA supplements to enhance eicosanoid balance — in fact, he states that it is best not to use nutritional supplements at all.

But how many people want to live that way? I don't want to eat that carefully, and I bet you don't either. I'd rather improve my eicosanoid balance *radically* by limiting my insulin levels and exercising, and then take EPAs and GLAs to adjust it as needed. On any of the programs outlined in this book, your eicosanoid balance — and your health — should improve dramatically!

The Careful Carb Diet

The genesis of the *Careful Carb Diet* was a nutritional discussion with some online email pals. The discussion turned to nutrition, and I mentioned that fructose — fruit sugar — has been proven to raise triglycerides. One member of the group, Rob Douvres, posted back:

"This is *not* what I want to hear when I'm force feeding me fruit every day and my triglycerides are over 1200." Over 1200!?

Thus began a *very* long email discussion!

It turned out that Rob's health was *very* fragile. After seven years — *seven years!* — of trying to improve his health by eating a low fat diet, with lots of fruit — 6 to 8 pieces a day — low fat cereal, skim milk, pasta and grains, only lean proteins, no eggs or cheese, and very little red meat, his condition remained very serious. He had total cholesterol of 425, triglycerides at a whopping 1260 (anything over *200* is bad, and it's beginning to appear that it's best to have them below 100). He'd fought a weight problem since youth, and his blood pressure had been high since his teens. Furthermore, at the age of 44, he'd already had two strokes from severe blood sugar drops! It was clear that Rob was as carbohydrate intolerant as they come.

However, I couldn't put Rob on a strict low carb diet. He had another health problem: terrible kidneys. Rob had only 20% of normal kidney function, and between this and the high blood pressure, took three different diuretics (water pills) daily. While it is untrue that a high protein diet damages kidneys — Rob's damage came from a long habit of heavy drinking, which he had quit years before — for someone with Rob's kidney troubles, an unlimited protein ketogenic diet would have been risky.

But we *had* to get his insulin levels down! So I wrote a diet just for Rob. And we didn't have to wait long to see if we were on the right track. Because of his serious health problems, Rob gets bloodwork done every three months — and he was scheduled to have blood drawn just two weeks after he started on the program I wrote for him. His bloodwork stats hadn't changed much in years, so we knew that any improvement — or, God forbid, deterioration — would be due to the new diet.

And it worked!! Here's an email Rob posted to our online discussion group after *one week* on what I'm now calling *The Careful Carb Diet:*

"My blood pressure has been about 140/100 for years and nothing would work to repair it. I've been on BP pills on/off since 18. Yesterday at the drug store, after 1 week on "Dana's Miracle Cure Diet for Life", I weighed in with a 10 lb. loss and my BP was 121/83!!!!!!!! My weight was down to begin with but was stuck for 6 months. I could never get under that weight on the "no fat diet". My low blood sugar problems are gone, the vertigo is gone, I never have hunger pains, and I cheat a little most evenings and don't tell Dana!! It's hard to eat all the "evil" food but it sure is fun!! My blood report will tell me more. I'm more interested in lowering cholesterol/triglycerides than losing weight."

Another wonderful thing that happened to Rob was that his legs stopped aching. You see, Rob retained so much water — despite all the diuretics — that it made his legs ache terribly every night. He would have to take both prescription pain killers and prescription

sleeping pills to get any shut-eye at all. Yet in less than two weeks, I received this post:

"I'm up and at 'em since 8:30. I went to bed at 1AM and was asleep in minutes with an over the counter nonaddictive sleeping pill and NO Xanax.

I'm just speechless. You have no idea how wonderful it is to simply go to sleep."

Still, the big test would be the bloodwork.

Just 16 days after Rob started on *The Careful Carb Diet,* the verdict was in. His cholesterol was down 90 points, his triglycerides were down over *600 points.* His blood pressure was normal, even a little low. His oh-so-important cholesterol/HDL ratio had improved by 7 points. Maybe best of all, his creatinine — a measure of kidney function — had improved for the first time in five years. And 15 pounds were gone — with no hunger. All of this by *adding* eggs and meat and cheese *back* to Rob's diet — but dramatically *lessening* the quantity and *improving* the quality of the carbohydrates he was eating.

Since then, Rob has gotten bloodwork again, and all of his stats continue to improve. He's not completely well yet, and due to his kidney damage will always have health problems. But he feels better than he has in *years,* and his weight has stabilized at 20 pounds down — around his high school weight. Rob continues to rave about how much better he feels, how un-hungry he is, how much energy he has. And Rob tells everyone who will listen about how a low fat diet turned out to be part of his problem, and a low carb diet, the solution.

Since then, I have recommended a similar program for a number of people — largely those who cared about health first, weight loss second, since weight loss tends to be less dramatic on *The Careful Carb Diet.* The results have been excellent!

My friend Charlotte, who had been plagued by severe fatigue and horrible mood swings, contacted me four days after she began the *Careful Carb* program — using one of the shakes I describe in the next section as one of her carbs everyday — to say that she hadn't felt so good since she was a teenager. Charlotte runs a beauty school, and needs all the energy she can get — and now she has it! She's lost a dress size, and her moods have leveled out. Further, her blood pressure, which had always been high even with medication, has come down, and her doctor is very pleased. She's very happy!

A friend of my husband's called me, begging me to talk to his mother, who had multiple health problems, including high blood pressure, severe asthma, dangerous obesity, and some very ugly mood swings. After a few weeks on *The Careful Carb Diet,* she told me that she was down a size for dresses and underwear (she's heavy enough that she can't weigh herself on her bathroom scale). Her energy and moods were far better, she was healing faster than she could ever remember, her blood pressure was improving, and her asthma had abated to the point where she'd been able to drastically reduce her use of corticosteroid.

(Here's the cautionary tale: When I talked to her several weeks after that, she told me she'd grown lax about following the diet — and her asthma and blood pressure were troubling her badly again. This stuff only works if you continue to do it!)

So what is *The Careful Carb Diet*? Well, it's a hybrid diet — one that allows some carbs. Further, unlike the Mini-Binge approach, it allows you to snack, and to spread your carbs, and other food, throughout the day. *However* — those carbs must be chosen from a rather limited list of what I call *"low impact carbohydrates"*.

What's a Low Impact Carbohydrate?

A low impact carbohydrate is a carbohydrate that has a relatively small effect on blood sugar levels. In general, the faster and higher blood sugar goes up, the faster and harder it comes down. Therefore, low impact carbs are less likely to cause a severe insulin release, with all its bad effects. The official medical name for these carbs is "low glycemic index" carbs, but that's a little technical, don't you think?

How do we know which carbs are low impact? Since the concept of the glycemic index originated, many tests have been done —

We've been told that starches are not hard on the body the way sugar is, because after all they break down more slowly, and give us "sustained energy." Piffle!!

and what tests!! Medical researchers feed a large group of subjects — some with diabetes, some without — a carefully measured portion of a particular carbohydrate food. These portions are calculated to be exactly 50 grams of carbohydrate worth, not just a certain number of grams of the food. (In other words, a subject would eat a *lot* more cucumbers than they would spaghetti.)

Once they've eaten the food, their blood is drawn, and their blood sugar measured, every half-hour for six hours. All of the blood tests of all the different subjects are averaged, so they can get a clear idea of how the *average* person will react to these foods. Then the foods are rated against an "index food" — usually glucose, but sometimes commercial white bread. Whichever index food the researchers choose is rated a 100. All the other foods are assigned a number higher or lower that indicates that food's relative impact on blood sugar.

I've looked over some fairly extensive tables of these results, and I find them fascinating! There's some real surprises.

For instance, for the past twenty years or so, we've had "complex carbohydrates" — starches — pushed at us. We've been told that they're not hard on the body the way sugar is, because after all they break down more slowly, and give us "sustained energy."

Piffle!! Table sugar, poisonous as it is (and I'm convinced it's as deadly a drug as heroin or cocaine — seems like those white, crystalline powders from plants are just a bad idea, period!), has a much lower impact on blood sugar than does the dieter's darling, the baked potato. In fact, potatoes come in at a whopping 98, just two points lower than glucose!! Rice cakes — you know, those nasty, flavorless styrofoam things you've been eating all these years because you thought they were good for you — are a 77. No wonder they never filled you up! And almost all cold cereals are sky-high, even the ones that don't have a ton of sugar added.

So complex carbohydrates are *not* necessarily easier on your body than sugar is.

Science has not yet determined all the factors that affect the impact of carbohydrates. But we do know a few things. Carbohydrates that contain a lot of fiber tend to have a lower impact than those that have the fiber taken out. Apparently, the fiber acts a little like a sponge, slowing the absorption of the carbohydrate a bit. This probably explains why whole or very coarsely ground grains have a milder impact than those that are finely ground — in fact, the less processed the grain, the better. We also know that eating a food with a fairly high impact along with a lot of low impact foods, especially protein and fat, will lessen its impact on your blood sugar.

. . . .

Complex carbohydrates are *not* necessarily easier on your body than sugar is.

. . . .

But there are some things we can't explain: For instance, whole wheat pita bread has a lower impact on blood sugar than regular whole wheat bread. Why? You got me! It just does, that's all. And barley and rye have a far lower impact than rice or wheat; again, why that should be so is anybody's guess. But the nice thing is that we don't have to totally understand this principle to put it to work!

Here's the Plan

Here's how *The Careful Carb Diet* works: Just as with the other diets, you build your plan around *protein*. You should aim at getting right around your daily protein requirement, or a little higher, every day. Don't drop below your protein requirement, but unlike on the Basic Low Carb Diet, it is recommended that you don't exceed this amount by a whole lot, either. Your protein should be divided up between at least three meals a day — more, if you like — but you should always get *at least* 14 grams of protein for breakfast, and 21 isn't excessive. (Why not 15-20 grams? Because an egg or an ounce of meat has about 7 grams of protein, of course! So we're talking two or three eggs, or two or three ounces of meat or cheese, or any combination thereof.)

Once you've had your breakfast, don't eat again until you're hungry! And only eat when you're actually hungry, rather than because it's "time to eat", or you're bored, or there's food in front of you. But when you're hungry, eat! Just make sure that when you do, *you include some of your protein ration for the day each time.*

You may have all the low carb vegetables you like, and moderate quantities of "borderline" vegetables — see the list in the Game Rules.

Fat intake should be moderate, but not restricted. What do I mean by that? I mean that it's okay to eat the fats that come as part of protein foods — meat and eggs and chicken skin — but that you should use separated fats — oil, butter, mayonnaise, sour cream, heavy cream — in modest quantities. A tablespoon of oil on your salad, a teaspoon or two of butter to fry your eggs, a dollop of mayo in your tuna fish, or a splash of cream in your coffee, fine. Just don't go nuts. It's also probably best to choose leaner meats rather than fattier ones.

It's also wise to use cheese and nuts in moderation. This is, again, a hybrid diet — some carb control, some calorie control — and cheese and nuts are *very* calorically dense. And if you're like

You may, if you like, choose reduced fat products IF — and this is a big "if" — they aren't loaded with sugars, starches, and chemicals.

me, it's easy to go through 500 calories worth of nuts without even thinking about it! It's a good idea to buy your nuts and seeds in the shell — if you have to crack each one to eat it, it's hard to go too far overboard.

You may, if you like, choose reduced fat products *IF* — and this is a big "if" — they aren't loaded with sugars, starches, and chemicals. For example, reduced fat cheeses will probably be okay, but most low fat salad dressings most definitely are not. Remember that list of ingredients in the fat-free Ranch dressing! Those fat-free salad dressings are mostly sugar.

Don't assume that you can substitute any old carbs for the ones on the list; you'll end up in trouble as sure as you're born.

On the other hand, remember that your body needs healthy fats! Don't be afraid to use a little olive oil, avocados, fatty fish. Believe it or not, there are fats that are essential to fat burning!! Don't make this into a low fat diet. It's a *moderate* fat diet.

Now, for those carbs. On *The Careful Carb Diet*, you may have 1 to 3 *small* servings of low impact carbs a day. Choose them from the list provided. You *must always* eat your carbs in the context of a meal, with protein. If you try eating 3 servings of low impact carbs a day, and don't lose weight, try cutting back to 1 or 2. If that still doesn't work for you — and remember, this is too much carb for my own personal body — you'll do better to try the Basic Low Carbohydrate Diet, instead.

If you include one of the low impact carbs with a meal, and you're hungry and/or tired within 90 minutes or so, that particular carb isn't good for you. Try a different one and see how you react. And don't assume that you can substitute any old carbs for the ones on the list; you'll end up in trouble as sure as you're born. There's a *huge* difference between 100% whole grain rye bread from the health food store and commercial rye bread from the grocery store — the commercial kind is mostly "enriched" white flour, and will spike your blood sugar just like white bread does. If you don't know for *sure* that a carb food has a low impact, *don't eat it!*

It is HIGHLY RECOMMENDED that you choose sweet carbs, *fruit included*, no more than once a day, and less is better. Despite the fact that fructose — fruit sugar — has a low glycemic index, it still has some not-so-great effects. It can cause high triglycerides, and some researchers feel that it stimulates fat formation more than any other kind of sugar. If you want more fruit than that, try cantaloupe, honeydew, strawberries, or raspberries, all of which are very low in total carbohydrates.

As you can see, this is the closest of any of these diets to being the traditional "balanced diet". Enough protein, probably more than you're used to eating, will give you energy and fill you up. The carbs that are allowed shouldn't trigger severe blood sugar swings, with their hunger and cravings and fatigue. Your insulin levels should stay moderate, though not as low as on the Basic Low Carb Diet. And you'll be getting enough fat to make you feel satisfied, and provide the essential fatty acids your body needs.

Interestingly, since I came up with this diet for Rob almost a year ago, Dr. Bob Arnot (medical dude for NBC News) has come out with his *Revolutionary Weight Control Program*, which focuses on lean proteins and low impact carbs! Not that far from the *Careful Carb Diet*. I have a few differences with Dr. Arnot — he feels that we should eat a fairly large amount of these low impact carbs, especially beans. He also feels that we should avoid egg yolks and red meat and such, and that fat intake should be quite low — it's as if he's straddling two paradigms.

Personally, I'm convinced that for the vast majority natural, unprocessed fats are harmless in moderate amounts, that for most of us the yolk is the most nutritious part of the egg (not to mention the tastiest!), and, most importantly, that grains and beans are relative newcomers to the human diet, and that their safety in large quantity is highly suspect. But I see Dr. Arnot's diet as a big step in the right direction for the low fat folks!

Game Rules for the Careful Carb Diet

1) You must consume your minimum protein requirement every day!
   Allowed proteins include meat, fish, poultry, eggs and egg substitutes, tofu, tempeh, sugar-free protein powder, brewer's or nutritional yeast. Eat a *minimum* of 14 grams of protein at breakfast. You *must* have protein at every meal, and you may divide your protein up so that you have snacks too, if you like. Leaner proteins are better than fattier proteins — with the exception of fatty fishes, such as salmon, mackerel, herring, and sardines, which are wonderful! Do not exceed your protein requirement by more than 20 grams a day.

2) Eat healthy fats in moderation, but do not use excessive quantities of added fat, or of very high fat foods, such as nuts and cheeses. A tablespoon or two of mayonnaise or olive oil is okay, a half a cup is not!

3) *Eat low carbohydrate vegetables freely;* the more the better.

LOW CARB VEGGIES ARE:

Alfalfa sprouts	Endive
Artichokes	Escarole
Arugula	Kale
Asparagus	Lettuce, all kinds
Avocado	Mushrooms
Beans—green,	Okra
wax, and snap	Olives
Beet greens	Peppers
Bok Choy	Pumpkin
Broccoli	Radishes
Brussels sprouts	Sauerkraut
Cabbage	Spinach
Cauliflower	Summer squashes
Celery	— zucchini, crookneck
Chicory	Turnip greens
Cucumber	Water Cress
Eggplant	

4) Eat melons, berries, and borderline vegetables in moderation. Borderline vegetables are onions, garlic, rutabaga, beets, turnips, tomatoes. As a guideline, not more than a half a large onion, or one large tomato, or a couple of cloves of garlic at a meal.

5) Eat between 1 and 3 servings of the allowed Low Impact Carbohydrate foods per day. Start with two servings per day, and see how your hunger and your weight react. If you're doing great, you may add one serving per day. If you're not losing, and/or you're still hungry, drop one serving a day. If you still have trouble, you may be so severely carbohydrate intolerant that you'd do better on the Basic Low Carb Diet. Low Impact Carbs *must* be eaten in combination with proteins, *not* by themselves. DO NOT eat *any* other concentrated carbohydrate foods!

LOW IMPACT CARBS

Grains and other Starches

- Whole grain barley (cook and use like rice) 1/2 - 3/4 cup
- Steel cut oats (NOT rolled oats) 1/2 - 3/4 cup
- Protein enriched pasta (Contadina makes a good one) 1/2 - 3/4 cup
- DeBoles Jerusalem artichoke pasta 1/2 - 3/4 cup
- Whole wheat pasta 1/2 - 3/4 cup
- 100% whole grain rye bread (no sugar, corn syrup, or honey added — available at health food stores) 1 small slice
- Whole wheat pita (no sugar, corn syrup, or honey added — many grocery stores have this) 1/2 round loaf
- Yam or sweet potato 1 small
- Peas 1/2 - 3/4 cup
- Kidney beans 1/2 - 3/4 cup
- Navy beans 1/2 - 3/4 cup
- Butter beans 1/2 - 3/4 cup
- Chick peas 1/2 - 3/4 cup
- Lentils 1/2 - 3/4 cup
- Black beans 1/2 - 3/4 cup
  (oh, heck, all the dried beans except limas) DO NOT eat canned baked beans or pork and beans — they're loaded with sugar!!
- Hummus 1/2 cup
- Winter squash (butternut, acorn, hubbard, spaghetti) 1/2 - 3/4 cup
- All Bran, Fiber One, and other spaghetti-shaped bran cereals
- Split pea, lentil, or bean soup 3/4 - 1 cup
- Chili with beans (no sugar, corn syrup or honey added) 3/4 - 1 cup
- Hominy 1/2 cup
- Brown rice 1/2 - 3/4 cup

Fruits
You already know the low carb fruits
— berries, cantaloupe, honeydew

Most other fruits may not be very low in carbohydrates, but have a fairly low impact on blood sugar. Exceptions are kiwi, bananas, pineapple, raisins, grapes, watermelon. Consider all other fruits to be an okay Low Impact Carb choice. DO NOT EXCEED TWO FRUITS A DAY.

Other Low Impact Carbs

- Milk (1 cup)
- Tomato soup (1 cup)
- Super premium ice cream (Hagen Daaz, etc)
  NO CHUNKY VARIETIES
- Sugar-free or plain yogurt (Sugar-free has aspartame)
- Peanut M&Ms
- Snickers
- All-fruit type jam or jelly

It is HIGHLY RECOMMENDED that you do NOT make all of your Low Impact Carb choices from the sweet carbs — i.e., ice cream, M&Ms, Snickers, and fruit. This is NOT a license to eat these things in an uncontrolled fashion!!

6) Permitted beverages include tea, coffee, unsweetened sparkling waters, both plain and flavored, sugar-free soda, sugar-free fruit drinks, herb tea.

7) You may have a glass of dry wine or a light beer with dinner. Read labels on light beers and look for one with 4 g of carb or less per can — some "light" beers have as many as 9 g per can! Be aware that for some people, alcohol will prevent weight loss, and pay attention to your body. If you're not losing, you may need to trade one of your Low Impact Carbs for your drink, or abstain from alcohol altogether.

8) Avoid eating for entertainment! If you've had your breakfast at 7:30, and you're not hungry at noon, wait till you are hungry!

The Low Carb Liquid Semi-Fast

A perennially popular approach to dieting is the replacement of meals with "diet shakes". From Metrecal and Slender in the '60s to Ultra Slim Fast today, many dieters like the idea of simply drinking most of their meals, partly for convenience's sake, partly for the easy portion control it offers, and partly because it lets them have something sweet for several meals a day!

Unfortunately, most of the diet shakes on the market today are as bad as they are over-advertised. The most highly advertised brand — *you* know which one — proudly crows that their shake provides "energy from carbohydrates", which is a sneaky way of saying that the stuff is simply *loaded* with sugar. You might just as well drink a fast food shake and take a vitamin pill! *(Don't you dare!!)* If you're carb intolerant, ongoing use of these shakes can lead you into a nasty downward spiral, blood sugar crashing harder and harder, energy going lower and lower, getting more irritable by the day. And of course, all your insulin-based health problems will be getting worse. Not good.

There's only one pre-packaged diet shake that I know of that's really very low carb — Dr. Atkins markets it. I haven't tried it, because it costs $30 for a can of the mix, but I'm sure it's fine. There are also *Zone*-inspired 30-30-40 shakes available (also 30-30-40 bars). I still find them pretty expensive, and they have more added sugar than I want.

 **Most of the diet shakes on the market today are as bad as they are over-advertised.**

But you don't need a pre-packaged shake. Anyone who has a blender can make a diet shake! Dr. Michael Eades, of *Protein Power* fame, wrote a book in 1989 called *Thin So Fast*, in which he details a low carbohydrate diet in which one drinks homemade low carb shakes three times a day, and eats a low carb meal of real food for dinner. His formula for the shakes calls for instant powdered milk, protein powder, a tiny amount of fructose, and some "lite salt" for the potassium. One combines these ingredients, then mixes them with diet pop, sugar-free Kool-Aid, Crystal Light, whatever. I believe *Thin So Fast* is out of print, but any public library should be able to get it for you through Inter-Library Loan, if you'd like to read it.

But as I've mentioned elsewhere, I'm a bit iffy about Nutrasweet (aspartame). I don't drink soda, Kool-Aid, or Crystal Light, almost at all. I wanted a shake that didn't have artificial stuff in it.

Luckily, there's a completely natural carbohydrate-and-calorie-free sweetener available. It's called *stevia*, and it's an extract from the leaf of a Brazilian shrub. The Brazilian natives have used stevia leaves as a sweetener *forever*, and in Japan, everything that's sweetened with aspartame here, is sweetened with stevia instead. You can't buy food that's pre-sweetened with stevia in the USA, but you can buy stevia itself, and use it in things. The best form is a white extracted powder, of

Luckily, there's a completely natural carbohydrate-and-calorie-free sweetener available. It's called stevia.

which you use only very tiny quantities at a time. I pay $85.99/lb. for stevia in bulk at my health food store, which sounds alarming, but isn't. Since you use such tiny quantities, you don't need anything like a pound of the stuff!! I bought a small jar for four or five bucks, and it's lasted for months. So it's not expensive to use.

There's another odd ingredient that is optional in this recipe: guar gum. What the heck is guar gum? Sounds icky! Actually, guar is in lots of your favorite processed junk foods, so how horrible can it be? Guar is a kind of fiber extracted from beans, and it adds a nice thickness to the shake without altering the flavor at all. Like stevia, guar is used in tiny little quantities. The first time I experimented with guar, I did a one-for-one substitution for cornstarch — and it grabbed the spoon right out of my hand! I could have used the stuff to surface roads! I learned but *fast* to use guar sparingly, and used that way it's very helpful in replacing high carb thickeners in our diet. I bought a 1 lb bag of guar gum powder at a health food store over 10 years ago, and I haven't used it up yet — so again, this is not an expensive ingredient to use, and it makes the shakes nice and thick and creamy.

Here's the recipe for your

BASIC SUGAR-FREE PROTEIN SHAKE
- 1/3 cup instant dry skim milk
- 2 heaping tablespoons protein powder, or more if desired. (This must be a protein powder with *no carbohydrates*. I recommend unflavored, or if you like, vanilla — which blends nicely with most other flavors.)
- 1 teaspoon cold pressed safflower oil. (DON'T substitute inexpensive oil from the grocery; the label should read either "cold pressed" or "expeller pressed". Hain brand is good, and has a very mild flavor. Store this in the refrigerator! You can leave out the oil if you add lecithin, flax seeds, or peanut butter.)
- 1/4 teaspoon white stevia extract powder, or more or less to taste. If you prefer, you can use artificial sweeteners.
- 3/4 - 1 cup cold water
- 3 - 5 ice cubes
- 1/4 teaspoon guar gum (optional, but gives a thicker texture; available at health food stores)

Then you choose a flavoring. My favorite is a rounded tablespoon of unsweetened cocoa powder, plus a little instant coffee. My

> **Lecithin is quite nutritious, good for your nerves, brain and skin, and for lowering cholesterol — and has a reputation for helping even out fat distribution on your body and improving fat burning.**

husband likes a heaping tablespoon of natural peanut butter, plus a little vanilla in his — but keep in mind that this adds both a few carbs and substantial calories. If you're drinking two or three shakes a day, better go easy on the peanut butter. Berries are great in a shake — strawberries, raspberries, blueberries, whatever. Use about a half-cupful. Again, this adds a few carbs — but also adds fiber and some potassium. Chocolate raspberry or chocolate strawberry are both wonderful! You might like a coffee shake — just add instant coffee powder, either regular or decaf, to taste — start with a scant teaspoonful, then taste. If you like vanilla best, and didn't buy vanilla protein powder, add at least a good teaspoon of real vanilla extract. You can make a vanilla shake taste richer by adding a smidge of salt, too, and a little cinnamon or nutmeg might be nice!

Of course, your grocery store offers scads of flavorings and extracts for you to play around with. How about adding a drop of mint extract to a chocolate shake to get chocolate mint? Or how about rum extract? Orange? Almond? No need to get bored — but to be honest, I usually make good old chocolate!

You can, if you like, add extra nutritional ingredients to your shake; I often do. For instance, I usually add *lecithin*. This is a substance found in egg yolks and soybeans that is used as an *emulsifier* — that is, to make oil and water combine. It's the lecithin in egg yolk that makes mayonnaise and hollandaise sauce thicken and hold together. Lecithin is also what makes non-stick cooking spray work. Lecithin is quite nutritious, good for your nerves, brain and skin, and for lowering cholesterol — and has a reputation for helping even out fat distribution on your body and improving fat burning. Whether this last is true, I have no concrete evidence, but I know it's good for me, and it improves the texture of the shake — makes it very creamy

— without changing the flavor, so I usually add a big tablespoon of the stuff. By the way, you'll find lecithin at your health food store, in liquid, capsules, or granules. The granules are what you want for shakes — the liquid is as thick as 40-weight on a January day. Store 'em in the frig.

Another thing I sometimes add is *bee pollen*. This is, of course, the male reproductive part of flowers, and is *loaded* with vitamins, minerals, protein, enzymes, phytonutrients and such. It has a little carb in it, but so much nutrition that it seems worth it to me. Don't buy dried bee pollen, or tablets — look for a store that sells fresh bee pollen granules, and stores them in the cooler. Unlike lecithin and guar, bee pollen does have a flavor — but the flavor is just sort of mildly sweet and flowery. I use maybe a heaping teaspoon per shake. And of course, if you have a severe pollen allergy, you'd want to be very, very careful if you tried pollen, right? (Some people claim that eating bee pollen, starting with just a grain or two, will build up an immunity and get rid of the allergy. I have no idea if this is true or not. I'd be *very* careful. Or just leave it out altogether.)

Flax seeds are an excellent source of the same healthy fats you get in fish. They can help with inflammation and pain, lower cholesterol and blood pressure, and there's some evidence that they help with fat burning.

You can also add flax seeds to a shake! These will add thickness — they're *loaded* with fiber — and also will add very healthy oil. Flax seeds are an excellent source of the same healthy fats you get in fish. They can help with inflammation and pain, lower cholesterol and blood pressure, and there's some evidence that they help with fat burning. Of course, the fiber will help with any irregularity you might have. Flax seeds will grind up in the shake; I haven't noticed that they hurt the flavor much. Up to you! I'd use about a tablespoon.

Then there's two things I sometimes add a tiny amount of — I add them because they're very, very nutritious, but I add tiny amounts because they taste *godawful*. I wouldn't mind at all if you left them out, but I often add just a scant teaspoon of nutritional yeast (loaded with B vitamins and minerals and protein), and maybe an eighth of a

Be aware that the vast majority of soy milks have sugar added in the form of barley malt syrup or rice syrup, both of which have a much higher impact on blood sugar than the lactose in milk.

teaspoon of spirulina, a very nutritious algae. Both of these are available at health food stores, but if you have really sensitive tastebuds, these may not be for you.

Anyway, put the water in the blender *first* — this will help prevent the dry ingredients from caking at the bottom. Then add all your dry ingredients, your flavorings, extra nutrition stuff, etc. Turn on the blender, and drop in the ice cubes, one at a time. I like to let mine whip at high speed for a few minutes; makes it pretty thick. Speaking of which, people often ask if they can just use a cup of fluid skim milk instead, and the answer is yes, but the powdered skim whips up better for some strange reason. I think it's a lot better. It's cheaper, too, and easier to store.

You could also use soy milk, if you're lactose intolerant, or avoiding milk for some other reason. If you choose to do this, be aware that the vast majority of soy milks have sugar added in the form of barley malt syrup or rice syrup, both of which have a *much* higher impact on blood sugar than the lactose in milk. You'll need to look for soy milk with no sugar added. There are a few on the market; read the labels carefully. I've tried this stuff, and I find it unappealing; kinda chalky and beany. However, the no-sugar-added soy milk has only a third of the carbs of milk, so I often use half soy milk, half powdered skim milk, which is okay. I like the taste better with all powdered skim, though — which I use depends on whether I'm more concerned that day with flavor, or keeping my carb intake as low as I can.

Depending on what you use to flavor the shake, it will have somewhere in the neighborhood of 15 to 20 grams of carbohydrate, most of it from the milk. Fortunately, lactose has a fairly modest impact on blood sugar levels, and shouldn't cause a major crash. So long as you're not terribly carb sensitive, and keep your intake of carbs from other sources very low, this shouldn't be a problem. Depending on your protein powder, your shake should have 25-35 grams of protein, enough to keep you going for *hours*. And unless you use peanut butter or another high-fat flavoring, it will be quite low in calories, too. (Still, peanut oil is a healthy fat — if you like peanut butter shakes, use natural peanut butter, not Skippy or Jif, which have hydrogenated oil and sugar in them! — and if using peanut butter in your shake fills you up for longer, and you need one less shake a day, then you can have a *few* more carbs with your dinner!)

You can use one of these shakes as an occasional meal replacement, if you like. I drink them for lunch fairly often. If you're on the Basic Low Carb Diet, you'll have to subtract the carbohydrate grams from some other meal, of course. The shakes don't really fit into the Mini-Binge Program, since they aren't low carb enough for a low carb meal, and why would you have one at your Reward Meal?

If you're one of those folks who just can't handle cooked food in the morning, a shake is perfect for you! You can even drink it in the car. Hey, make a coffee shake and you won't even have to slow down to drink your coffee!

A good use of shakes is for breakfast. If you're one of those folks who just can't handle cooked food in the morning, a shake is perfect for you! And if you put all the stuff (except the ice cubes, of course) in the blender jar the night before, and store it overnight in the refrigerator, you can then throw in the ice, turn on the blender, go brush your hair or throw on your clothes, and breakfast will be ready to go. You can even drink it in the car. Hey, make a coffee shake and you won't even have to slow down to drink your coffee!

If you're one of the minority who have the 50/50 cholesterol reaction to low carbing that I mentioned earlier — your triglycerides go down and your HDL goes up, which is good, but your LDL goes up too, which is bad — shakes can be a very good idea for you. Soy is often effective for lowering LDL, and flax seeds are excellent for improving blood values, so if you use a soy-based protein powder and add some flax seed, for its heart-healthy fats and fiber, and a heaping tablespoon of lecithin, for its cholesterol-dissolving properties, a shake a day can be a *big* part of the solution.

But the real value of the shakes is this: If you like a simple, shake-based diet because it's a no-brainer, you can drink two or three of these shakes during the day, and you'll feel full, have high energy, and be getting both reasonably low carbs *and* low calories — again, a hybrid diet — and, depending on what extras you add, a *ton* of nutrition as well. (You can take a shake to work in a thermos for lunch, of course. Shake it up well before you open the thermos.) Then — and this is *essential* — for dinner you *must* have a low carb dinner of *both* meat, fish, poultry or eggs, *and* plenty of low carb vegetables. This is to supply the nutrients that are missing from the shake. Since you're getting a fair amount of low impact carbs in the shake, keep your dinner very low carb, okay?

Since you're not eating as much "real food" on this program, you should be very careful to take your vitamins, and also to take a potassium supplement, unless you have the health problems I mentioned in chapter 8.

Chapter Fourteen
Wrapping It Up

So there's the diets. And now that you've read through them all, you should have a pretty good grip of the basics of low carb dieting: Get enough protein, eat only healthy fats, treat carbohydrates with *extreme* caution. You'll want to choose one of these approaches and try it for a few weeks or months, and see how it fits *you* — your personality, your body, your lifestyle. If one doesn't fit you quite right, try another! That's why I haven't given you a one-size-fits-all diet plan — I want you to find the path that's right for you; the Way Of Eating that will see you through a healthy lifetime.

Further, there's no reason you can't mix and match to find what's best for you, so long as you're *very* careful about keeping your carb load low. For instance, you could try doing a Mini-Binge approach where you only ate Low Impact carbs at your Reward Meal, for a

I haven't given you a one-size-fits-all diet plan — I want you to find the path that's right for you; the Way Of Eating that will see you through a healthy lifetime.

faster weight loss and better control of your hunger, and faster improvement of your bloodwork. If you entertain a lot on the weekends, and want to be able to eat all the foods you cook for others, you could do the Basic Low Carb Diet or the Liquid Semi-Fast during

The vast majority of Americans would dramatically improve their health, sense of well being, appearance, and waistlines if they simply quit eating anything with refined, processed, valueless carbohydrates — sugar and corn syrup, white flour products, cold cereals, all that garbage — and made sure they got enough protein at every meal.

the week, and then switch to a Mini-Binge diet on the weekends — or you could serve only Low Impact carbs at your dinner parties! You could do a Cyclic Ketogenic Diet where you used only Low Impact carbs during your carb-up. You could do a Cyclic Ketogenic Diet where you only do a carb-up when you stop going into ketosis easily, then carb up for three or four days before heading back into ketosis for another month or two. Or, as I do, you could do a Basic Low Carb Diet most of the year, and switch over to a Paleolithic Diet when the fruit is ripe in the summer, to sneak in a few more cherries and nectarines.

Something you should absolutely *not* do is combine the Careful Carb Diet with the Mini-Binge Diet — eating snacks and Low Impact Carbs all day, and then having a Reward Meal with lots more carbs — even High Impact Carbs — once a day. You'll be sorry if you do! And if you're eating the Mini-Binge diet, you don't ever get to do the 12-to-24-hour carb-up from the Cyclic Ketogenic diet, either!! You may be able to fool yourself, but you can't fool your body.

That being said, the vast majority of Americans would *dramatically* improve their health, sense of well being, appearance, and waistlines if they simply quit eating anything with refined, processed, valueless carbohydrates — sugar and corn syrup, white flour products, cold cereals, all that garbage — and made sure they got enough protein at every meal.

The point is, I want you to understand the principles, so you have tools to work with. With all these different approaches, I think you have those tools.

In review, here's a quick rundown of the basics of taming your runaway insulin and losing weight permanently:

• **Be afraid — be VERY afraid!** — of added sugar in all forms: sugar, corn syrup, malt syrup, fruit juice concentrate, honey, molasses, brown sugar, maple syrup, Sucanat, turbinado, fructose, dextrose, maltose, or anything else ending in -ose. **THERE IS NO SUCH THING AS "GOOD SUGAR"**. (*Many* products labeled "No sugar added" have honey, fruit juice, or malt syrup. These are sugar!!) Be wary even of the natural sugars in fruits. Remember: If it tastes even a little bit sweet, and it isn't artificially sweetened, it's got some kind of sugar! Also, be aware that some "sugar-free" products are made with "sugar alcohols", such as sorbitol, mannitol, and xylitol. These *are* carbohydrates.

• Avoid grains, including bread, crackers, rice, pasta, cereal, pizza crust, biscuits, muffins, etc.
    Avoid dried beans and other starchy legumes, and starchy or sugary vegetables, such as potatoes, corn, peas, and carrots. IF YOU WISH TO BREAK THIS RULE, IT IS BEST TO EAT THE LEAST PROCESSED, HIGHEST FIBER, HIGHEST NUTRIENT CARBOHYDRATES THAT YOU CAN. Coarsely ground whole grain rye bread, steel cut oats, and homemade black bean soup will cause you far less harm than white flour bagels, sugary cold cereal, and (corn syrup-laced) canned pork and beans. We won't even *talk* about rubbish like marshmallow squares and fake canned biscuits.

• The more strictly you are willing to cut out carbohydrates, the less you will have to concern yourself with portion control or calories. If you wish to keep some of the less damaging carbs in your diet, you may well have to control portions and/or limit calories as well. There are some hard choices to be made here; make them with your eyes wide open!

• Eat plenty of unprocessed, carb-free protein foods. Eat protein at every meal. If you choose to eat a carbohydrate food, eat protein with it. Protein is the cornerstone of your diet; all other foods are secondary. Eating your protein will increase your metabolism, and keep you feeling full and energetic longer than any other kind of food.

• Eat only fresh, unprocessed, natural fats. Don't use polyunsaturated oils for cooking — safflower, soy, corn, sunflower, etc.; they break down rapidly and become unhealthy when heated. Olive, canola, and peanut oils are all right for cooking, as are butter and fresh meat fats (chicken fat, pork fat — don't use purchased lard; it's heavily processed and hydrogenated). Do not eat margarine, vegetable shortening, or other "hydrogenated" fats.

• Get plenty of high fiber, low carb foods, especially low carb vegetables. Nuts and seeds are excellent foods, high in fiber, protein, minerals, and valuable fats, but they are also very high in calories, so eat them with at least a bit of restraint. With almost all of these plant foods, raw or only lightly cooked is best.

• Eat a high protein breakfast every day. If you're not hungry when you get up, take some protein food to work with you, to eat in the car or at your first break. And stop eating so heavily at night! If you eat less at night, you'll wake up with an appetite. Why lay in a bunch of food just before going to sleep?

• Drink plenty of water!

• Learn to listen to your hunger, which on a low carb diet you should be able to trust. I didn't say this elsewhere, but it's important to point out: Americans have been trained to munch mindlessly for hours on carb-y junk food that never fills them up, what I call the "hand-to-mouth routine". There's very little in the way of low carb food that you can do this with, for the very simple reason that low carb foods are *filling*. The big exception, of course, is low carb vegetables, which you may munch on to your heart's content. Other "entertainment" foods are sunflower seeds or pumpkin seeds in the shell — because you have to crack each shell, and each kernel is so small, it's hard to eat too many. (I sneak sunflower seeds into the movies with me!) Pork rinds are no-carb — unless you get them barbeque style or with other flavors; READ THE LABEL — and mostly air, so you can munch on these, too. (Personally, I reach my pork rind limit after about four. But some people adore the things.)

If you try to eat most low carb foods — meat, cheese, nuts, eggs — endlessly, you'll make yourself sick to your stomach! A sugar-junkie was at my house one day, uninvited, and wanted me to feed her lunch when I was busy. I threw her a bag of nut and seed mix. That afternoon, she complained of being nauseated. When I picked up the bag of nut and seed mix later on, and discovered she'd eaten well over a *pound* of the stuff, I understood why she felt sick! Again, learn to listen to your hunger.

• Read the labels on *everything* you put into your body. Most people do far more research before buying a car or a VCR than they do on what they put into their own bodies. **"You are what you eat" is literally true — all your body has to make itself from is what you put in your mouth. If you give your body junk, you'll be made out of junk, and you'll feel and look like it.**

• Make the best choice possible given any particular circumstance. What do I mean? If you're at work, and the vending machine has cookies, crackers, chips, candy and peanuts, the peanuts are the best choice, even if they're not completely carb-free. When you're genuinely hungry, and faced with foods which are not ideal for the diet, choose the food that will screw you up the least — and don't be afraid to pick off breading, eat only the cheese and toppings off the pizza, etc.

• Buy a food counter book, one which lists not only carbohydrates and calories, but also fiber, so you can subtract the grams of fiber from the grams of carbohydrate. If you're not absolutely certain that a food is low in carbs, LOOK IT UP!!

• Take a high-quality, broad-spectrum multiple vitamin and mineral supplement every day. This should be a supplement that requires that you take more than one tablet a day — 6 is not excessive, depending on how big or small a tablet you can swallow.

Don't Become Dependent on the Scale!

One other tip — don't become too dependent on your scale. Yes, we've been talking all along about "weight loss", but now might be an appropriate time to mention that actually, weighing yourself is a pretty lame way to determine how fat you are. Why? Because a scale weighs all of you, fat and muscle, bones and blood and skin and hair. How do you know what part of you is getting heavier or lighter?

To put it another way, if you wanted to buy the leanest steak in the grocery store, you wouldn't just pick the lightest one, would you? Of course not.

A scale weighs all of you, fat and muscle, bones and blood and skin and hair. How do you know what part of you is getting heavier or lighter?

Or, think of it this way: Arnold Schwartzenegger is *far* heavier than average for his height. Do you think he's fat? For that matter, I still weigh fairly heavy for a woman of my height and percent body fat, largely because I'm quite muscular, and muscle weighs much more than fat. (For this very reason, you may gain a pound or two if you start working out. Don't panic; you're exchanging fat for muscle, a good bargain no matter how you look at it!)

So use your scale, but don't consider it the ultimate judge of how fat or slim you are, or whether you're losing fat. Here's a better way: Most of us have on hand some piece of clothing that doesn't fit us anymore — something we've kept, hoping to fit back into it some-day. Jeans are probably the best. Try on that too-small pair of jeans, or dress, or whatever. Then try it on again each week as you diet. See how much closer you are to being able to fasten it. At first, the zipper may be 5 inches apart in front. Then four inches. Then three. One day, you can fasten the button! Pretty exciting.

Or, you can use a belt, and see where it fastens each week — if you use an old one, you can mark it with a magic marker to show your progress. Or you can be truly revolutionary, and use a tape measure!

❖ ❖

Use your scale, but don't consider it the ultimate judge of how fat or slim you are, or whether you're losing fat.

❖ ❖

It's not uncommon, by the way, for inch loss to occur even when weight loss does not. In fact, I've talked with a few low carbers who find that when they're losing pounds, their size stays pretty much the same. Then their weight will plateau for a week or so, but they'll be losing inches all the while. Odd, but true.

It's not uncommon, by the way, for inch loss to occur even when weight loss does not. Pay attention to what size you are, in addition to what you weigh. It's a far more accurate way to gauge your progress.

In any case, pay attention to what *size* you are, in addition to what you *weigh*. It's a far more accurate way to gauge your progress.

Chapter Fifteen

Odds and Ends

Now, let's talk about a very important subject:

CHEATING!

I'm not naive. I know you're going to cheat! It's a-gonna happen. You know it, I know it. So let's talk about it here and now! After all, a good offense is the best defense.

In fact, I *plan* to cheat — and that's what I want you to do. I don't even call it cheating — I call it an "Indulgence".

I like this term far better, because the word "cheating" implies that you're going to get away with something. I remember my father coming into the kitchen an hour after dinner and eating ice cream out of the container — he'd get this look on his face that screamed "Aren't I a cute, mischievous little boy? Look what I'm getting away with!" But he didn't get away with a thing.

A good offense is the best defense.

He was fat. And he was hospitalized with heart disease at the age of 55. *There is no cheating; you can't fool your body. You don't get away with a thing.*

 There is no cheating; you can't fool your body. You don't get away with a thing. So don't even try to cheat. Plan to Indulge, instead. Then you have the power!

So don't even try to cheat. Plan to Indulge, instead. Then *you* have the power!

How often do I have an Indulgence? Not as often as you might think! As I write this sentence, it is mid-June — and I haven't had a dessert (except for low carb ones) since February. Pretty good, huh? But I've reached this level after *three years* of low carbing. I'm not deliberately being good; I've just reached a blessed state of not caring about carbohydrate foods! In fact, I went to a huge wedding over Memorial Day weekend, and had every intention of eating a dessert at the reception. They had a fabulous sweet table, so there were all kinds of choices — but I was way too busy dancing to slow myself down with sugar. I just never got around to it. If you had asked me as a kid if I would ever be having too good a time to get around to eating sugar, I would have thought you were nuts!

You're not at that point yet. So think ahead — what are the times when it will really, I mean *really*, be important to you to eat carbs? The holidays spring to mind — I eat whatever I want on Thanksgiving Day and Christmas Day. And I expect you to do the same! You might want to add your birthday to the list of Indulgence Days. How about your anniversary? Give yourself between five and eight occasions during the year — and they don't have to be fixed occasions like holidays. If you're going to a party and you know the host is a

* *

If you had asked me as a kid if I would ever be having too good a time to get around to eating sugar, I would have thought you were nuts!

* *

marvelous cook, you might choose to make that one of your Indulgences. Or maybe you're going on vacation and know that you'll be visiting a five-star restaurant — Indulgence time!

BUT! Remember there is *danger* here! I spoke to small club of low carb dieters in my town, and one woman said she *had* to eat cake that night because it was her daughter's birthday. It is all very well to decide that *your* birthday is an Indulgence Day. It is quite another thing to decide that *everyone's* birthday is an Indulgence Day! If you have an Indulgence on your birthday, your husband's birthday, your mother's birthday, your father's birthday, your sister's birthday, your brother's birthday, each of your kids' birthdays, your office mates' birthdays, you're not having an Indulgence, you're fooling yourself. And you'll stay fat, tired and sick.

It is all very well to decide that your birthday is an Indulgence Day. It is quite another thing to decide that everyone's birthday is an Indulgence Day!

Likewise, there is a HUGE difference between deciding that on Thanksgiving Day and Christmas Day you may have an Indulgence, and deciding that "It's the Holiday Season", so you can make like a Hoover at all the holiday parties and cookie exchanges for the whole month from Thanksgiving till Christmas. If you do that, you'll be shopping the post-Christmas sales for new clothes in a larger size!

Beware the lesser holidays! If you have an Indulgence every time Hallmark comes out with new cards, you'll never get there! Groundhog Day, St. Patrick's Day, Columbus Day — these don't count! And it's one thing to have chocolate on Valentine's Day, if you've chosen that for an Indulgence day. It's another thing to sweet-talk your honey out of a five pound *box* of chocolates, and nosh on them for a few days. Okay?

So pick and choose your Indulgences, and NEVER HAVE AN UNPLANNED INDULGENCE. If you're confronted with a carb food and you haven't planned an Indulgence, leave it alone!

Let me make another suggestion about Indulgences: Think hard to yourself about which carbohydrate foods *really* matter to you. For instance, at our traditional family Thanksgiving dinner, the carbohydrate foods include mashed potatoes, stuffing, candied sweet potatoes, creamed onions (flour in the cream sauce), gravy (again, flour as a thickener), cranberry sauce, banana-nut bread, oatmeal-molasses bread, pumpkin pie, and apple pie. Quite a list! But which of those foods do I *really* care about?

> **Decide which carb foods really matter to you, and only eat those carbs.**

I couldn't care less about candied sweet potatoes, creamed onions, banana-nut bread, or pumpkin pie. Accordingly, I don't eat those things at all. Mashed potatoes are okay, I only have a little — maybe a spoonful.

But I *love* stuffing, especially with gravy, so I have a full-sized portion. I have a half-slice or so of mom's oatmeal-molasses bread, cranberry with my turkey, and apple pie for dessert. I only eat the carbs that are *truly desirable* to me. Your priorities will be different, but the process is the same: decide which carb foods really matter to you, and *only* eat those carbs.

This is a good strategy in general: Why eat anything that's *not* what you want? For instance, since I hadn't had a dessert at that wedding Memorial Day weekend, when I went to a terrific restaurant a couple weeks later I thought I might Indulge. But they only had fruit cobblers for dessert, and I really had my heart set on something chocolate. I passed on the Indulgence — and I still have one coming! I also am planning an Indulgence of Jalapeno Krunchers Potato Chips, the hottest and crunchiest potato chips on the planet. I haven't had them in over two years, and that's what I want at my next Indulgence. Don't know quite when I'll do it, yet, but sometime this summer for sure.

Another important thing to remember is that even at Indulgence meals, you *must* eat your *protein!* You are *never* excused from eating your protein. (Okay, if you have food poisoning or stomach flu, you're excused. But you won't be eating carbs, either!) For instance, on Christmas morning at my mom's house I eat a piece of her traditional coffee cake — but I also have a substantial serving of scrambled eggs and bacon. And at that Thanksgiving dinner we just passed I also have plenty of turkey and low carb vegetables, like green beans, plus I'll have had my usual eggs for breakfast, so I'm not hitting the dinner table ravenous. Eating your protein will take the edge off your hunger for the carbs, limiting how much of them you're likely to eat. Also, the protein will help soften any blood sugar crash, with subsequent cravings — making it much easier to go right back to low carbing the next meal or the next day.

This picking and choosing what to have for your Indulgence leads me to another thought: Don't let other people buffalo you into eating something high carb that isn't what you want. Diet saboteurs are everywhere; some of them well-meaning, some of them just plain malicious. They'll say things like, "Just a little taste won't hurt!" and "I made this just for you — you *have* to eat it!" But a little taste *can* hurt — it can unleash hunger and cravings, make you feel lousy and depressed, and add 5 pounds of water overnight. And unless you're a politician on the campaign trail, you don't *have* to eat anything you don't want to. Ever.

I've gotten to the point where I'm not even a little apologetic about this business of not eating stuff that's bad for me. No one else has to live with my fat, work through my mood and energy swings, pay my doctor bills, fight my cravings, or face my family history of heart disease and cancer. If people insist, I can get a little testy. One family member is a case in point: A couple of years back, we were going to visit this relative around my birthday. She decided to cook me a birthday dinner; very nice — except she asked my husband what I could and could not eat, and after being told I didn't eat sugar or starch, proceeded to serve me potatoes and ice cream cake. She was very hurt and angry that I simply would *not* eat them. But why should I give in to that kind of emotional blackmail? She knew in advance that I didn't eat sugar or starch; I can only see serving them to me as a deliberate act. Don't give in to this kind of thing; Indulgences are far too precious to waste on what other people think you should eat.

> **I've gotten to the point where I'm not even a little apologetic about this business of not eating stuff that's bad for me. No one else has to live with my fat, work through my mood and energy swings, pay my doctor bills, fight my cravings, or face my family history of heart disease and cancer.**

If someone — usually a family member — is genuinely trying to sabotage your diet, repeatedly, it may call for either strong action,

Indulgences are far too precious to waste on what other people think you should eat.

or serious sneakiness. This happens far more often than you would believe! In particular, spouses often feel very threatened when their partner starts to change their eating habits and lose weight. They may feel pressured to change themselves, or they may feel that if their spouse becomes more attractive, they'll have more options and leave. Either way, it can get ugly. In a low carb discussion on the Internet, a woman complained that her husband would deliberately open a box of chocolates and leave them next to her on the couch! Since this woman was not only dangerously obese, but also a diabetic, this was a very, very serious act. She chose to become sneaky; she'd keep a baggie in her pocket and slip a few chocolates into it so her husband would think she was eating them, then throw them away later.

Maybe you have that kind of willpower; many do not. Personally, faced with this situation, I would have asked *once*, nicely but firmly, that he stop trying to feed me candy. After that, the next time the box of chocolates appeared, I would have marched them to the bathroom and flushed them all down the toilet. After a few times of wasting his money on chocolates to feed the septic tank, I suspect the husband would have given up. In this situation I would also have insisted on marriage counseling, to try to understand the insecurity and hostility that would drive a husband to treat his wife in a way that quite literally threatened her life.

Now and then there's a situation where you're faced with days and days of temptation. For instance, one friend went on a two-week cruise, with hot-and-cold running food, and a fantastic dessert bar every night. In this situation, there's a few possibilities. One, you could decide that whatever program you've been doing up until then, for the interim you're on a Mini-Binge diet — and allow yourself to have that Indulgence once each day. If you're like me, you won't lose weight while doing this, but you shouldn't gain much, either. Another possibility would be to go on the *Careful Carb Diet*, and only eat plain super-premium ice cream from the dessert bar, as one of your carb servings for the day.

What if you *really* screw up? What if you walk into the office one day, and there's a big box of Dunkin' Donuts on the table, and despite the fact that you didn't plan any kind of Indulgence — after all,

STOP HATING YOURSELF!

Tuesday is hardly an occasion — you eat *three* of them. Now what?!

Well, first of all, *stop hating yourself!* This is not a moral issue here! I once had a low carb cyberpal tell me she'd been "bad" — and I told her that unless she'd eaten the neighbor's child, she might have been unwise, but she hadn't been *bad.*

And don't bother playing little games with the scale! We all do this — moving it around on the floor, standing on the outsides of our feet, whatever. It doesn't change your true weight one iota, and you know it. You need to know the bad news — or the good news! Be honest with yourself; it's the path to success.

Next, go eat some protein! It will modify the crash, and make it hurt less. And it *will* hurt, believe me!

Oh, I didn't warn you about that, did I? Yep, once you've been low carb for a few weeks, off the sugar, you'll find that you notice the drug-like effects of the stuff. You'll feel lousy, and you'll have a hangover! You'll wonder how you ever ate so much of that stuff, and each time you do it, it will become less and less appealing. Here's a quote from an email I got from Tina, who I taught to cut her carbs for energy — she titled the post "Walking Death!"

"BLAH!!! I have just managed to get off my couch for the second time in 24 hours. I got home yesterday at 1:30 pm from partying on Saturday night and have been like walking death ever since.

Dana, you didn't warn me that after having not consumed enormous amounts of sugar that I would get ill if I DID consume sugar again!"

I'm not making that mistake with you. Consider yourself warned! Once you've given up sugar and other nasty, blood sugar-wrecking carbs, you will feel anywhere from mildly hungover to downright

> **Be honest with yourself; it's the path to success.**

sick if you load up on them again. You'll also very likely find that the stuff just doesn't taste as good as you remembered. Most of the sweets I used to love now taste far, far too sweet to me, and I just can't eat them, even at an Indulgence.

And *that*, my friend, is how you eventually learn not to miss sugar!

Nutritional Supplements

Let's talk about nutritional supplements. I should make it clear from the start that I am a person who believes in vitamins. I take a large number of vitamins, and have for a very long time. I am more and more convinced that they are worth the money, and then some. In fact, I consider them the best investment I've ever made.

Why can't we get all our vitamins and minerals from our food? A few hundred years ago, people probably could, and did, if they had access to good food. If you ate fresh free-range meat, lots of vegetables grown on composted soil, some seeds and nuts that you sprouted and didn't roast, and some fruit in season, you would probably get most of what you needed to deal with a world with little pollution.

However, that is hardly the case now. As long ago as the 1930s, the Congress officially stated that our soils were mineral depleted, and people who ate food grown on those soils would have mineral deficiencies. Minerals are lacking to begin with, and vitamins are lost in transit, on the shelf, or in the freezing or canning process, and during cooking.

Add to that the garbage in our air and water, and even such unquantified stressors as living under artificial light, and our dramatic reduction in exercise, and supplementation looks like a pretty good bet.

So what should you take? And in particular, what can you take to help with your diet?

First of all, in my opinion EVERYONE should take a strong, **full-spectrum multiple vitamin and mineral.**

Further, I feel that the highly advertised drugstore or grocery store multiple vitamins are close to worthless — first of all, they're not very well absorbed, and secondly, while they have okay doses of the vitamins that they do include, they are missing some of the vitamins entirely, and have very low doses of a lot of minerals. Minerals, especially **calcium and magnesium,** take up a *lot* of room. Tablets which contain *only* calcium and magnesium usually require you to take 3 to 6 daily to get your RDA. If the necessary dose of just those two minerals won't fit in one tablet, think about all the vitamins and the other minerals you need and you'll see that a one-a-day type supplement just isn't enough.

I would *strongly* recommend that you get a good, high potency, three-to-six-tablet-or-capsule-a-day multiple vitamin with minerals that includes at least 100% of your RDA of calcium and magnesium. Alternatively, you can get a multiple vitamin that requires only one tablet a day, and also buy a good, broad-spectrum multiple mineral formula (just minerals), and take them together. Another possibility is the "pack vitamin" — little packets with four to six different tablets in them that you take every day. There are many good brands at health food stores, and many of the network marketing companies also have excellent formulas. What should you get for your money?

I would look for at least 10,000 units of **vitamin A**, and 25,000 isn't excessive. I know that **beta carotene** is very "in" right now, but I feel that **fish liver oil A** is excellent as well. I wouldn't buy a supplement that supplied less than 200 units of **vitamin E**, and feel that 400 units is better. Any supplement which is adequate in these is likely to be adequate in **vitamin D** as well. If you find a supplement which includes **vitamin K** — which most people haven't even *heard* of — that's a clear sign the manufacturer is working to make it as complete as possible.

I would suggest that you buy a supplement that gives you good big doses of **all the B vitamins**. 50 units of each is great, but even 25 units is a healthy dose. (I say "units" here because some B vitamins are measured in milligrams (mg) while others are measured in micrograms (mcg). B vitamins should include **thiamin (B1), riboflavin (B2), niacin or niacinamide (B3), pantothenic acid or pantothenate**

(B5), **pyridoxine (B6)**, **cobalamin or cyanocobalamin (B12)**, **folic acid**, sometimes called folate or folacin (this is an exception, by the way; a supplement should include *200* mcg of folic acid) **biotin, choline**, and **inositol**. It's these last three that most often get left out. If you look for a supplement which includes choline and inositol, again, that's a sign that it's pretty complete.

B vitamins are water soluble, so you can't overdose. But you *can* get an imbalance, since supplementing one or two of them can cause your body to eliminate all of them faster. This happened back in the early 1980s, when it was publicized that B6 was a diuretic (would make you lose water). Women started taking truly frightening doses — as much as 1000 mg — of B6, without taking anything else. They, you should pardon the term, peed out all their other water soluble vitamins, and got good and sick. That's why I think it's best that you get your Bs from a good, complete multiple — you'll stay in balance.

Vitamin C is water soluble too. Did you know that human beings are one of a very, very few animals who don't make vitamin C in our bodies? Us, guinea pigs, coho salmon, and some fruit bat somewhere, and that's about it. That's why your dog doesn't need vitamin C. Not only do most animals make their own vitamin C, but they make it in quantities far larger than the government recommends for human beings — the equivalent of an adult taking at least a few grams a day. I certainly would recommend that you take a minimum of 500 mg of vitamin C per day; I take *far* more — about 6,000 mg a day. If you smoke, you need more than a non-smoker — that 500 mg a day will just *barely* offset what you lose by smoking a pack a day, with none left over. (This is one of the reasons smokers age so fast!) If you're taking aspirin regularly, you'll need more, too.

It's easy to tell if you're getting more vitamin C than your body can use. If it's giving you gas and diarrhea, you're getting more than you need, and your body is throwing off the excess. If you're not getting these gastrointestinal symptoms, you're not getting too much. In fact, many nutritionists feel that you can best find your optimal dose of vitamin C by pushing your dose up until you start to get gas, and then backing it off just a bit. That's how I hit on a dose of 6,000 mg (6 grams) a day for my body. I've found, too, that when I get ill, I can take far, far more, as much as 25 grams a day (25,000 mg), and never get gut trouble. Tells me my body is using all of it. As soon as I'm well, I have to drop back to 6 grams a day, or I'm running for the john!

Anyway, get at least 500-1000 mg of vitamin C a day, okay?

Then there are the minerals. I'm not going to list every single mineral you should look for — most supplements that are adequate in the ones I do talk about will have the others, too. But there are a few minerals that everyone needs to be careful to get enough of, and a couple of minerals that are especially important to us low carb dieters. I harp on minerals a lot, but I think they've been neglected — and I think they're truly vital, especially to dieters. Farmers know about a problem called "cribbing" — when cattle start chewing on strange things, like metal or rock. They know that if they give the cattle mineral supplements, the problem will go away. Well, in humans the same problem is known as pica, and causes near-uncontrollable cravings. Sometimes people eat really strange things, like paint chips or dirt! I had one online low carb buddy who had horrible sugar cravings every single day, and absolutely hated vegetables — until she threw out her grocery store, one-pill-a-day supplement and bought a high potency multivitamin and mineral from the health food store. Within a week, her cravings disappeared, and lettuce started to taste okay to her. Pretty dramatic. *So get your minerals!*

First, as I mentioned before, make sure you're getting at least your RDA of **calcium**, which is one gram, or 1000 milligrams a day. Since milk is quite high in carbohydrates — 12 grams in 1 cup — you really can't drink the quart of milk a day you'd need to get your calcium. (Did you know it took that much? I know lots of people who drink a glass of milk a day and think they're covered.) There are some good low carb sources of calcium — sardines (just about as good a food as you can get, if you like them), tofu, almonds, some of the dark green leafy vegetables, like collards and turnip greens. Broccoli has more calcium in the leaves than in the stems and flowers, did you know that? Which means that if you buy frozen broccoli, you'll get a little more calcium in the cheaper chopped broccoli than in the more expensive broccoli spears, because they put the leaves in the chopped kind.

It's funny but true that the cutting edge in calcium supplements is something called "hydroxyapatite", which is calcium in the form it appears in bones. Fifty years ago, nutrition pioneers, along with recommending a low carbohydrate, high protein diet, were recommending bone meal. I guess everything old really is new again!

Historically, people got a great deal of their calcium from *bones*. When people gnawed every last bit of meat off of a bone, they got a little of the bone, too. Calcium! (And the gristle is good for you too, builds strong joints.) As we grew more civilized, bones were saved for making soup, and some of the calcium dissolved out of the bones into the broth, especially if some kind of acid, like vinegar or wine, was added. I save all my chicken bones in a bag in the freezer and make soup from them.

It's funny but true that the cutting edge in calcium supplements is something called "hydroxyapatite", which is calcium in the form it appears in bones. Fifty years ago, nutrition pioneers, along with recommending a low carbohydrate, high protein diet, were recommending bone meal. I guess everything old really *is* new again!

Most of us aren't willing to eat sardines every day, or make soup from bones, or eat enough broccoli leaves to get all our calcium. Yet calcium remains as vital as it ever was. Osteoporosis is no joke! Thousands of people die of the aftermath of hip fractures every year. Take your supplements.

You should get at least half as much **magnesium** as you do calcium — among other things, magnesium keeps calcium from forming stones in your kidneys. Also, magnesium is important for proper nerve function, and can be calming — and who couldn't use that? Also, many people find that magnesium help reduce carbohydrate cravings a *lot*. In particular, magnesium has a reputation for calming chocolate and sugar cravings. So that's at least a gram a day (1000 mg) of calcium, and at least 500 mg of magnesium, right off the top.

Be careful about **iron**; it's possible to get too much, and if you're eating red meat, you're getting a fair amount in your diet. Excessive iron has been implicated in heart disease. Don't buy a supplement with more than the RDA of iron, and if you're eating red meat several

> Be careful about iron; it's possible to get too much! If you're a man, or a post-menopausal woman, be aware that you're at a greater risk for iron overdose.

times a week, you might look for one of the new iron-free supplements. If you're a man, or a post-menopausal woman, be aware that you're at a greater risk for iron overdose.

Be sure you're getting enough **iodine**. It's essential for thyroid function, and if your thyroid function is low, you'll have a very hard time losing weight. If you're not using iodized salt, or eating fish several times a week, you might want to take kelp tablets — very inexpensive, a good source of iodine, and nutritious all the way around. I take 6 to 8 a day, myself. Seaweed is a staple of oriental diets, and very good for you — but not to my Western tastes!

Chromium is essential for carbohydrate metabolism, and a deficiency can destabilize blood sugar and cause sugar cravings. There is a lot of debate as to whether one form of chromium is better than another — the two most often recommended are GTF Chromium (also called Chromium Polynicotinate) and Chromium Picolinate. I take a product that has three kinds of chromium in it! Either GTF or Picolinate should be okay, but make sure you're getting at least 200 micrograms a day, and 400 mcgs won't hurt you. **Zinc** seems to help chromium do its job, so be sure you're getting it, too. By the way, the classic sign of too little zinc in your body is white spots on your fingernails. 30 to 60 mg of zinc is fine.

Vanadium, and especially a form called vanadyl sulfate, has been getting a lot of press lately because of its ability to fix insulin resistance to some degree. 25 micrograms should be plenty.

Chromium picolinate and **vanadyl sulfate** have been touted recently as "super fat burners" — I would consider this a *huge* exaggeration. However, I do think they can strengthen your carb metabolism and help your diet a lot — and taking them over the months that you're actively losing may mean that when the time comes for maintenance, you can afford a few more grams of carb a day than you would otherwise. Anything that allows you 60 or 70 grams a day of carb, instead of 30 or 40, is worth taking!

By the way, you want to look for minerals that are "**chelated**" — which means they're bound to a protein to help them cross the intestinal lining and be absorbed. These chelated minerals are VASTLY superior to the cheap mineral supplements, which are little more than ground rock.

As I mentioned earlier, some of the top of the line supplements are now using a form of calcium called "**hydroxyapatite**". This is the form calcium takes in your bones, and is very absorbable — it's naturally protein-bound. I take a hydroxyapatite-type calcium supple-

 Chromium picolinate and vanadyl sulfate have been touted recently as "super fat burners" — I would consider this a huge exaggeration. However, I do think they can strengthen your carb metabolism and help your diet a lot

ment myself. You can also take bone meal, if you like. I keep powdered bone meal on hand and add it to meat loaf and other ground beef dishes. You'd never know it was there!

Let me remind you again of a mineral I mentioned back in the section about the Basic Low Carb Diet — **potassium**. If you were feeling really good on a very low carb diet, and then all of a sudden felt tired and wrung out and weak and achy, you might need a potassium supplement. Because of the fast water loss in the first few weeks, and because a low fat/high carb diet encourages your body to throw off potassium at the same time it causes sodium retention, many people take a little while to balance out the sodium/potassium thing. You can add two or three potassium pills through the day — that's assuming they're the common 99 mg dosage — or you can buy Morton's Lite Salt, which is about half potassium chloride, and tastes pretty okay. Multiple vitamins do not contain appreciable amounts of potassium.

CAUTION: There are high blood pressure medications which are "potassium sparing", which means they keep your body from throwing off excess potassium. If you are on one of these medications, you should NOT take potassium supplements! If you are not certain, call the pharmacy and ask; they'll know. DON'T TAKE A RISK HERE! Too little potassium can kill you, but so can too much.

When you find a multiple vitamin and mineral, or a multiple vitamin with minerals and a multiple mineral formula which gives you all these things — enough A and E, plenty of C, *all* the Bs in ample doses, all of the calcium, magnesium, zinc, chromium, and vanadium you need, in well-absorbed chelate form — you can feel fairly confident that it will be adequate in other nutrients — **manganese, copper, zinc, selenium**, etc. — as well.

Other supplements you should know about — if you're feeling a bit constipated, you may certainly take **fiber supplements** on a low carb diet. Fiber Con tablets are fine, as is sugar-free Metamucil, or any fiber product that has no sugar in it. READ YOUR LABELS! Probably your best choice for extra fiber is, as mentioned earlier, flax seed. If you're eating plenty of low carb vegetables, constipation shouldn't be a problem, but if you're having trouble warming up to lots of salad and broccoli, you may well need some help.

Also, I personally have had good results with the newest "wonder supplement", **DHEA**. DHEA is a hormone precursor — that is, a substance your body uses to make a whole bunch of different hormones, including estrogen and testosterone. Levels are naturally high in your twenties, and then decline after age thirty. DHEA supplementation in lab animals caused them to lose fat and gain muscle, have less heart problems, more energy, and a higher sex drive. It's had about the same effect on me — within three days I found myself dancing in the kitchen, I had so much extra energy, and I lost 7 lbs in the first week or so that I was on it.

Youngsters don't need DHEA — I wouldn't recommend it much before age thirty-five — and I would stick with what are called "replacement dosages", which is to say just enough to approximate youthful levels. That would be from 5 to 50 milligrams a day. (I take 25 mg per day.) Body builders are using it in huge doses as a steroid replacement, and it seems to work well, but I wonder about the safety of increasing hormone levels that dramatically for long periods of time. You should know that DHEA is controversial — please be cautious.

However, at this writing, I'm experimenting with another hormone precursor called **"pregnenelone"** instead. Pregnenelone can be differentiated into a wider variety of hormones than DHEA — indeed, your body can make DHEA and all its resultant hormones from pregnenelone. But it can also make progesterone, the other female hormone, from pregnenelone, which it cannot do from DHEA. I have read a fair amount about the disadvantages of estrogen "unopposed" by progesterone, and suspect that pregnenelone may be better, especially for women, for this one reason alone. Also, pregnenelone seems to have mood elevating and memory-enhancing properties that DHEA lacks. Too, pregnenelone was widely used as a safe, effective treatment for arthritis before steroid drugs were invented.

Bottom line, I would strongly recommend that you take a high potency multiple, with plenty of chelated calcium and magnesium, at least 200 micrograms of GTF chromium or chromium picolinate, and 25 micrograms of vanadium or vanadyl sulfate. Even better would be a product with a broad spectrum of chelated minerals. Make sure you're getting enough iodine. I also take a colloidal trace mineral product – 66 different minerals in tiny amounts.

If you want to maximize your good eicosanoids, adding an EPA and a GLA supplement couldn't hurt. And I personally swear by DHEA, but it's controversial enough that I'd recommend that you do a little research on your own before you decide it's right for you. *The Super Hormone Promise,* by Dr. William Regelson, is a good place to start!

Plateaus

Oh, the dreaded plateau! Not just part of low carb dieting; everybody who's ever been on any kind of weight loss diet has hit a plateau from time to time. Low carbers are no different. Plateaus are discouraging, no question about it. When you're being "good", it's almost more than a body can bear to have your weight loss stall for a few weeks, or even a few months.

So what to do?

Well, first, take a mental inventory of any other benefits you've noticed from your low carb diet: improved energy, better bloodwork, reduced allergies, less hunger, clearer mind, better moods, whatever. These, for me, were the biggest reason I never seriously considered quitting during my plateaus, some of which lasted waaaay too long, to my way of thinking! I was unwilling to gain back what I had lost, or to go back to feeling tired and logy and hungry, so I stuck it out.

Get really honest with yourself and make sure you've really been sticking to which ever program you've chosen.

Second, If you're on the Basic Low Carb diet, get out the food count book and count your carb grams for a week, to be sure you're not getting more than you think you are. Remember that food labels allow manufacturers to fudge a bit; count foods that say "0 g per serving" as 0.5 g, and foods that say "less than 1 g per serving" as 1g. And if you haven't been vigilant about reading labels, start! If you've been on a Mini-Binge plan, be sure you haven't been eating between meals, or stretching that hour for the Reward Meal. In other words, be sure that you're really plateaued, rather than cheating.

If you're sure you're not slipping on the diet, and a plateau lasts more than a few weeks, it may be time to try changing something. What? There's a whole lot of adjustments you can make, and different changes help different people.

Your Milage May Vary

That's the phrase we use on the Internet to summarize the concept that different things have different effects on different people.

All of the things in this section have a very large effect on some people, and a much lesser effect — or no perceptible effect — on others.

First of all, with this book in hand, you're well prepared to try a different approach to low-carbing. So do it! If you've been doing the Mini-Binge, try the Careful Carb program, or go to a Basic Low Carb diet. If you've been doing the Basic Low Carb plan, eating three meals a day, try it eating six smaller meals, or try a day or two of carb-up. If you've been eating a whole lot of extra protein, and not a lot of fat, try eating more healthy fats, and only your minimum allowance of protein. If you've been eating just the minimum of protein, and a lot of fat, try switching that. You get the picture.

But only change one thing at a time, okay? Otherwise you may never know what worked. And remember that your body is a remarkable thing, and can adapt to almost anything; throwing it a curve now and then can be a good idea.

Here, in no particular order, are some things that affect some people's weight loss a lot, and others not at all.

Artificially Sweetened Beverages

Roughly half of low carb dieters find that artificially sweetened beverages interfere with their ability to lose weight, or will act as a "trigger" — something that makes them hungry. Why this should be is a matter of controversy. Some say that aspartame (Nutrasweet, Equal) has a negative effect on your body's ability to burn fat — Dr. Robert Atkins among them. Dr. Atkins used to allow aspartame; you'll find it in his book. But since then, in his newsletter, he has stated that he feels that aspartame is dangerous, and that it interferes with fat burning on a chemical level.

Others state that some people are so hypersensitive to carbohydrates that even the *taste* of sweetness will cause an insulin surge — the Hellers have said this — while still others say this has never been demonstrated in clinical tests.

Still another camp feels that the aspartame is not the problem; that instead the problem is citric acid, widely used in beverages and other processed foods. Apparently it can interfere with ketosis, that state of rapid fat burning. Citric acid shows up in most diet beverages — both sodas, and other beverages like Crystal Light and diet

Roughly half of low carb dieters find that artificially sweetened beverages interfere with their ability to lose weight, or will act as a "trigger" — something that makes them hungry.

iced tea mix, and even unsweetened, unflavored bottled iced tea. Some iced tea at fast food joints has citric acid, too — if you've ever gotten iced tea that had a strange, sour undertaste, that was citric acid. It also can be an ingredient in sugar-free gelatin desserts.

If you're having trouble losing, or you're still hungry and craving, on your low carb program, and you're certain you've been good about cutting out the carbs, try cutting down, or cutting out, the artificially sweetened beverages. Drink iced tea sweetened, if you need it, with saccharine (Sweet'n Low) or stevia, the natural sweetener I mentioned in the Shake Diet section.

Thyroid

If you have a slow thyroid, all efforts to lose weight will be in vain. You may also well be tired, chilly, depressed, have a low sex drive, brittle hair, constipation, headaches, cloudy thinking, and you'll heal slowly and have a poor immune system. Not fun.

There's a safe, easy, free way to find out if you're hypothyroid (have low thyroid function): Take your temperature in your armpit first thing in the morning, before you get out of bed. It's best not to do this during the first couple of days of a menstrual period, which affects temperature. Tuck a thermometer in your armpit, and leave it there for ten minutes. If it reads less than 97.8, you just might be hypothyroid. If it reads under 96.8, chances are very high. (This is called the Broda Barnes Basal Metabolism Test, by the way.)

Go see a doctor you trust, and insist that he or she take this seriously. Be aware that there is such a thing as "sub-clinical" hypothyroidism — a low level deficiency that doesn't show up on lab tests, but will cause a low temperature — and keep you from losing weight and feeling well. If you have the symptoms listed above, and your morning temperature tests low, find a doctor who will help! Insist on T3, T4, and TSH tests.

If you're pretty sure that borderline low thyroid is a problem for you, and you can't find a doctor who'll take you seriously, be aware that health food stores often carry thyroid support supplements, and "desiccated thyroid gland" tablets, which can help some. I take a thyroid support supplement myself, since low thyroid runs in the family.

The Pill, and Estrogen Replacement Therapy

It is very, very common for women to gain weight when they start taking the birth control pill or estrogen replacement therapy (ERT). I've seen friends balloon by 25 pounds in a matter of months!

This is because estrogen encourages fat deposition and water retention. That's why women have a much harder time losing weight than men! It's also why farmers give beef cattle artificial estrogens; it makes them weigh more.

Also, estrogens are usually given without progesterone, the other most abundant female hormone, to balance them. Too much estrogen, without progesterone, will slow down thyroid function — and as we just discussed, slow thyroid function will give you a slow metabolism. Some doctors now feel that many of the health problems which have been blamed on low estrogen levels are actually symptomatic of low progesterone levels instead. For instance, there have been bone-density scans done on post-menopausal women given solely progesterone, showing an increase in bone density from the treatment.

 **It is very, very common for women to gain weight when they start taking the birth control pill or estrogen replacement therapy (ERT). I've seen friends balloon by 25 pounds in a matter of months!**

What can you do? First of all, if you can possibly tolerate a birth control method other than those which affect hormones — the Pill, Norplant (very much like the Pill in effect) or Depo-Provera — your body will thank you for it by losing weight. These all are unbalancing, and have weight gain as a side effect. (I use a diaphragm, have for years, and have no problem with it.)

If it is *essential* that you use hormonally-based birth control — for instance, pregnancy would be disastrous, but you're deeply morally opposed to abortion — you might consider supplementing progesterone as well. You can consult your doctor, if you like. If you do, insist on being given natural progesterone, NOT "progestin", which does not have the same beneficial effect! Or, assuming your health is not fragile, you might try one of the many natural progesterone creams on the market — progesterone has been shown to be easily absorbed through the skin, and is usually given in a transdermal cream form.

Another possibility for those who take ERT is to consider taking pregnenelone instead. As mentioned before, this is a hormone "precursor"; — a substance your body uses to make many different hormones from. When you take this precursor, your body decides just how much estrogen it wants to make, how much progesterone, how much testosterone (yes, ladies, women have testosterone too; it's responsible for our sex drive), and how much of the other hormones. This strikes me as a far more balanced, more natural approach to hormone supplementation. Since your body makes DHEA from pregnenelone, you could, if you like, get a DHEA saliva test from your doctor to see if you really need it, or you can simply try a small dose — maybe 10-30 mg — in place of your ERT for a few months to see what the results are. DON'T TAKE THE PREGNENELONE — OR DHEA — ALONG WITH THE ERT!! Overkill! And *do* let your doctor know what you're doing, and why.

Caffeine

Caffeine can cause a rise in blood sugar! It triggers the adrenal glands to release hormones that in turn release stored sugar into the blood stream. This is why many low carb diets ban caffeine.

On the other hand, I have a cup of tea — with caffeine — in front of me as I write this. And many, many folks find that they do just fine on a low carb diet without ever giving up caffeine. Further, caffeine is recommended by some as a "thermogenic" to stimulate fat burning! Confusing, huh?

I wouldn't be in a huge hurry to drop caffeine, but if you find that you're hungry within an hour of drinking a caffeinated beverage, you may be sensitive. The solution, of course, is to give it up.

> I have known low carb dieters who have added
> extra fat to their diets and improved their weight
> loss. I also have known low carb dieters who cut
> back a bit on fat and improved their weight loss! Talk
> about Your Milage May Vary!

Easier said than done! Caffeine withdrawal can be a real bear, causing *killer* headaches. If you feel that caffeine is limiting your weight loss, I would suggest that you start mixing regular and decaf coffee, or regular and decaf tea, and over the space of a few weeks slowly decrease the level of caffeine, tapering off gradually. If you're a cola drinker, you could alternate caffeinated diet cola and decaf, until you're drinking all decaf.

I drink half-caf tea myself, except for first thing in the morning. Now that I don't eat carbs, my energy level is so high I can't tolerate fully caffeinated tea all day like I used to.

Fat Intake

Wouldn't you know it, level of fat intake is controversial even in low carb circles! Some, like Dr. Robert Atkins, Dr. Herman Taller, and Dr. Richard MacKarness, feel that more fat is better, that it suppresses appetite, deepens ketosis, stimulates fat burning. Dr. Taller in his 1962 book recommended that his readers drink an ounce of safflower oil before every meal! MacKarness actually named his 1958 low carb book *Eat Fat & Grow Slim*. And Dr. Atkins, one of my heroes, recommends eating plenty of fat, especially in the first few weeks, because it encourages ketosis. He even outlines a "Fat Fast" for those who have a great deal of trouble losing — 1000 calories a day, 900 of which are pure fat! He feels that the fat fast is the fastest way to burn fat, faster than eating nothing at all. Not much fun, though, unless you're awfully fond of macadamia nuts and cream cheese.

Others are more moderate. The Eades don't want you to *avoid* fat, but they don't push it, either. And the Hellers give instructions on how to make their program both carb controlled and low fat if you want to, though they don't specifically recommend this.

I have known low carb dieters who have added extra fat to their diets and improved their weight loss. I also have known low carb dieters who cut *back* a bit on fat and improved their weight loss! Talk about Your Milage May Vary!

One thing I'm pretty sure of: The more you are willing to do without carbs, the more fat you can afford to eat. On the other hand, a low fat/high carb diet has been disastrous, overall, to the health of the nation! So don't decide to eat protein, low impact carbs, and no fat. *Bad* idea. Even Anne Louise Gittleman, former nutrition director at The Pritikin Center, has now stated that good fats are essential for health — and for fat burning. Don't let your fat intake drop an inch below 30% of your calories.

**So don't decide to eat protein, low impact carbs, and no fat.
Bad idea!!!**

All I can suggest is experimentation. If you're trying to break a plateau, you might try adding some healthy fats — or you might try switching to lean meats, fewer nuts, seeds and cheeses, and less added fats (oils, butter, etc.). Whichever you try, give it a week or two to see how it works.

Also be aware that there are fats that stimulate fat burning. Most notable among these are GLA (gamma linoleic acid) and EPA (eicosapentanoic acid). It now appears that the reason drinking safflower oil made Dr. Taller lose weight is because in individuals of normal metabolism, the linoleic acid in the safflower oil is converted to GLA, which stimulates fat burning. One of the *many* biochemical differences between those of normal weight and the chronically obese may be that obese people's bodies do not perform this conversion. In clinical studies, supplements of GLA resulted in fat loss for many subjects. You can buy GLA as capsules of either evening primrose oil or borage oil. I take 6 evening primrose oil capsules daily.

Another oil that has been helpful for fat burning in many people is flax seed oil. Unfortunately, flax seed oil is very perishable, and is downright dangerous unless very fresh. There's an easy solution, however: Take flax seeds instead! Flax seeds are available at health food stores. You can grind a few days worth into a coarse meal in the blender — this makes it easier for your body to digest them — and

---

just swallow a spoonful or two of the meal with a big glass of water. It's kind of gritty, but very mild tasting. The added bonus to this is that flax seed is a fabulous source of fiber, and will take care of any constipation problems you might have!

Alcohol

As I have mentioned, I have a couple of glasses of dry wine or a couple of light beers every evening. However, I don't consider this optimal for weight loss, whether on a low carb diet or any other diet.

Despite the fact that my wine and beer have only 3 to 4 grams of carbohydrate per serving, and distilled liquor has none (one popular low carb diet of the '60s was called *The Drinking Man's Diet* because it allowed distilled liquor, on the theory it had no carbs), they're still a *major* luxury. Why? Because chemically speaking, alcohol is closer to carbohydrate than it is to anything else. There's little question that alcohol slows metabolism, making it harder to lose weight. I'm quite certain if I gave it up I'd drop more weight.

But I *like* my wine and beer! And especially where the wine is concerned, there's a lot of evidence that it has other beneficial effects on health — even some evidence that dry red wines improve insulin utilization!

This is another one where you'll have to see how your body reacts. If you like alcohol, and you can have a little (notice the word *little!*) and still lose weight, great! If you include alcohol in your diet and you're not losing, it's one of the most likely culprits.

Watch out which wines and beers you choose! Dry wines include chablis, rhine, pinot noir, gewurtztraminer, sauvignon blanc, cabernet sauvignon, burgundy, merlot, chianti. If you're not *certain* that a wine is dry, ask the liquor store clerk or the waiter. Sweet wines can have a *lot* of sugar in them! And even the dry wines can vary in carbohydrate content quite a lot from brand to brand. If you can't find the brand you want in your carb counter, consider calling the company. I did this with Franzia vineyards, and they were very helpful. Just explain that you have a medical condition that requires that you avoid carbs.

Alcohol on any diet has to be considered a luxury. Be aware of that, and choose accordingly.

Light beers vary tremendously in carbohydrate count. Most of them are so high in carbs I won't drink them — 7 grams a can or so — which, high as it is, is still only *half* of what most regular beers have! But there are a few light beers which run between 3 and 4 grams per can. *Those* are the ones you want. Do I have to say it again? READ THE LABEL!! (If you're ordering a light beer while out, remember that Miller Light has far fewer carbs than Bud Light.)

Most plain distilled liquors have no actual carbs in them — whisky, scotch, vodka, gin, tequila and rum fall into this category. Beyond these, however, danger looms! Just about all liqueurs, cordials, schnapps, etc., have a *ton* of sugar in them. So do most mixers — whiskey sour mix, marguerita mix, daiquiri mix, pina colada mix, orange juice, you name it. And wine coolers are right out!! If you want a mixed drink, try a gin and tonic made with *diet* tonic water (yes, tonic has sugar!), or a rum and cola made with diet cola. A bloody mary now and then is *just* passable; tomato juice is lower in carbs than fruit juices.

Club soda and sparkling water are carb-free, of course, so you could have a scotch and soda. Or you could have my favorite "tall" drink, a wine spritzer. I put about 3 ounces of burgundy in a tall glass with ice, and fill it up with berry flavored sparkling water. This actually tastes sweet to me, despite the very low carb count.

Still, alcohol on any diet has to be considered a luxury. Be aware of that, and choose accordingly.

Food Allergies and Sensitivities

A year after I went low carb, my husband and I went on a camping trip. Thinking I could avoid preparing lunches, I bought a big bag of peanuts in the shell, reasoning that the shells would force me to eat them more slowly than shelled peanuts, and that with the exercise I would get while camping (we walk several miles a day while camping, as a rule) the few carbohydrates in the peanuts wouldn't be a big problem.

Imagine my chagrin when I got home after a three day trip — and had gained seven or eight pounds!

I continued to eat peanuts, although I was careful about quantities. It wasn't until about six months ago that I realized that quantity wasn't the problem!

One night while watching TV, a few hours after dinner, my husband brought out a can of peanuts. I had two small handsful — and within *minutes* I was wheezing slightly. I could feel my waistband cutting into me uncomfortably, and suddenly my wedding ring was tight. I was allergic to peanuts!

I cut the peanuts out of my diet entirely — a sad thing to do; I love them. But I found that I had far fewer sudden swings in weight after I eliminated them from my diet.

Hidden food allergies can torpedo your weight loss. They can also be the source of *fierce* food cravings. There is a phenomenon

> **Hidden food allergies can torpedo your weight loss. They can also be the source of fierce food cravings.**

called "Allergic-Addiction". What this means is that the foods you are most likely to be allergic to are the ones you crave most and eat most often! (I was eating a nut and seed mix with peanuts in it almost every day.) The uncomfortable symptoms of the allergy — headaches, fatigue, spaciness, depression, etc. — start to set in as you withdraw from the food, and you crave the food to stop the symptoms. But it can only make you worse in the long run, just like sugar.

The most commonly allergic/addictive foods are the grains (corn, wheat, rye, oats, rice), soy, milk and dairy products, yeast, eggs, citrus fruits, shellfish, nuts, and chocolate. However, you can be sensitive to anything! (Along with peanuts, I am allergic to almonds. They don't make me blow up, however, they just make me wheeze quite badly. A shame; they're a *very* nutritious low carb food.)

An alternative indicator can be a change in handwriting after eating a suspected food!!

If you're quite sure you've got your carb intake under control, but you still have unpleasant symptoms an hour or so after eating, and can't lose weight, you may have a food sensitivity.

How to find out? The simplest way is to drop the suspected food — and remember, it's likely to be the foods you eat and crave the most — from your diet for three or four weeks and see how you feel. Then, if you like, you can add it back and see if the symptoms reappear. You may be surprised! It's not uncommon for people to feel heavily drugged when they eat an allergenic food after not having it for a while.

Another way to find out is to eat the suspected food, all by itself, on an empty stomach. Wait several hours from your last meal. Then, before you eat the suspected food, take your pulse. (Find it at your neck or wrist, count it for fifteen seconds by the clock, then multiply by four.) Eat a moderate sized portion of the food you're testing. Remain seated, and take your pulse again at five minutes, ten, and fifteen. What you're looking for is a speeding up of your pulse. If you get one, that's a clue that that particular food may not be great for your body.

An alternative indicator can be a change in handwriting after eating a suspected food. Once again, you test after fasting for several hours. Write your name as clearly as you can, eat the suspected food, wait ten or fifteen minutes, and write your name again. If there is a deterioration in your handwriting, I'd drop that food, fast!

You can, of course, talk to a doctor about this. If you do so, be aware that most doctors only accept a certain kind of sensitivity — to be technical, one that is "IgE antibody mediated" — as a true allergy. Most food sensitivities don't fall into this category. Tests for "IgG antibody" response, or "cytotoxic" testing, are likely to be closer to the mark. You may have to search to find a doctor who will do these tests. Don't let yourself be intimidated! Remember, doctors work for *you!*

But I'd start by paying attention to which foods you crave most, and noticing how your body reacts when you eat that food alone, on an empty stomach.

Chapter Sixteen
Enhancing Success

For Emotional Eaters — St. John's Wort, 5-hydroxytryptophan, Niacin

Is there anybody left who doesn't know that St. John's Wort is a natural, herbal antidepressant? Prescribed twice as often as pharmaceutical antidepressants in Europe, and proven effective in clinical tests. Fairly cheap, too!

Why mention this antidepressant in a diet book? Because there's a pretty fair argument to be made that one of the things that makes people crave carbohydrates is the fact that taking on a big load of starch and/or sugar will rapidly raise brain levels of a chemical called "serotonin". And serotonin is a mood elevator — the way Prozac and similar drugs work is by raising brain levels of serotonin.

Unfortunately, the effect on serotonin from eating carbs is short-lived, just like the blood sugar rush, and you're left tired, irritable, and craving for more. Not good!

So raising your brain levels of serotonin in *other* ways can be a good strategy for you if you're prone to stress- or depression-related binging. All three of the substances in the heading — **St. John's Wort**, **5-hydroxytryptophan**, and **niacin** — can do that for you.

They work in different ways, and I know people — me occasionally included — who take all three.

> There's a pretty fair argument to be made that one of the things that makes people crave carbohydrates is the fact that taking on a big load of starch and/or sugar will rapidly raise brain levels of a chemical called "serotonin". And serotonin is a mood elevator — the way Prozac and similar drugs work is by raising brain levels of serotonin.

St. John's Wort, it's beginning to appear, works in a similar fashion to Prozac. Prozac falls into a class of drugs called "SSRIs", which stands for "Selective Serotonin Reuptake Inhibitors." Let me explain.

Each of your brain cells has a microscopic space, called a *synapse*, between it and the next cell. Messages are sent from one cell to the next by chemicals, called *neurotransmitters*, that flow in and fill the space, and then are immediately pumped back out again so they can be reused. Serotonin is one of those neurotransmitters. Prozac and other SSRIs slow down the pumping out/recycling mechanism, so that serotonin, which makes us feel cheerful and calm, stimulates the brain cells longer. It's beginning to appear that St. John's Wort works in much the same way.

Be aware that high doses of St. John's Wort may cause photosensitivity — in other words, you'll burn more easily in sunlight. If you decide to try it, keep this in mind, and don't forget to protect yourself.

Then there's 5-hydroxytryptophan. This is what your body uses to make serotonin out of, so taking it, especially on an empty stomach, can increase brain levels of serotonin. Good to take before bed; it can help you get a good night's sleep, with no hangover.

You may remember tryptophan, which was on the market in the '80s. Tryptophan is an amino acid — a protein building block — which your body can use, among other things, to make serotonin. Tablets of tryptophan became very popular for self-treatment of insomnia and depression, and studies showed very similar results with tryptophan or Prozac.

Then came the epidemic — hundreds of people became ill from taking tryptophan; a few died. Tryptophan was taken off the market, and rightly so, pending investigation. However, the investigation showed that everybody who got sick had taken tryptophan made at the same factory, in the same batch — and that that factory had just changed their production methods. It wasn't that the tryptophan was dangerous, the tablets from that batch were contaminated!

Yet until recently tryptophan remained off the market, as illegal as cocaine or marijuana. Just recently, tryptophan has been approved for use again — but only as a very expensive prescription *drug*. If I were a conspiracy theorist, I'd wonder if the producers of Prozac and other pharmaceutical antidepressants had a hand in this.

Recently, however, 5-hydroxytryptophan has hit the market, and it does just about the same things that tryptophan did. The way I understand it, your body turns tryptophan into 5-hydroxytryptophan, and *then* into serotonin — the 5-HTP is the intermediate step. So the difference in effect is minimal. I've spoken to one researcher, a fella by the name of Rick Handel, who runs a big vitamin manufacturing business. Rick feels that 5-hydroxytryptophan is the most important nutritional product for helping depression currently on the market, and a lot of researchers seem to agree with him.

5-hydroxytryptophan is the most important nutritional product for helping depression currently on the market.

Then there's niacin. Niacin is a B vitamin, B3 to be exact. Niacin has some profound effects on brain chemistry, to say the least! For instance, Dr. Abram Hoffer worked with schizophrenics, and found that for many of them, huge doses of niacin would completely eliminate the psychosis. He theorized that many schizophrenics simply had an abnormally high need for niacin.

For that matter, it was common folk wisdom in the 1960s and 1970s that if someone was having a bad acid trip, you could pull them right out of it by giving them a big dose of niacin. Set their scrambled brain chemicals right, fast!

Niacin also can lessen cravings for nicotine. The proper, scien-

Niacin is a fairly potent cholesterol-lowering substance, proven in many clinical trials.

tific name for niacin is "nicotinic acid", and its calming effect on the brain is not unlike that of tobacco.

All of these effects seem to relate to niacin's ability to increase brain levels of serotonin. You see, when you eat tryptophan in food (remember, it's an amino acid, and it's present in many protein foods we eat), your body can use that tryptophan to make *either* niacin or serotonin. If you're short on niacin — and evidence is that different people can need different amounts — your body uses the tryptophan for niacin, not serotonin. If you take plenty of niacin, your body is more likely to use the tryptophan for serotonin.

One warning about niacin: Vitamin B3 comes in two forms, niacin and niacinamide. They both have about the same effect on your moods. The difference between the two is that niacin causes a "flush" — about fifteen to twenty minutes after you take niacin, all your surface blood vessels dilate, and you become hot, red, and itchy all over!! This flush lasts for about 15 minutes, and is harmless. Personally, I kinda like it! But some people find it very irritating, or even frightening. When I ran the health food store, I used to have people return niacin, explaining that they were terribly allergic to it!

The niacin flush has some benefits. First of all, what causes the flush is the same chemical that causes allergic reactions: histamine. (When you have allergies, you take antihistamines, right? That's because allergic symptoms — runny nose, itchy eyes, hives, sneezing — are caused by histamine.) The niacin flush is like a temporary case of the hives. By deliberately dumping histamine stores on a daily basis, some people find that their allergies become milder!

Also, only niacin, with its flush, will lower cholesterol. And niacin is a fairly potent cholesterol-lowering substance, proven in many clinical trials. However, it only seems to have an effect on cholesterol in very big doses, between a gram and three grams a day — for comparison, I take 100 mg, or a tenth of a gram, daily. If you're blue *and* have high cholesterol, you may want to try niacin in large

Don't be a dope! It's your brain you're playing around with here, for heaven's sake!! So take care.

doses. But DON'T DO IT WITHOUT YOUR DOCTOR'S SUPERVISION. At doses of 1-3 grams a day, niacin is more a drug than a vitamin, and has been known to cause liver inflammation in susceptible people.

For purposes of raising your serotonin levels, I'd stay with 100-250 mg, once or twice a day. And for this purpose, you can take niacinamide instead, and avoid the flush entirely.

All three of these substances — St. John's Wort, 5-HTP, and niacin — are pretty darn safe. But don't be a dope! It's your brain you're playing around with here, for heaven's sake!! So take care. If you're under treatment for profound depression, for goodness' sake don't try to go off of your antidepressant drugs and switch over to any of these three without a doctor's input!

Also know that for every substance in the world, there's someone who reacts badly to it. I used to babysit a little boy who was allergic to breast milk! The point is, if you start taking one or more of these substances and feel worse, instead of better, pay attention!

None of these three serotonin-raising, mood-elevating substances will actually speed up your weight loss. But they can make it far easier to go low carb and stick to it! If you find yourself reaching for candy or bread or ice cream when you're feeling blue, these three substances may be for you.

Thermogenics

Remember what I said about naturally skinny people having bodies that simply turned up the heat and burned off excess calories? Guess what! There are over-the-counter drugs and herbal preparations that will up your body temperature slightly, and help burn off fat. We call these products **"thermogenics"**. And my experience is that they *do* work — but that there are some real dangers involved, so caution is essential.

The most commonly used thermogenic agent is called **ephedrine**. Ephedrine has been widely used for decades for asthma — it's a major ingredient in Primatene tablets — and as a decongestant. It is also popular as an over-the-counter pep pill. I often see it at truck stops, since truckers use it to stay awake on long runs. Interestingly, the brand I see most often at truck stops is called "Mini-Thin" — a reference to the thermogenic effect. Ephedrine also is sometimes sold by the tablet on the black market as cheap speed, called White Cross, a reference to the double-scoring, or cross mark, on the tablets.

Ephedrine is currently pretty controversial stuff, largely because a few morons have gotten stupid with it. Kids looking for kicks will take outrageous doses, and illegal drug labs will combine it with other chemicals, including *Drano* for heaven's sake, to produce much more powerful and dangerous forms of speed, including methcathinone and methamphetamine. (On its own, ephedrine is *much* milder than either of these illegal drugs.) There has been some talk of removing ephedrine from the market, or making it available only by prescription. I have noticed that it now seems to be combined with guafenisin, a drug that loosens up phlegm, whenever I see it. Apparently this prevents people from misusing it somehow.

How does ephedrine work? It's a *sympathomimetic*, meaning that it mimics the effects of adrenaline in the body. It increases heart rate, opens up the breathing passages (which is why it's effective for asthma and colds), and makes you feel energetic or jittery, depending on how much you take. It also increases the metabolic rate of fat tissue, which is what we like about it! Some adrenal hormones encourage fat burning; there's speculation that one of the differences between people who are naturally slim and those of us who gain easily may be in levels of adrenal hormones. Again, ephedrine increases your body temperature very slightly (not enough to notice; you won't be sweating all the time or anything), so you burn off more calories, even when you're sitting still.

Side effects include increased blood pressure, insomnia, anxiety, and reduced appetite. In most people who use moderate doses, the insomnia, anxiety, and appetite suppression wear off in a week

> I feel that ephedrine and ma huang can be useful adjuncts to your low carb diet, to maximize fat burning and increase energy. However, these are *powerful drugs* — yes, even the herbs are drugs — and must be used with sense and caution!

or so. However, the thermogenic (fat burning) effect remains. Some even feel the fat-burning effect increases with time!

Ephedrine works best in combination with two other drugs you're familiar with: caffeine and aspirin. I don't understand the chemistry, but all the clinical studies show that these two drugs increase the fat-burning effectiveness of ephedrine quite a bit. This combination of drugs is usually referred to as a "stack", or "ECA stack". The most commonly recommended dose is 20-25 mg of ephedrine (most tablets are this strength), a cup of coffee or one No-Doze or Vivarin tablet, and one aspirin (some feel a baby aspirin — a quarter of an aspirin — is enough), three times a day.

Personally, that's too much for me!! I've taken the stuff, and I've found that a full 25 mg ephedrine tablet is enough to make me want to jump out of my skin! Furthermore, taking it in the morning and afternoon is okay, but if I take an evening dose, no way am I going to sleep! When I've used pharmaceutical ephedrine, I've taken three-quarters of a tablet (about 19 mg), with a pot of tea and a half an aspirin. Tea, by the way, not only has caffeine, but theophylline, which is itself a thermogenic.

If you want to buy plain old pharmaceutical ephedrine, in double-scored white cross tablets, don't go buying it at a truck stop; it will be *wildly* overpriced. About $30 should buy you 1,000 tablets, enough to last you a very, very long time. Living in a college town, I can find ephedrine retail — students buy it to stay awake to cram for exams. If you can't find it in stores near you (most pharmacies don't handle it), you might consider mail order. You can find ads for ephedrine in many exercise magazines. If you want to increase effectiveness by "stacking", add to that a bottle of baby aspirin, and some source of caffeine, whether a beverage, or No-Doz or Vivarin tablets.

There's an easier way to do this, although it's not quite as inexpensive. *Many* companies now put out herbal versions of the ECA stack, with all three substances in one tablet, often with other ingredients included. The herbal version of ephedrine — which, of course, was the original, and which has been used in herbal medicine for centuries — is called **ma huang** (pronounced mah wong) or **ephedra**. It is the main ingredient in many herbal pep pills, and most herbal diet pills. In most herbal thermogenics, **guarana** is used to supply caffeine, and **willow bark** is used to supply an aspirin-like compound. These products work about the same as the ephedrine/caffeine/aspirin combo, but many people are more comfortable with the idea of taking herbs.

There are also herbal ephedrine products which include some herbal diuretics, like uva ursi. Since a low carb diet will itself reduce water retention, I don't consider these necessary for us. Some products also include herbal laxatives like cascara sagrada, which I also consider superfluous. And I've seen one or two products which combine ma huang with St. John's Wort, to speed fat burning *and* cut emotional carb cravings. This may be useful.

There is some feeling that prolonged use of ephedrine can be hard on the adrenal glands; some of the herbal products include herbs like licorice that supposedly prevent this effect; probably not a bad idea, though I'm not knowledgeable enough to be able to say whether this is effective or not. Also, there is some feeling that it is best to cycle on and off thermogenics, taking them for a week, then taking a day or two off, and then starting again. This is said to prevent some of the weakening of the adrenal glands, and to prevent your body adapting to the ephedrine and losing effectiveness. I do this myself.

I feel that ephedrine and ma huang can be useful adjuncts to your low carb diet, to maximize fat burning and increase energy.

 These are powerful drugs! If you use them recklessly, they can make you very uncomfortable, or even kill you. So don't be stupid.

However, these are *powerful drugs* — yes, even the herbs are drugs — and must be used with sense and caution! If you use them recklessly, they can make you very uncomfortable, or even kill you. *So don't be stupid.*

> **Do NOT decide that if a little ephedrine is good, a lot will be better!**

First of all, if you have high blood pressure, heart disease, clots, *any* cardiovascular condition at all, ephedrine/ma huang is NOT FOR YOU. It could give you a heart attack or a stroke. If you are taking MAO inhibitors, or any other prescription medication, for that matter, I'd avoid it. If you're prone to seizures, it's a bad idea as well — I knew a young man who was seizure-prone who gave himself a seizure by taking large doses of ephedrine. If you have glaucoma, it's a no-no. And, like any drug, ephedrine should not be taken during pregnancy, or if you are breast feeding. (Tangentially, breast feeding will dramatically speed weight loss after pregnancy, especially in your butt and thighs. It's not just much better for your baby, it's much better for you, too.) Furthermore, you shouldn't take ephedrine or ma huang if you have thyroid disease, or if you're a man with prostate trouble.

Do NOT decide that if a little ephedrine is good, a lot will be better — again, it is not unknown for people — even healthy young people — to die of overdoses of the stuff, just like any other drug, and the fact that it's available without a prescription or a "natural, herbal" product doesn't change that. I would *strongly* caution you not to take any product that gives you more than 25 mg of ephedrine in a dose, and I personally would not take more than three doses in a day. (That being said, at this writing I have on hand a popular herbal thermogenic from a network marketing company. It contains 22 mg of ephedrine activity per capsule, and the instructions suggest taking two at a time. I won't do it, no matter what their label says. I'm sure I'd drop weight if I did, but I consider it risky, and anyway, I'd never be able to sit still and write this book!)

Having now effectively scared you to death, let me say that ephedrine and ma huang are substances which have been used safely for centuries. Ephedrine has been classified as a non-prescription drug for decades, and authorities have only been deeply concerned about it in the past ten years or so, when people have started abusing

Used with caution and good sense, I feel that for healthy people, ephedrine can be a safe and effective diet aid.

it. Used with caution and good sense, I feel that for healthy people, ephedrine can be a safe and effective diet aid.

There is an alternative to ephedrine/ma huang, however. Recently, bitter orange has been found to have chemicals which have a similar effect to ephedrine/ma huang — they cause thermogenesis and fat burning. Since the FDA has become alarmed about ephedrine abuse, some herbal and nutritional supplement companies have been switching over to the bitter orange thermogenics. Bitter orange extracts are felt to be less stimulating or "speedy", but to still be effective for fat burning. I plan to try a bitter orange-based thermogenic soon. The same precautions that apply to ephedrine products also apply to bitter orange products.

Exercise

What would a weight-loss book be without the obligatory lecture on exercise? You know it's good for you, you know you should — but statistics say you probably don't do it. This is my attempt to change that!

Exercise will give you energy, raise your spirits, create glucagon to help you release fat for burning, speed your metabolism, and all around improve your life. It will make you feel better about yourself, your body, and the world. It will, to a large degree, slow and even reverse the aging process, since much of what we think of as the ravages of aging is really the result of gradual muscle loss. If God hadn't invented exercise, some big corporation would be charging you $60 a shot to take a walk!

Or as one wag put it, "We've found the magic anti-aging pill. It just takes 20 minutes three times a week to swallow it."

But forget that stuff. Here's the bottom line: Exercise will improve the way you *look* about a thousand percent. For most of us, that's our real motivation for doing any of this. When I've lectured on low carb dieting, it's been very clear that the people who came to

**If God hadn't invented exercise, some big corporation would
be charging you $60 a shot to take a walk!**

hear me were concerned about appearance first, with health a distant second.

We want to be attractive. We want to be appealing. We want to be noticed. We want to be *sexy*.

Maybe people shouldn't judge each other by the way we look. But we do. We do. And we all live with it. Women in particular — we're constantly comparing ourselves to surgically augmented, airbrushed supermodels (most of whom work out, by the way!) and we have the nasty suspicion that the rest of the world is, too — and all too often, they are. We women obsess about our weight because on some level it stands for our whole sense of self-worth as a woman. Men do diet, do worry about their weight and their looks, but it's not the same desperate feeling women have.

(For the men reading this: If you'd like to understand why we women are so psycho about our weight, try to imagine growing up in a world where every magazine, every TV station, all your life, told you over and over that if you just had "willpower" and "strength of character" and "self-esteem" enough to torture and starve yourself the rest of your life, you could make your penis bigger. Now imagine it in a society where your penis was on display every time you went out of the house. Get it?)

**"We've found the magic anti-aging pill. It just takes 20 minutes
three times a week to swallow it."**

Exercise *shows*. Everything pulls up and in. You move better. Your skin looks healthier. You stand with more confidence. You move with purpose. You feel sexy. You *look* sexy! (Not while you're doing it; in between times!) Everyone notices on some level.

Your posture improves. Standing straight and tall, torso lifted up out of your hips, shoulders square, stomach taut, neck long, gets rid of ten pounds and ten years, at least! But you can't do it — and

> Exercise shows. Everything pulls up and in. You move better. Your skin looks healthier. You stand with more confidence. You move with purpose. You feel sexy. You look sexy!

feel comfortable with it — without exercise. Your muscles simply won't be up to the task.

You probably know all of this. Yet the chances are good that you're *still* not exercising! Especially if, like me, you've had weight problems and energy problems all your life, gym class was probably the most humiliating part of your childhood. So here's a little

Peptalk for Gym Class Dropouts

I am one of you. When I was fifteen, and a high school sophomore, I cut an entire semester of gym. Didn't even go to day one. Got a "C", too, though only God (and the bureaucracy) knows how! (Ridgewood High, please don't call!) I was a reader and a talker, not an athlete of any kind.

Sports, games, exercise — to me these were NOT fun; they were sheer humiliation. The phrase I heard over and over and over again on the elementary school playground, as sides were chosen for dodgeball or kickball or prison, was, "And you get Carpender!" Not pretty.

(To any elementary school teachers reading this: If you are still using the "choosing up sides" method of establishing teams, I implore you to *cut it out!* I am sure that this torture alone is responsible for thousands of adult sports-phobics. Have 'em count off, one-two, one-two, instead.)

I was, as I have said, fat by the age of 8 or 9. I was not — still am not — very coordinated. I was the kid who could never make it up the rope. I was the kid who missed the easy throws, and took a softball in the eye. I was the kid who was too fat and slow to get away from the dodgeball. I was the kid who never really understood the rules of any game, and made stupid, embarrassing mistakes as a result.

Yet at the age of 40, I am fit. I exercise regularly, and I actually *enjoy* it. I am convinced that anyone can do the same. There are just

---

three things you need to understand to make exercise a part of your life.

Number one: If you, like me, have associated all things athletic with severe humiliation, you need to know a very important fact: No one is going to make fun of you if you're not a great athlete!! Maybe you'll want to avoid team sports — I do — but as far as the world of adult exercise goes, the simple fact that you're *trying* is enough to make you one of the gang, one of the elite. Effort counts for everything; skill for very little. No one cares how you look in your workout clothes, either. I promise you, I have never been to a gym where people were even the tiniest bit mean about people who weren't as athletic as they. Really.

No one is going to make fun of you!

You don't have to play a game, *ever*, to get in shape. And you never have to compete with anybody but yourself. Furthermore, I've gone to aerobics class as a size 18, in shiny pink spandex, and not a single person made fun of me. Not one! Grownups, thank God, are kinder about these things than kids are.

Number two: Anything that keeps you moving around at a pretty good clip counts as exercise! You don't have to join a gym if you don't want to, although I go three times a week. You simply need to move around! If you rake your yard for 45 minutes — assuming you keep moving, instead of stopping and starting — *that's* an aerobic exercise. So is walking. So is dancing. If you spend all Saturday lifting rocks and putting them into place for a patio or rock garden, that's both aerobic and strength training! You may not want to get on a stair climber, but how about going out country western line dancing a couple of times a week? The trick is to come up with something that you actually find not hideously unpleasant, and then *do* it. Regularly!

Anything that keeps you moving around counts as exercise!

Number three: Exercise will make you feel great! And it will make you look better, fast. I'm not making it up. Really. One of the great things about exercise is that it's the only totally reliable thing I know: If you do it, it works. Period. Not, if you do it and the weather holds out, it works, or if you do it and your boss approves, it works, or if you do it and you can get the funding, it works. If you exercise, you *will* get stronger. And stronger *feels* and *looks* better.

Exercise will make you feel great!

Stronger is not panting as you hustle up the stairs. Stronger is being able to carry in the groceries in two trips, not four. Stronger is being able to dance for hours! Strong is sexy! (All the stars you think of as "naturally" gorgeous are working out, never doubt it!) Stronger is breaking into a trot as you cross the street, just because you feel energetic. Strong IS energetic. And lack of energy is the single greatest health complaint Americans have! If you've been avoiding exercise because you don't have the energy, you're taking exactly the *wrong* approach!

And here's the kicker: If you haven't been exercising at all, you will get *far* more good out of starting even a modest exercise program than a professional athlete would get out of adding another several hours a week! That's right. All of the research shows that the jump in health when you go from no exercise to just twenty or thirty minutes, three or four times a week, is the single greatest gain you can get. Adding another few hours will increase the gain, but not by as much. And for a serious athlete to get any real increase in fitness, they'd have to add many, many hours, and a great deal of intensity. You're going to get the greatest exercise benefit of all!

So all you have to do is decide which form of exercise is for you. It has to be something you'll actually do — no use buying some expensive piece of equipment and ending up using it as a clothes rack. (Been there, done that!)

What is the best kind of exercise? I could talk about the advantages of resistance (weight) training versus aerobics versus anything else — and I will, a bit — but here's what for me is the bottom line:

> ## The best exercise is the one you will do!

It doesn't matter if stairclimbing machines burn more calories than walking; if you find walking fun, and stairclimbers about as enjoyable as root canal, you'd better go for a walk. I, for one, would rather give a speech to a thousand people dressed only in my old underwear than use a stationary bicycle. This just means that stationary bikes are not for me!

There are three basic **classes of exercise: aerobic, resistance or muscle training, and stretching.** These categories can overlap; for instance, many aerobics classes now incorporate work with powerbands or weights, to strengthen muscles. Some stretching programs also strengthen. And weights can be done as "circuit training", where you move from exercise to exercise fast enough that your heart rate doesn't drop, creating aerobic benefits.

Which is most important? Oh dear. Such a hard call, but I'd like to put in a strong pitch for strength training. During the seventies and eighties, aerobics were king. Everyone considered them the most important form of exercise, especially for people who wanted to lose weight. Then new research came in about resistance exercise ("resistance" and "strength" exercise are the same thing — overloading your muscles so that they make themselves stronger as a result) and the picture started to change. We discovered that while aerobics increased your metabolism while you were doing them, and for a little while after, weight training would increase your metabolism *twenty-four hours a day,* even while you're sleeping, by increasing your muscle mass.

Bottom line is that aerobics alone will never reshape your body. Just won't happen. Resistance exercise — weights or powerbands — will. If you want the most results in the least amount of time, plus the greatest increase in your metabolism, you'll get that from resistance training. Furthermore, you'll never have to increase the amount of time you work out to increase your results — you just increase the weight, or use a heavier band. I love this about resistance! If I wanted to increase my results with a walking program, I'd have to walk more

We discovered that while aerobics increased your metabolism while you were doing them, and for a little while after, weight training would increase your metabolism twenty-four hours a day, even while you're sleeping, by increasing your muscle mass.

miles, which would take more time. With my weight lifting routine, I get stronger and fitter and better looking without ever increasing the length of my workout.

Further, a clinical study was done with the elderly. A group of subjects, with an average age well over 80, was put on a program of progressive resistance exercise. The results? Every single one of them showed an improvement in their ability to stand, walk, balance, climb stairs, get in and out of chairs. Some who had used walkers for years were able to abandon them! Pretty impressive stuff.

And no, you won't end up looking like a man, or even like a female body builder. Women who look that way work *incredibly* hard, and usually take steroids, to get there. You'll just get shapelier. Promise.

Gym Versus Home

Should you go to the gym, or should you work out at home? Again, a tough call. I've done both, and there's pluses and minuses to each.

Obviously, a good gym is going to have equipment you don't have at home, including any and all weight training stuff you might need. Gyms can offer a lot of camaraderie, and most of them now have child care. If you've tried to work out at home, but the kids keep interrupting, joining a gym may be the solution. Please don't think you have to have fancy, sexy workout wear to go to a gym. I have one cotton/lycra unitard my mom gave me for Christmas; I alternate wearing it with wearing ancient elastic waist shorts and old, beat up tee shirts. There are some "meat market" gyms where everybody dresses up, but in my experience they're few and far between. Just wear something comfortable, and good gym shoes.

Many people join gyms to go to aerobic classes of various kinds. Almost all gyms will have classes ranging from beginner to advanced,

If you decide to take aerobics, please be aware that everybody looks dopey the first few times they do it.

many of which now include some strength work with weights or powerbands, too — if you're going to take aerobics, I would heartily recommend that you take a class that includes strength training. (I like step aerobics with weights and powerbands, myself.) If you decide to take aerobics, please be aware that *everybody* takes a while to catch on to the commands in aerobics class. Everybody looks dopey the first few times they do it. There's no shame in missing your footing, or in taking a few weeks to figure it all out. Just keep moving — as my trainer friend BJ would say, "Your heart doesn't know if your feet are doing it right". I did step aerobics for a long time, and I never got to the point where I got every move right. Big deal. Just keep moving!

I think this dopiness factor is why you don't see a lot of men in aerobics classes, despite the opportunity to scope out women in spandex — they're too embarrassed to do something athletic badly in front of a whole room of women who are doing it well! Also, I can honestly say that one of the things I like about step aerobics is that I'm bad at it. I have to concentrate so hard on the steps, there's no time for watching the clock! By the time I catch on to the day's routine, I'm done!

Another big plus for **gyms**: You'll find knowledgeable people who can show you the ropes. If you're intimidated by the specialized equipment — many people are — this is a big help! I have three weight routines that I do in rotation that BJ put together for me, and I like them a lot. Once you've gone through your routine a few times, it's not complicated at all. It's also very helpful to talk to people who are certified in athletic training if you have concerns about physical limitations; they can help you put together a program which is safe and effective for you.

If you get bored with the same routine fairly quickly, a gym lets you change your type of workout a lot, without spending extra money for new equipment. You can take aerobics for six weeks, then switch over to the stairclimber and some weight training for a few weeks, then go for a stationary bicycle and a stretch class. If you did that at home, you'd be spending more money on new equipment and videos every few weeks!

One other thing you can do at a health club that you probably can't do at home — **swim**. If you have arthritis or any other joint problem, or if you're extremely heavy, and afraid for your knees and your back, having access to a pool can be a real lifesaver. Water aerobics are excellent for anyone with these concerns, and they're fun, too! I was surprised to discover when I tried water aerobics that they use dumbbells — only they're made out of styrofoam, so the resistance comes from forcing them under the water! Water running is another exercise that's catching on — you wear a flotation belt and run in place in the water. Excellent!

Be aware, though, that while swimming will improve your heart and lungs, and up your energy, it's not great for burning fat. Your body seems to know what kind of exercise you're doing, and shapes your body for that particular stress — and in swimming, a bit of fat is of benefit, both for buoyancy, and as insulation. Accordingly, swimming won't slim you down like some other things — just look at the women who swim the English Channel. Fit? You bet. Skinny? No. But swimming and other water exercises can help you get in good enough shape to do some other things! (Because of the resistance training they incorporate, water aerobics are likely to get you in better shape than just swimming laps.) If there's no health club with a pool near you, try calling some of the local hotels. Often they'll let you pay a monthly fee to use their pool; a friend of my mother's did this for years.

On the negative side, working out at a gym — unless you live right next door — takes more time than working out at home. Dur-

Working out at a gym — unless you live right next door — takes more time than working out at home.

ing some very busy periods of my life, I have taken to walking with hand and ankle weights instead of going to the gym, because I could

Beware the lifetime gym contract!!! I bought a lifetime contract with the biggest, most widely advertised health club chain in America, and rapidly discovered that since they had my money, and didn't have to worry about me taking my business elsewhere, that any complaint I had was totally ignored.

walk out the door, do my 3.5 mile circuit of my neighborhood, get back home, showered and changed, in the time it would take me to get to the gym, change clothes twice, and get back — my gym is across town from my home; it takes twenty minutes to get there and another twenty to get back, plus changing time. In this busy day and age, time is a big issue for a lot of us.

If you're extremely shy about working out in public, a gym can be kind of scary. You might look for a gym that has classes just for people who are overweight; there are some out there. There are also "ladies only" gyms for women who are uncomfortable working out in front of men.

Also, of course, joining a gym costs *money*. For the cost of a month or two at a gym, you could buy a good aerobics-with-weights video, and a few dumbbells, and get good results at home. Further, your video and weights would then be paid for, but with most gyms, you pay a fee every month.

(Beware the lifetime gym contract!!! I bought a lifetime contract with the biggest, most widely advertised health club chain in America, and rapidly discovered that since they had my money, and didn't have to worry about me taking my business elsewhere, that any complaint I had was totally ignored. Better to keep the clout that comes with the option to vote with your feet. If you've been going to the same gym for quite a while, and are certain you're satisfied, you *might* consider the lifetime contract, if it's a good buy — but gyms change hands, and will you like the new management?)

Here's what my trainer/gym owner friend BJ Baxter has to say about choosing a gym:

"Back in the 1960s, most gyms were mostly 'meat head' gyms (catering to male body builders). The '70s brought a surge of women into the fitness industry due to the popularity of aerobics. The '80s unfortunately saw the incorporation of high pressure sales techniques, especially at big-name fitness chains.

For those in the fitness industry, the 1990s have been spent learning to survive the severe competition, and erasing the ugly reputation that was brought about by the big chain fitness clubs' less-than-honest sales techniques. Here are some tips on what to look for when seeking a good fitness facility:

You will be happy to know that the days of high-pressure sales are gone. Any gym worth even an ounce of your attention will offer you not one free day, not one free week, but one free *month* to try the gym before you purchase a membership. You want to become familiar with the ambiance of the club as a whole. Is it clean? Is the staff friendly, knowledgeable, and helpful? Do they offer the equipment, training, and/or classes that fit your needs?

> **Any gym worth even an ounce of your attention will offer you not one free day, not one free week, but one free month to try the gym before you purchase a membership.**

Make sure the staff takes the time and effort to learn your name and use it every time you walk into the club. On your initial visit, they should take the time to find out *your* goals, *your* interests, and what results *you* want to see with *your* body. They should be able to explain how they are going to help you make it happen.

Don't get me wrong, the expression "You can lead a horse to water but you can't make him drink" is very true of exercise; you have to do the work yourself. But what is the point of joining a gym if they are not going to offer every means possible for you to get the results you want? At my gym we offer two memberships: one for those who are already at their goal, or are experienced enough to know how to reach their goal on their own; and a membership that incorporates five different components facilitated by a team of professional trainers who completely eliminate all guesswork, so the beginner can get maximum results for their efforts. We *guarantee* results.

> If the potential club you're scoping out does not give you a substantial amount of time to "try before you buy", or does not provide quality service and attention to you in every way appropriately possible, this is either not the gym for you — or the only gym in town.

Purchasing a fitness membership at any health club should be nothing but a win-win situation."

Couldn't have said it better myself.

How about working out at home? Certainly it's very possible to get into good shape at home, and you don't have to spend a ton of money on fancy equipment to do it. If you have a television and a VCR, your local video rental joint is likely to have all the **exercise videos** you could ever need! Again, I'd recommend that you pick one that includes weights, and invest in a few sizes of dumbbells; they're inexpensive. Rent a video and try it for a few days, then try another, until you find a few you really like. *Then* you can purchase! An ideal home fitness video library contains aerobics, strength training, and stretching-type videos, all three.

(I would like to say here that the very best workout videos I've ever done are put out by a company called *The Firm*. I like their #3 and #4 videos best. They're just "dance-y" enough to be fun, but not so much so that this klutz can't keep up. They do an excellent job of incorporating weights into the workout, so that you get strength training at the same time you get your aerobic workout, saving you precious time. They're clear and easy-to-follow — a virtue not to be underestimated — and, by using heavier or lighter weights, or none at all to start, they can be adapted for just about any level of fitness. *The Firm* videos, in my opinion, are the best of the best.

On the other hand, I'd also like to put in a word for Richard Simmons' *Sweatin' to the Oldies* series. They're not as rigorous or complete a workout as *The Firm* videos, by any means, but they're *approachable*. The people look *real*, it's music you know and love, and it doesn't matter if you mess up the steps a little — you're just dancing, after all. People find these videos *fun*, and that's a big plus.

One other video series, and then I'll stop making unpaid plugs: *Callanetics*, a series of stretching and strengthening exercises, is superb for improving posture, flexibility, and bearing. As a massage therapist, I have recommended these tapes many, many times for people with posture-related pain problems. Improving your posture will make you look slimmer almost overnight. Start with either the original *Callanetics* tape, or the Beginner tape. Don't underestimate these seemingly low-key exercises; they're a lot tougher than they look!)

If you'd like a near-unlimited supply of great exercise videos for almost nothing, check out a show called *Body Electric*, broadcast on many public television stations. Margaret Richards, who creates and leads the show, does a terrific job of mixing up strength, stretching, and some aerobics, and is never dull. You can, of course, tape the show if it comes on while you're at work. You could end up with an excellent fitness video library this way, for just the cost of the blank cassettes.

Of course, videos aren't the only way to get in shape at home. There's a million **machines** on the market, both for aerobic conditioning and strength training. In my day, I've had a ski machine, which I didn't much like, and a rowing machine, which is excellent, especially for flattening the stomach. At this writing, I'm lusting after a machine called a Total Gym, which allows for both aerobic and strength training. BJ greatly admires a strength training machine called the Bowflex. I think most of the well-made machines are worthwhile if you *use* them, and they let you do your workout while watching television. (By the way, if you're thinking "I don't have time to work out", but you watch even an hour of television a day, you're making excuses. Cut it out.)

> **If you're thinking "I don't have time to work out", but you watch even an hour of television a day, you're making excuses. Cut it out.**

Which machine is best? Once again, the answer is "the one you'll use". Keeping that in mind, there is a real edge to any home exercise machine that lets you vary your workout. The more different things you can do on it, the better. Also, the more muscles get used,

You could just go for a good, long, brisk walk several times a week, and it would do you a world of good, and not cost you a penny.

the better the workout. A stationary bike uses your legs; a rowing machine uses your legs, your back, your shoulders, your arms, and your stomach muscles. Guess which will get you in better shape, faster? On the other hand, if you like the bike and hate the rowing machine, get the bike!

Beware what one fellow has termed "Post Purchase User Neglect Syndrome" — the strong tendency to use exercise machines as expensive coat racks. And *don't* buy the cheapest machine you can find. Almost invariably the cheap exercise machines are worth even less than you pay, because they're clumsy and uncomfortable to use, and break easily. I'll never forget the Saturday when I saw three cheap plastic "shuffle"-type ski machines — they had been aggressively advertised on TV — for sale in less than an hour of yardsaling! Tried one — what junk!

The way to get around the expense of buying a decent machine is to *harness* Post Purchase User Neglect Syndrome, by buying used! It's a rare day of yardsaling that I don't see at least one or two decent exercise bikes or "rider" machines, even the odd stairclimber or two. (I often see dumbbells and ankle weights at yard sales, too — that's where I got mine.) These things are also advertised in the classifieds every day. Almost always you can get the seller to let you try the machine first. Do try it to make sure it's a good fit, not too noisy (I *hate* noisy exercise machines!), has smooth action, and feels kinda fun to you.

Or you can take advantage of the many second-hand sporting goods stores popping up around the nation. You'll get a better selection, but the price will be higher. And should you make a mistake buying a machine, and fall victim to Post Purchase Neglect Syndrome yourself, the used sporting goods store will gladly take that machine and give you partial credit toward another.

You don't have to have a video or a machine either, of course.

You could just go for a good, long, brisk **walk** several times a week, and it would do you a world of good, and not cost you a penny. I like to use handweights when I walk (these are special dumbbells, made to be comfortable to carry for long periods of time; they have straps that go across the backs of the hands, so there's no need to grip them strongly), and pump my arms hard, to increase my "burn". Another benefit of handweights is that they made me feel far safer back when I used to walk in the city! Walking is everyone's exercise; it's cheap, it requires no equipment beyond comfortable sturdy shoes, you need no special training, you're extremely unlikely to get injured, and it's fun, especially if you have a friend along. How about finding a diet and walking buddy? A personal cassette player can also make walking more fun. You can play music, of course, but I often have played books on cassette, instead. (Don't buy them; they're terribly expen-

> **We find a way to do what is important to us. NO EXCUSES!!**

sive. Your public library no doubt has a fine selection for free!)

I don't want to hear that you have nowhere to walk! In my day, I've walked in circles around parking lots on my lunch break, around the lobby of the building I worked in, all sorts of places. You know and I know you're making excuses. We all do what we really want to do — what we decide is important to us. We find a way, if we really want the benefit. There's a fellow who works out at my gym, mid-40s-ish I'd guess, who has a withered leg, a heavy limp, one hand that curls in and is clearly not fully functional, along with a withered forearm on that side. I have no idea whether it's from an accident or disease or birth defect — but I do know that he's at the gym regularly, and in terrific shape. Every muscle not affected by his disability is toned and defined. Then there's my friend Cory, who after a catastrophic car accident at age 17 spent years *crawling* around the track at the local YMCA, getting her strength back so she could learn to walk again. Cory now swims several times a week. For that matter, I've had the good fortune to hear Art Berg, perhaps America's finest motivational speaker. Art is a quadriplegic — and did a 325 mile super-marathon in his wheelchair! We find a way to do what is important to us. NO EXCUSES!!

Of course there's the *weather*. I live in the Midwest, where we definitely have weather, rather than climate! I have walked in all sorts of weather, and have learned a few things. The hardest weather condition for walking is ice. If the sidewalks and roads in your area are icy, you may as well forget walking outside; it's foolhardy. Cold, on the other hand, is not a big deal. All you have to do is dress for it. The most important thing I've learned about walking in cold — and I've walked extensively in weather as cold as zero degrees — is to wear something under your trousers. In very cold weather, you'll need long johns, but even a pair of old nylons will make a *big* difference to your comfort when it's chilly. And wear a hat, will you? It never ceases to amaze me how many people refuse to wear hats, no matter how cold it is.

If you live where the weather is severe, or in an iffy neighborhood, it's good to know that many malls now welcome "mall walkers". My mother takes advantage of a mall near her that opens its doors an hour early every day for walkers; no doubt they hope folks will stay and shop. This lets Mom walk in a controlled climate, in safety. Call your local mall and ask if they allow mall walkers — or just go walk. I did this when I was in Dallas for ten days in the summertime, and it was about a zillion degrees in the shade. I went to the nearest mall and walked, every day. Even took my hand weights with me! No one said a word.

How about **running**? The tendency of your body to shape itself for a particular type of stress is why running seems to be the best sport for slimming down. You lose upper body mass as your body tries to lighten the load it has to carry. But I can tell you after 14 years of professional massage experience that running has one of the highest injury rates of any sport. If you really like it, and have great feet and knees, go for it. Just be sure you have the best possible shoes; cheap running shoes are a bargain you can't afford. But for the general population, I'm not sure the drawbacks of running don't outweigh the benefits.

What else can you do at home? How about pulling the blinds, putting on music, and **dancing** like a lunatic for a half hour every day? Bet you could even get any little kids who are home to join in, solving the "how do I watch the kids while I work out?" problem. Dancing's a gas! Who cares if you're not Paula Abdul? Just move around and have fun. You could get a basket for your **bicycle** and pedal to the convenience store instead of taking the car. You could use a **push mower** instead of a ride-on job. You could go to the **playground** with your four-year-old and do every single thing they do!

Then there's always good old basic **calisthenics** — jumping jacks, crunches, leg lifts, all that stuff you did in PE class as a kid. Pushups, in particular, are terrific; they build your chest, back, and arms all at once. Calisthenics are free, take no equipment, and can be done in your living room, while watching television or listening to music. What more do you want?

Another cool way to exercise at home is the **mini-trampoline** or rebounder. This is a trampoline three feet across, and about eight or ten inches high. You can bounce on it, jump on it, jog on it, do jumping jacks, whatever. It's very easy on your joints, and a lot of fun! Good ones — you don't want a cheap one; who wants a trampoline to give out under them? — are not cheap, about $200. But this is another item often found used — I got mine for ten dollars at a yard sale. I really enjoy the thing! I can run and jump on my mini-tramp for a half an hour, forty minutes, and I'll get off feeling more energetic than when I started.

I've read something really interesting about the mini-tramp — that the benefit of using a mini-tramp is not just that it gives you a low impact way to run or jump in place. According to the theory I read, the real benefit of a mini-tramp has to do with the shift in gravity when you bounce on it. Think of your body as a big pile of water balloons, which isn't that far off — each of your cells has a flexible wall, filled mostly with fluid. If you were to bounce those water balloons, each of the rubber walls would flex and stretch with every bounce — it would be *stressed*. And with exercise, stress is the name of the game. The whole point of exercise is to stress your body a bit, so that it makes itself stronger for next time. And by shifting gravity — from 3-5 times your normal weight when you "bottom out" on the mini-tramp to a brief moment of weightlessness just as you start to come down — dozens of times every minute, you can stress every single cell in your body! You're not just working out your legs or your lungs or your heart, this article said — you're working out your liver, and your spleen and your eyeballs too; *everything!* I don't know how true this is, but it made instinctive sense to me. I'm guessing that's why I feel so good after I "bounce".

Right here, after the section on bouncing, might be a good place to put in a plug for the *sports bra*. I don't know about you, but I'm a D cup (unlike so many women, I didn't lose an *inch* off of my bust when I lost weight!), and a good underwire sports bra makes all the difference for me between exercising comfortably and causing myself pain. If you're a woman with a large chest, go to a store where they have people who know how to fit bras properly, and get a good sports bra that supports you comfortably. I even know a woman who wears two — a fitted underwire one under one of the unfitted, "compressive" ones that doubles as a top. Very helpful, especially if you do aerobics, running, or jump on a mini-tramp.

If you want to do strength training at home, you can, of course. Buy some **dumbbells**; they're not very expensive. You'll want more than one size — I have three pounders, fives, tens, and eighteens. Then go to your local public library, and get a good book on working out with weights. It'll show you how to isolate your different muscles. Remember to work as many different muscles as you can; uneven muscle development can cause postural problems. Ever noticed how some body builders have shoulders that round forward, making them look a little gorilla-like? That comes from working the big, showy muscles of the chest more than the smaller, less flashy muscles in the back. You can actually make quite a lot of progress by lifting weights at home.

Or, if you prefer, you can use **powerbands**. Powerbands are strips or tubes of rubber, some with handles, some without, that you can use to give resistance instead of weights. There are a lot of advantages to powerbands! First of all, they're inexpensive. Secondly, with one band you can work out just about every muscle in your body — it can be difficult to do lower-body weight lifting without machines. Third, they're very light, so you can take them with you when you travel. (As a person who has carried weights in her luggage, I can tell you that this is an advantage not to be underestimated!) Or you can carry one in your purse, so you can get in a few minutes of exercise on a lunch hour or coffee break. Powerbands are available at sporting goods stores and some health clubs. Insist on powerbands that come with a booklet or chart describing and showing the exercises you can do with them.

What are the benefits of working out at home? It's cheap, or can be. It requires no travel time, and therefore may be easier to fit into a busy schedule. It allows you to start working out in private, if you're uncomfortable being seen. It can, in some cases, let you include your family in your working out, which wouldn't hurt them a bit. It lets you use your television time productively, which for some people is no small thing. And there's more opportunity to get your exercise outside in good weather, which can be wonderful!

The phone rings, your spouse wants something, the dog needs to go out, the kids want your attention — it can be easy to get suckered into feeling that all that stuff is more important than your workout, especially if you're iffy about working out in the first place!

What are the drawbacks? It's very easy to get off-track. For most of us, home is the place where we go to relax, to *stop* working; it can be hard to make yourself get off that couch. It's easy to get distracted, too. The phone rings, your spouse wants something, the dog needs to go out, the kids want your attention — it can be easy to get suckered into feeling that all that stuff is more important than your workout, especially if you're iffy about working out in the first place! If you want camaraderie at home, you'll have to make it yourself, by inviting a friend over, or getting a family member to work out with you — and then they can encourage you to skip a day by skipping a day themselves! There's only whichever machines you've decided to pay for and give houseroom to; no switching off now and then to crosstrain and prevent boredom. And of course, there's no staff with fitness certification to give you advice and work out a program for you.

One other thing to keep in mind: BJ assures me that after about 9 weeks of doing the same exercise routine, it will start to lose its effectiveness. Your body, clever thing that it is, starts to adapt, and doesn't think of that exercise as a stress anymore. You not only will stop making progress, you can even start to slip back a little! (This is why aerobics instructors stay up nights devising new routines — it's not just to entertain you, it's to keep you progressing.) Now, this doesn't mean that you'll regress all the way to where you were before you started, or our ancestors, who walked long distances all the time, would have eventually had no muscles at all! If the only exercise you can stand to do is walk (or bicycle, or whatever), it still beats the heck out of nothing, despite this 9 Week Rule. But the 9 Week Rule does mean that it's a very good idea to change what you're doing every couple of months. Buy a new video, try some new moves with the weights, try a different machine. If you've been walking on a flat course, try one with hills. If you've been walking on hills, try doing sprints of fast walking on a flat course. Throw your body a curve now and then. Okay?

Chapter Seventeen
A Word to the Wise

I genuinely feel that the advice I have given you in this book is safe and sound for the vast, vast majority. But there are exceptions to every rule, and when one is dealing with health, it's important to be careful. I'd hate for you to be the exception!

Accordingly, here are a few cautions. Please pay close attention, and take me at my word.

First and foremost, please remember that I am *not* a doctor, nor am I a registered dietician. I am a layperson with a longtime interest in nutrition, who has rediscovered a time-honored way of losing weight and improving health that has worked beautifully for me and my friends. If you have health problems, you *must* be under a doctor's supervision while shifting over to a low carbohydrate diet.

This is *especially* true if you have any of the health problems that I talked about being associated with hyperinsulinemia. I am not qualified to diagnose, prescribe, or treat any ailment, and this book is NOT intended to do so; it is for your information only. If you have high blood pressure, and are on medication for it, you *must* be supervised — your blood pressure may well drop so fast on a low carbohydrate diet that your medication will need adjusting. This is a good thing, but we don't want anyone fainting at the grocery store!

If you are diabetic, once again, you may very well need an adjustment in your medication — I have one cyberpal with type II diabe-

> If you have health problems, you must be under a doctor's supervision while shifting over to a low carbohydrate diet. This is especially true if you have any of the health problems that I talked about being associated with hyperinsulinemia.

tes who is medication-free so long as she sticks to her diet. Again, this is a good thing, but you *must be monitored.* Insulin shock is no joke.

As for people with cholesterol and triglyceride problems: Triglycerides tend to drop *very* quickly on a low carbohydrate diet, and for most people cholesterol does too. But, as I mentioned, there is a minority that will experience a rise in LDL cholesterol, as well as an increase in HDL and a drop in triglycerides, whether from saturated fats or arachidonic acid no one seems to be quite certain. Most of you will find that you can eat beef and egg yolks, and many other things, and keep your cholesterol low, so don't go assuming that you have to have whites-only omelettes. However, you need to be aware of your own blood stats, so you can catch it if you're one of that minority. Don't fly blind! Get tested, regularly.

Then there are people with kidney damage, like my friend Rob. Most people should have no kidney trouble with this diet — there has been a recent, well-documented, peer-reviewed medical study that shows no difference in kidney function between people who have eaten high protein diets for years, and people who have eaten low protein, high carbohydrate vegetarian diets. However, high protein levels are still *very* controversial for people with malfunctioning kidneys. If you have this problem, you will need to calculate your minimum protein requirement, and stay at that level, adding fats to get more calories. Once again, you should certainly be under a doctor's supervision, and be tested frequently for kidney function. I would recommend that you try the Mini-Binge or Careful Carb approach, rather than the Basic Low Carb Diet, if you have *any* kidney trouble at all.

As I mentioned, many people will find their mental health greatly improved by this diet; I've heard it over and over. And if you're

 **Bottom line: Use your brain, take care of yourself! Good advice no matter what you're doing.**

fundamentally healthy, psychologically, I see no reason not to try St. John's Wort or 5-HTP, in moderation. But if you are being treated for depression, or any other mental problem, *do not* attempt to adjust your medication without your doctor's input, or give up treatment in favor of the diet, figuring that it will take care of everything for you. If it doesn't — and mental illness is still very poorly understood — you could pay for it with your happiness, your sanity, your relationships, or even your life. Doesn't mean you can't go low carb; doesn't even mean it won't help your mental state. It just means that you don't know *what* it will do if you have a real chemical imbalance, and you need expert help to adjust that biochemistry.

By the way, don't expect your doctor to be excited about this, or to even be accepting. But remember — there is NO nutrition requirement to get through medical school in this country. It is unlikely that your doctor is aware of the medical research backing up this form of dieting — although I do hear, now and then, about a doctor prescribing a low carb diet for cholesterol trouble, high blood pressure, or diabetes; it's just starting to happen. I would suggest that you tell your doctor you would "like to try it" and want him/her to monitor your progress for your own safety. The results will speak for themselves. But if you have any health problems at all, *do not* decide to bypass your doctor and go it alone. "Better safe than sorry" didn't become a cliche for no reason, you know.

Finally, don't make the mistake one girl I know did. She had been on low fat, high carb, but she saw my success with low carb. She decided to add fat back into her diet — but kept pigging out on low fat cookies and chips. She GAINED weight. Bad idea. Low carb only works when it's really low carb.

Bottom line: Use your brain, take care of yourself! Good advice no matter what you're doing.

Chapter Eighteen

The Rest Is Up to You!

I was trying to figure out what to say to you to wind up this book, when fate stepped in. My husband is a member of a fraternal order, and we went to the annual fair at the retirement/nursing home funded by and for members of the order and their families. It was a real down-home event, in a small midwestern town — people of all ages, lots of crafts for sale, a tractor pull, a parade, many prayers and invocations, several bands, a merry-go-round and camel rides for the kids — and, of course, food.

They cheerfully feasted on what they no doubt considered good, down-home cooking, and never once made the connection between the quality of the food they ate, the quality of their health, and the quality of their lives.

Bad food. Dangerous food. Barbeque beef made with shreds of beef in a barbeque sauce as sugary as pancake syrup, served on white flour buns. Pork tenderloins, breaded and deep fried, also on white flour buns. Sugar-loaded baked beans. Cole slaw with so much sugar, it was an insult to the cabbage. Lovely ripe red strawberries — sliced and sugared till they were syrupy. Elephant ears — big rounds of fried white flour dough sprinkled with cinnamon sugar. Oceans of

Nutrition isn't just about what size jeans you can fit into, although you'll never catch me complaining about having to buy smaller ones. Nutrition is about life, your life.

soda pop. In fact, there was only one food item I would have been willing to put in my body — the green beans. I didn't bother; I had a glass of iced tea, and just enjoyed the activities. Needless to say, I'd had my eggs for breakfast.

But here's the point of all this: At a conservative estimate, 75% of the people there were obese. Just about everybody over forty was not only obese, but looked unwell. Even the kids were overweight; every single one of the girls in the teens' club had a double chin — they looked about 17 years old and they were already on the road to ill health, the misery of obesity, and an early death.

I don't mean to cut these people down. It was a *lovely* crowd, happy and friendly and family-oriented, good and kind and reverent. They were a pleasure to be around. That is why it hurt me, really hurt me, to see so many of them looking so unhealthy; to see the children well on their way to a lifetime of ill health. They cheerfully feasted on what they no doubt considered good, down-home cooking, and never once made the connection between the quality of the food they ate, the quality of their health, and the quality of their lives.

How many wives will bury their husbands at all too early an age, struck down by a sudden heart attack? How many women will bury their own sexuality because they hate their own bodies? How many men will be impotent in their prime, from diabetes or just from impaired circulation? How many chi2ldren will cry themselves to sleep at night from the humiliation heaped on the overweight kids at any school? How many marriages will be ruined by neglect born of simple fatigue? How many family vacations will be cancelled because the money is needed for doctor bills? How many deadly drug and alcohol habits will grow from the poisoned soil of sugar addiction? How much simple human misery will result from the thoughtless consumption of "food" that doesn't even merit the title?

Nutrition isn't just about what size jeans you can fit into, although you'll never catch me complaining about having to buy smaller ones. Nutrition is about life, *your* life. You genuinely *are* what you eat, and the quality of your health, your thoughts, your work, your moods, your *life* is not just related to what you eat, it is directly dependent on it.

Life is full of choices; that's what freedom is all about. Choices make life both interesting, and often maddeningly difficult. You have the choice before you now to change your life dramatically for the better — not just to lose weight and look better, but to be happier, more energetic, sexier, healthier. To live longer, and *far* better. It's a free choice, completely up to you. All you have to do to get started is *choose*.

How much simple human misery will result from the thoughtless consumption of "food" that doesn't even merit the title?

But, it's not just a choice you can make *now* and have done with it. That would be a lot easier!! It's a choice you'll have to make again, and again, and again, every meal, every snack, every time you're confronted by the garbage that passes as food all over this grand land of ours. Once you've learned how good it feels to feed your body right, that choice becomes easier and easier, but it's still a choice — a choice between eating what you've become habituated to, and eating real food that will make your body and mind as well as they can be. And should you make a choice one day which you later decide was a mistake, all it takes to get back on track is to make a different choice with your next meal.

I know how hard it is to imagine not eating the food you grew up on. I've been there; not so long ago I ate cold cereal for breakfast every morning and pasta for dinner three or four nights a week. But I chose to try a low carbohydrate diet for just a few weeks, to see how it worked and how I felt — and it changed my life so dramatically for the better, I've been choosing to continue every day, every meal, ever since. I sincerely hope that you can find the extraordinary improvement in your life that a low carbohydrate diet has brought me and mine.

May all your choices be wise and beneficial, and bring you health and happiness.

Appendixes

Appendix One: Basic Low Carb Principles

My dear friend Lilo Schuster, a chiropractor of no small ability, was kind enough to read my manuscript for me, and she made the valuable suggestion that I should pull together all the basic low carb principles and the game rules of the various programs into a single appendix, for quick reference. I thought it was a great idea! So here they are.

1) Be afraid — be VERY afraid! — of added sugar in all forms: sugar, corn syrup, malt syrup, fruit juice concentrate, honey, molasses, brown sugar, maple syrup, Sucanat, turbinado, fructose, dextrose, maltose, or anything else ending in -ose. THERE IS NO SUCH THING AS "GOOD SUGAR". (Many products labeled "No sugar added" have honey, fruit juice, or malt syrup These are sugar!!) Be wary even of the natural sugars in fruits. Remember: If it tastes even a little bit sweet, and it isn't artificially sweetened, it's got some kind of sugar! Also, be aware that some "sugar-free" products are made with "sugar alcohols", such as sorbitol, mannitol, and xylitol. These are carbohydrates.

2) Avoid grains, including bread, crackers, rice, pasta, cereal, pizza crust, biscuits, muffins, etc.
    Avoid dried beans and other starchy legumes, and starchy or sugary vegetables, such as potatoes, corn, peas, and carrots. IF YOU WISH TO BREAK THIS RULE, IT IS BEST TO EAT THE LEAST PROCESSED, HIGHEST FIBER, HIGHEST NUTRIENT CARBOHYDRATES THAT YOU CAN. Coarsely ground whole grain rye bread, steel cut oats, and homemade black bean soup will cause you far less harm than white flour bagels, sugary cold cereal, and (corn-syrup laced)

canned pork and beans.   We won't even talk about rubbish like marshmallow squares and fake canned biscuits.

3) The more strictly you are willing to cut out carbohydrates, the less you will have to concern yourself with portion control or calories.   If you wish to keep some of the less damaging carbs in your diet, you may well have to control portions and/or limit calories as well.   There are some hard choices to be made here, make them with your eyes wide open!

4) Eat plenty of unprocessed, carb-free protein foods.   Eat protein at every meal.   If you choose to eat a carbohydrate food, eat protein with it.   Protein is the cornerstone of your diet; all other foods are secondary.   Eating your protein will increase your metabolism, and keep you feeling full and energetic longer than any other kind of food.

5) Eat only fresh, unprocessed, natural fats. Don't use polyunsaturated oils for cooking — safflower, soy, corn, sunflower, etc.; they break down rapidly and become unhealthy when heated.   Olive, canola, and peanut oils are all right for cooking, as are butter and fresh meat fats (chicken fat, pork fat — don't use purchased lard; it's heavily processed and hydrogenated.)   Do not eat margarine, vegetable shortening, or other "hydrogenated" fats.

6) Get plenty of high fiber, low carb foods, especially low carb vegetables.   Nuts and seeds are excellent foods, high in fiber, protein, minerals, and valuable fats, but they are also very high in calories, so eat them with at least a bit of restraint.   With almost all of these plant foods, raw or only lightly cooked is best.

7) Eat a high protein breakfast every day.   If you're not hungry when you get up, take some protein food to work with you, to eat in the car or at your first break.   And stop eating so heavily at night!   If you eat less at night, you'll wake up with an appetite.   Why lay in a bunch of food just before going to sleep?

8) Drink plenty of water!

9) Learn to listen to your hunger, which on a low carb diet you should be able to trust. I didn't say this elsewhere, but it's important to point out: Americans have been trained to munch mindlessly for hours on carb-y junk food that never fills them up, what I call the "hand-to-mouth routine". There's very little in the way of low carb food that you can do this with, for the very simple reason that low carb foods are *filling*. The big exception, of course, is low carb vegetables, which you may munch on to your heart's content. Other "entertainment" foods are sunflower seeds or pumpkin seeds in the shell — because you have to crack each shell, and each kernel is so small, it's hard to eat too many. (I sneak sunflower seeds into the movies with me!) Pork rinds are no carb — unless you get them barbeque style or with other flavors, READ THE LABEL — and mostly air, so you can munch on these, too. (Personally, I reach my pork rind limit after about four. But some people adore the things.)

If you try to eat most low carb foods — meat, cheese, nuts, eggs — endlessly, you'll make yourself sick to your stomach!

10) Read the labels on *everything* you put into your body. Most people do far more research before buying a car or a VCR than they do on what they put into their own bodies. "You are what you eat" is literally true — all your body has to make itself from is what you put in your mouth. If you give your body junk, you'll be made out of junk, and you'll feel and look like it.

11) Make the best choice possible given any particular circumstance. What do I mean? If you're at work, and the vending machine has cookies, crackers, chips, candy and peanuts, the peanuts are the best choice, even if they're not completely carb-free. When you're genuinely hungry, and faced with foods which are not ideal for the diet, choose the food that will screw you up the least — and don't be afraid to pick off breading, eat only the cheese and toppings off the pizza, etc.

12) Buy a food counter book, one which lists not only carbohydrates and calories, but also fiber, so you can subtract the grams of fiber from the grams of carbohydrate. If you're not absolutely certain that a food is low in carbs, LOOK IT UP!!

13) Take a high-quality, broad-spectrum multiple vitamin and mineral supplement every day. This should be a supplement that requires that you take more than one tablet a day — 6 is not excessive, depending on how big or small a tablet you can swallow.

Game Rules for a Basic Low Carb Diet

1) Eat when you are actually hungry, and then eat enough to satiate your hunger, but not much more.

2) Eat all you wish of fresh meat, poultry, fish, and eggs. (By "fresh meat" I mean meat that has not been processed or flavored in any way.) Eat all you wish of cured meats (ham, bacon, sausages, cold cuts, etc.) only if they have 1 gram of carbohydrate or less per serving. Fresh (uncured) meats are nutritionally superior.
Use moderate quantities of cheese, and cured meats with 1 or 2 grams of carb per serving.

3) Use butter, oils, mayonnaise freely. Sour cream and heavy cream have about 1 gram of carbohydrate per ounce (2 tablespoons) — you can use them freely unless you're not losing. DO NOT USE MARGARINE, VEGETABLE SHORTENING, OR ANY OTHER HYDROGENATED OIL.

4) Eat at least two 1 cup servings a day of low carbohydrate vegetables — these include:

Alfalfa sprouts	Cucumbers	Okra
Artichokes	Dill pickles (NO sweet	Olives
Arugula	pickles)	Parsley
Asparagus	Eggplant	Peppers
Bamboo shoots	Endive	Radishes
Beans (green, snap or wax)	Fennel	Scallions
Bean sprouts	Greens (collard, turnip, beet,	Spinach
Broccoli	mustard)	Summer Squash (zucchini,
Cabbage	Kale	crookneck, etc.)
Cauliflower	Kohlrabi	Turnips
Celery	Lettuce (all kinds)	Watercress
Chicory	Mushrooms	

Onions, garlic, tomatoes, rutabaga, all are borderline vegetables, and may be eaten moderately — for example, half a small onion, or one or two cloves of garlic at a meal. **Avoid** carrots, lima beans, peas, corn, potatoes (white and sweet), winter squash (acorn, butternut, hubbard).

You may substitute a half-cup of berries (strawberries, blueberries, raspberries, blackberries) or a two-inch wedge of melon for a serving of veggies. These are the lowest carb fruits.

5) Nuts and seeds may be eaten moderately — stay below a half a cup a day, less if you're having trouble with losing. Avoid chestnuts — high carb. In a can of mixed nuts, the cashews and peanuts are higher carb than the other nuts — cashews are high enough that they should be considered an occasional treat, not a staple. Sunflower and pumpkin seeds, bought in the shell, are terrific munchy food, because having to shell each one slows you down!

6) You may have sugar free gelatin as desired — and you may top it with real whipped cream, artificially sweetened. (I find that just a little vanilla, no sweetener, is right for me.)

7) Beverages may include diet soda, sparkling water (watch out for colorless sodas, like Clearly Canadian — these are *loaded* with sugar!), sugar-free fruit-flavored drinks such as Crystal Light, tea — black tea, both regular and decaf, green tea or herb tea, coffee, and of course, water. About 40% of dieters find that diet beverages inhibit fat burning. This problem has been blamed both on aspartame (Nutrasweet) and citric acid, a common ingredient of beverages. If you are drinking many artificially sweetened beverages and not losing, this may be your problem. Drop them and see if you start losing.

8) Drink plenty of WATER. A gallon a day is not excessive.

9) DO NOT EAT SWEETS (anything with sugar, honey, fructose, malt syrup, concentrated fruit juice etc., etc., etc.). Products with trace amounts — so little that it shows up on the nutrition label

as 1 gram of carbohydrate or less — are okay in moderation. This would be things like commercial mayonnaise, worcestershire sauce, etc. Be aware that sugar lurks *everywhere!*

10) DO NOT EAT GRAIN PRODUCTS (bread, muffins, biscuits, bagels, pasta, cereal, etc.), CHIPS (fried pork rinds are okay! No carbs), or POTATOES. The exceptions to this rule are a few breads and crackers with so much fiber added that when you subtract it out, the carb count is negligible. Wasa Fiber Rye Crackers, for instance, have 2 g of usable carb per cracker (all the other Wasa crackers have far more, so READ THE LABEL). There are some "lite" breads which have enough added fiber that you can have a slice now and again if you like, as well. How do you know which? READ THE LABEL!

11) GET A FOOD COUNT BOOK, one that gives both carbohydrate counts and fiber counts. If it's not on the above list, and doesn't have a nutrition label, *look it up.* Remember that if you add 5 or 10 grams of carbohydrate from one source, you'll need to cut that number of grams somewhere else. Aim for less than 50 grams of carbohydrate a day, after you subtract out the fiber. Keep close track of your carbohydrates for a few weeks; after that you should be able to "eyeball" it — but if you plateau, you'd best start counting again!

12) Take a high potency, full-spectrum multiple vitamin daily. This should be a more-than-one-tablet-a-day product (you'll probably have to go to a health food store), and should give you a minimum of 1000 mg of calcium and 500 mg of magnesium a day. Minerals should be "chelated". It should also include at least 200 mcg of chromium, preferably in GTF, polynicotinate, or picolinate form. Vanadium is also a beneficial thing to have, if you find a multi that includes it. Another thing to watch for is a B complex that includes "folate", "choline" and "inositol". These are not the only things your multi should include — it should, of course, have Vitamin A, the Bs, C, etc. — but if you look for these things, the rest of what you need should be in there.

Mini-Binge Game Rules

1) For two meals a day, you must have a moderate portion of a protein food with no more than a gram of carb in it. Protein portions at these meals should be 4-6 oz of meat, poultry or fish, or two eggs, or 2-3 oz of meat plus an egg or 2 oz cheese. Along with the protein, you should have 2 cups of very low carb vegetables (listed below). If you can't stand vegetables at breakfast, you may skip veggies then, but you *must* have them with lunch and dinner. At these two low carb meals, you *must not eat* any foods but the protein and vegetables, plus very low carb fats and condiments (sugar-free salad dressing, mayo, sour cream, mustard, etc.)

LOW CARB FOODS —
If it's not on this list, don't eat it at a Low Carb Meal.

- All fresh meat, fish and poultry
- Many cured meats, such as ham, sausage or bacon — some have sugar, so READ THE LABELS
- Many luncheon meats — some have sugar or other fillers, so READ THE LABELS
- Many canned meats and fishes. READ THE LABELS
- Eggs
- Most cheeses — some have more carbs than others, especially the low fat kinds, so READ THE LABELS
- Fats and Oils, including all vegetable oils, butter, animal fats and mayonnaise. Avoid Miracle Whip.
- Some bottled salad dressings — many are LOADED with sugar, especially the low- and no- fat kinds. READ THE LABELS
- Sour cream

LOWEST CARB VEGGIES INCLUDE:

Alfalfa sprouts	Cabbage	Eggplant
Arugula	Cauliflower	Endive
Asparagus	Celery	Fennel
Bamboo shoots	Chicory	Greens (collard,
Beans (green, snap or wax)	Cucumbers	turnip, beet, mustard)
Bean sprouts	Dill pickles (NO sweet pickles)	Kale

Kohlrabi	Parsley	Summer squash (zuc-
Lettuce (all kinds)	Peppers	chini, crookneck, etc.)
Mushrooms	Radishes	Turnips
Okra	Scallions	Watercress
Olives	Spinach	

Onions and tomatoes are borderline — you are allowed up to two tablespoons chopped onion and/or one half a tomato at a low carb meal. Although the Hellers don't say so, I would say garlic falls into this category as well — only 1 clove at a low carb meal.

You may have sugar-free gelatin with REAL whipped cream (whip it yourself with sugar substitute) at a low carb meal.

You may have up to two ounces (4 tablespoons) a day of milk, cream, or half and half in coffee at low carb meals.

READ LABELS on condiments — many are loaded with sugar; ketchup, barbeque sauce, and relish especially. Herbs, vinegar, mustard (except honey mustard), salt, pepper, soy sauce, hot sauce, and some horseradishes are generally "safe". You may have small quantities of lemon and lime juice.

BEVERAGES:
- Diet soda, Crystal Light, other calorie-free beverages
- Sparkling water —be careful to choose those with NO SUGAR OR CORN SYRUP
- Club soda
- Tea
- Coffee

All other foods MUST BE SAVED FOR YOUR REWARD MEAL

2) NO EATING BETWEEN MEALS. Period. Full stop. No breath mints, nada. Calorie-free beverages *only*.

3) One meal a day will be your Reward Meal. The Reward Meal must last for NO MORE THAN ONE HOUR, by the clock.

Less is okay, but if you stop after 40 minutes, you can't have another 20 minutes later on. At the Reward Meal, you may eat any food you like. ANY food. However, you must eat roughly equal portions of protein, salad, low carb cooked veggies, and carbohydrate foods (starches and sweets).

4) Alcohol must only be consumed during the Reward Meal.

5) If, after a few weeks, you are losing very quickly, you may add a low carb snack (half the size of a low carb meal) if desired.

6) If, after a few weeks, you are not losing as well as you'd like, you should eat a large salad FIRST at your Reward Meal.

Game Rules for the Careful Carb Diet

1) You must consume your minimum protein requirement every day! Allowed proteins include meat, fish, poultry, eggs and egg sub-stitutes, tofu, tempeh, sugar-free protein powder, brewer's or nutri-tional yeast. Eat a *minimum* of 14 grams of protein at breakfast. You *must* have protein at every meal, and you may divide your protein up so that you have snacks too, if you like. Leaner proteins are better than fattier proteins — with the exception of fatty fishes, such as salmon, mackerel, herring, and sardines, which are wonderful! Do not exceed your protein requirement by more than 20 grams a day.

2) Eat healthy fats in moderation, but do not use *excessive* quan-tities of added fat, or of very high fat foods, such as nuts and cheeses. A tablespoon or two of mayonnaise or olive oil is okay, a half a cup is not!

3) Eat low carbohydrate vegetables freely; the more the better. Low carb veggies are:

Alfalfa sprouts	Asparagus	Beet greens
Artichokes	Avocado	Bok Choy
Arugula	Green, wax, and snap beans	Broccoli

Brussels sprouts	Escarole	Radishes
Cabbage	Kale	Sauerkraut
Cauliflower	Lettuce, all kinds	Spinach
Celery	Mushrooms	Summer squashes —
Chicory	Okra	zucchini, crookneck
Cucumber	Olives	Turnip greens
Eggplant	Peppers	Water Cress
Endive	Pumpkin	

4) Eat melons, berries, and borderline vegetables in moderation. Borderline vegetables are onions, garlic, rutabaga, beets, turnips, tomatoes. As a guideline, not more than a half a large onion, or one large tomato, or a couple of cloves of garlic at a meal.

5) Eat between 1 and 3 servings of the allowed Low Impact Carbohydrate foods per day. Start with two servings per day, and see how your hunger and your weight react. If you're doing great, you may add one serving per day. If you're not losing, and/or you're still hungry, drop one serving a day. If you still have trouble, you may be so severely carbohydrate intolerant that you'd do better on the Basic Low Carb Diet. Low Impact Carbs *must* be eaten in combination with proteins, *not* by themselves. DO NOT eat *any* other concentrated carbohydrate foods!

Low Impact Carbs

GRAINS AND OTHER STARCHES
- Whole grain barley (cook and use like rice) 1/2-3/4 cup
- Steel cut oats (NOT rolled oats) 1/2 - 3/4 cup
- Protein enriched pasta (Contadina makes a good one) 1/2-3/4 cup
- DeBoles Jerusalem artichoke pasta 1/2 - 3/4 cup
- Whole wheat pasta 1/2 - 3/4 cup
- 100% whole grain rye bread (no sugar, corn syrup, or honey added — available at health food stores) 1 small slice
- Whole wheat Pita (no sugar, corn syrup, or honey added — many grocery stores have this) 1/2 round loaf

- Yam or sweet potato 1 small
- Peas 1/2 - 3/4 cup
- Kidney beans 1/2 - 3/4 cup
- Navy beans 1/2 - 3/4 cup
- Butter beans 1/2 - 3/4 cup
- Chick peas 1/2 - 3/4 cup
- Lentils 1/2 - 3/4 cup
- Black beans 1/2 - 3/4 cup (oh, heck, all the dried beans except limas) DO NOT eat canned baked beans or pork and beans — they're loaded with sugar!!
- Hummus 1/2 cup
- Winter squash (butternut, acorn, hubbard, spaghetti) 1/2 - 3/4 cup
- All Bran, Fiber One, and other spaghetti-shaped bran cereals
- Split pea, lentil, or bean soup 3/4 - 1 cup
- Chili with beans (no sugar, corn syrup or honey added) 3/4 - 1 cup
- Hominy 1/2 cup
- Brown rice 1/2 - 3/4 cup

FRUITS You already know the low carb fruits —

- Berries, cantaloupe, honeydew

Most other fruits may not be very low in carbohydrates, but have a fairly low impact on blood sugar. Exceptions are kiwi, bananas, pine-apple, raisins, grapes, watermelon. Avoid these. Consider all other fruits to be an okay Low Impact Carb choice. DO NOT EXCEED TWO FRUITS A DAY.

OTHER LOW IMPACT CARBS

- Milk (1 cup)
- Tomato soup (1 cup)
- Super premium ice cream (Hagen Daaz, etc) NO CHUNKY VARIETIES
- Sugar- free or plain yogurt (Sugar- free has aspartame)
- Peanut M&Ms
- Snickers
- All-fruit type jam or jelly

It is HIGHLY RECOMMENDED that you do NOT make all of your Low Impact Carb choices from the sweet carbs — i.e., Ice cream, M&Ms, Snickers, and fruit. This is NOT a license to eat these things in an uncontrolled fashion!!

6) Permitted beverages include tea, coffee, unsweetened sparkling waters, both plain and flavored, sugar free soda, sugar-free fruit drinks, herb tea.

7) You may have a glass of dry wine or a light beer with dinner. Read labels on light beers and look for one with 4 g of carb or less per can — some "light" beers have as many as 9 g per can! Be aware that for some people, alcohol will prevent weight loss, and pay attention to your body. If you're not losing, you may need to trade one of your Low Impact Carbs for your drink, or abstain from alcohol altogether.

8) Avoid eating for entertainment! If you've had your breakfast at 7:30, and you're not hungry at noon, wait till you are hungry!

Basic Sugar-Free Protein Shake
- 1/3 cup instant dry skim milk
- 2 heaping tablespoons protein powder, or more if desired. (This must be a protein powder with *no carbohydrates.* I recommend unflavored, or if you like, vanilla — which blends nicely with most other flavors.)
- 1 teaspoon cold pressed safflower oil. (DON'T substitute inexpensive oil from the grocery; the label should read either "cold pressed" or "expeller pressed". Hain brand is good, and has a very mild flavor. Store this in the refrigerator! You can leave out the oil if you add lecithin, flax seeds, or peanut butter.)
- 1/4 teaspoon white stevia extract powder, or more or less to taste. If you prefer, you can use artificial sweeteners.
- 3/4 - 1 cup cold water
- 3-5 ice cubes
- 1/4 teaspoon guar gum (optional, but gives a thicker texture;

available at health food stores)

• Flavoring — 1 heaping T cocoa powder, or a teaspoon of instant coffee crystals, or a half-cup berries, or 1-2 t vanilla extract — whatever you like that is low carb.

• Optional — any or all of the following: 1 T flax seeds, 1 heaping T granular lecithin, 1 t bee pollen, 1/2-1 t nutritional yeast, 1/8-1/4 t spirulina

Put water in blender first, then other ingredients, saving ice cubes. Turn the blender on, and drop in the ice cubes one at a time. Blend until you can't hear the ice cubes racketing around inside the blender. Pour and drink.

You may substitute 1 cup fluid skim milk or no sugar added soy milk for the powdered skim and water. Sometimes I use 1/6 cup powdered skim, a half cup water, and a half cup no sugar added soy milk — lower carb than using all milk.

Use this shake as a quick breakfast or lunch, or drink 2-3 in place of meals, then eat a dinner of lean meat, fish or poultry, and a big low carb salad.

Appendix Two: Low Carbohydrate Vegetarian Meat Substitutes

I went to my local health food store and read the labels on all the vegetarian meat substitutes; here is a list of all the products that were suitable for a low carbohydrate diet. I don't know how many of these are available nationally, but this should give you some ideas. Your local health-food store should have many comparable products, and remember that most health food stores are wonderful about special-ordering things.

Note: As I mentioned, fiber, although technically a form of carbohydrate, is indigestible, and does not raise either blood sugar or insulin levels. Therefore, when reading labels, you may subtract the grams of fiber from the grams of carbohydrate, to find the "Effective Carbohydrate Count". (Eades and Eades) On this list, I have done this for you. All foods on the Great list have 5 or less grams of effective carb per serving. Be sure to pay attention not only to the carb count of vegetarian meat substitutes, but also to their protein content; many do not have as much protein as animal products.

Great

All forms of plain tofu
Natural Touch Vegan Burger
Natural Touch Okara Patty
Yves Veggie Wieners
Light Life Smart Dogs
Light Life Tofu Pups
White Wave Sea Veggie Tempeh
Yves Canadian Veggie Bacon
Yves Veggie Pepperoni
Yves Veggie Deli Slices
Light Life Foney Baloney
Light Life Fakin' Bacon
Garden Dog
Worthington Prosage Links
Worthington Stripples
White Wave Vegetarian Philly Steak

White Wave Fajita Strips
White Wave Baked Tofu Snack'n Savory Style
White Wave Baked Tofu Italian Style
White Wave Baked Tofu Thai Style
White Wave Baked Tofu Mexican Style
White Wave Baked Tofu Oriental Style
White Wave Hard Tofu
White Wave Tempeh
White Wave Seitan
White Wave Prime Burger
Tree of Life Savory Baked Tofu
Tree of Life Smoked Tofu
Tree of Life Smoked Tofu, Hot & Spicy
Tofu Rella Monterey Style
Tofu Rella Mozzarella Style
Soya Kaas Mozzarella Style
Soya Kaas Cheddar Style
Soy Mage Cheddar Alternative
Lite and Lean Veggy Singles American Alternative
Lite and Lean Veggy Singles Swiss Style

A Little High, But Okay Occasionally

Amy's Chicago Veggie Burger
White Wave Wild Rice Tempeh
Light Life Gimme Lean Beef Flavor
Light Life Gimme Lean Sausage Flavor

Available at Regular Grocery Stores

Green Giant Harvest Burgers
Garden Burgers
Plain Tofu, various brands

Appendix III: Cookbooks and Other Resources

The Low-Carb Cookbook, by Fran McCullough, 1997, Hyperion Press

For my money, the best low carb cookbook on the market today. Highly recommended.

Dr. Atkins' Quick & Easy New Diet Cookbook, by Robert C. Atkins, M.D., & Veronica Atkins, 1997, Fireside Books

I really liked the Hazelnut Torte recipe; I made two and filled them with low carb mocha custard. Who's dieting? These recipes are indeed quicker and easier than the rather complicated recipes in Dr. Atkins' previous cookbook.

Dr. Atkins' New Diet Cookbook, by Robert C. Atkins, M.D. & Fran Gare, 1995, M. Evans & Co.

Useful, but many of these recipes are quite complicated. The Tandoori Chicken is one of the most wonderful recipes I've ever tried, low carb or otherwise. If you like spicy, exotic food, it's a must. On the other hand, even the dog wouldn't eat the Gnocchi! And the bread recipes taste like baked scrambled eggs.

Everyday Low Carb Cookery, by Alex Haas, available from the author

Alex Haas
PO Box 7802
Talleyville, DE 19803-7802
USA
or through the Internet:
http://members.aol.com/alexhaas/index.htm

Many of the other low carb diet books on the market include recipes: *Protein Power, Dr. Atkins' New Diet Revolution,* and *Healthy for Life* all do. All of these books are available in paperback, and are most likely available through your library. If you check out the recipes in *Healthy for Life*, be aware that only the "Risk Reducing" recipes are low carb; the "Essential Balance" recipes are not.

Having listed these cookbooks, let me say that I get the vast majority of my recipes from regular cookbooks, and it's a rare cookbook in which I can't find a recipe that will work for a low carb diet. Even most vegetarian cookbooks have recipes that will work for us. Some recipes need minor modification, like leaving out a tablespoon of flour, or not serving them over rice. I prefer cookbooks written before the mid-80s, when everyone decided that pasta was God. Try checking out the cookbooks at used book stores. Old diet cookbooks often are useful.

Internet Resources

If you are online, you have access to reams and reams of great low carb information!! If you do a web search under "low carbohydrate diet", you'll find enough information to keep you busy for months. There are articles, support groups, discussion lists, recipes, etc., etc., etc. There are also low fat advocates explaining to you why low carb doesn't work; often these are well-nigh ludicrous. (My favorite of these is a dietician named Joanne Larson, who when a man asked her about his wife being on Protein Power, said it was a bad idea because, after all, she would gain back the weight when she went back to a low fat diet. As if one had to! Larson also objected to Atkins as a "600 calorie a day starvation diet", which is clearly ridiculous.)

If you don't have an Internet account, or even a computer, almost all public libraries have public computer terminals where you can access the Internet. If you don't know how to use it, ask a librarian to help you. (Can you tell that I'm a librarian's daughter?)

Here's a list of URLs (web addresses) to get you started:

The World's Biggest Fad Diet (A terrific article debunking low fat diets)   **http://www.syndicomm.com/lowfat.html**

Archives of the Low Carb Technical Discussion List (I subscribe to this list, and while it can be over my head, it's very interesting. A good place to send your doctor or other health professional for more information.) **http://maelstrom.stjohns.edu/archives/lowcarb.html**

Low Carbohydrate Diets Information Center (Check this one out! It will take you to a huge online low carb recipe archive, and also let you subscribe to the Low Carbohydrate Diets support list. If you are online, I strongly recommend you join the support group!! Very helpful. Also has a low carb FAQ — frequently asked questions list.) **http://people.delphi.com/elizjack/index.html**

Paul on Fat (One man's low carb diet story. Good stuff on breaking plateaus, and a list of links.) **http://www.split.com/fat/**

The Atkins' Diet (Dr. Atkins' Official Homepage. Lots of good medical journal quotes to show your doctor!) **http://www.atkinsdiet.com/diet101.html**

A Major Wellness Discovery: Above and Beyond Phen-Fen (A medical clinic's story of how they discovered that low carb was better for their patients than low fat/high carb.) **http://kindcare.com/hyperins.htm**

The Lowcarb Retreat (GREAT list of low carb links!!) **http://207.222.219.1541**

Adiposity 101 (Terrific, if long, article about obesity in general, and low carb diets in specific. Many other low carb sites link to Adiposity 101, with good reason.) **http://www.rdrop.com/users/caf/adipos.html**

All of these addresses were active as of this writing, but please keep in mind that web sites come and go, and that people change web addresses like they change phone numbers.

I have no connection with or interest in any of these sites, I just have found them interesting or useful myself.

Low Carb Food By Mail

D'lites Of Shadowood
9975 Glades Rd.
Boca Raton FL 33434
1-888-937-5262
http://www.lowcarb.com

Sells low carb cheesecake mix, bread and muffin mixes, fla-vored syrups, etc. by mail order. Sells many Atkins products. Also has a walk-in store, where you lucky locals can buy sugar-free cheese-cake, candy, and bread ready-made.

Bibliography

Books: Starred titles are highly recommended.

Adams, Ruth, & Murray, Frank, *Megavitamin Therapy*, 1980, Larchmont Books

*Atkins, Robert C., M.D., *Dr. Atkins' Health Revolution*, 1989, Bantam Books

*Atkins, Robert C., M.D., *Dr. Atkins' New Diet Revolution*, 1992, M. Evans & Co

*Audette, Ray, *Neanderthin*, 1997, Paleolithic Press

*Davis, Adelle, *Let's Get Well*, 1965, Harcourt, Brace, & World

*Dufty, William, *Sugar Blues*, 1975, Chilton Book Company

Eades, Michael R., M.D., *Thin So Fast*, 1989, Warner Books

*Eades, Michael R., M.D. & Mary Dan, M.D., *Protein Power*, 1996, Bantam

*Fredericks, Carlton, Ph.D., *New Low Blood Sugar and You*, 1985, Perigee Books

*Gittleman, Ann Louise, M.S., C.N.S., *Get the Sugar Out*, 1996, Crown Trade Paperbacks

Heller, Richard, M.S., Ph.D. & Rachael, M.A., M.Ph., Ph.D., *Carbohydrate Addicted Kids*, 1997, Harper Collins

*Heller, Richard & Rachael, *The Carbohydrate Addict's Diet*, 1991, The Penguin Group

*Heller, Richard & Rachael, *Healthy for Life*, 1995, The Penguin Group

Langer, Stephen E., M.D., & Scheer, James, *Solved: The Riddle of Illness*, 1984, Keats Publishing

MacKarness, Richard, M.D., *Eat Fat and Grow Slim*, 1958, Doubleday

Podell, Richard N., M.D., F.A.C.P., and Proctor, William, *The G-Index Diet*, 1993, Warner Books

Taller, Herman, M.D., *Calories Don't Count*, 1961, Simon and Schuster

Ulene, Dr. Art, *The Nutribase Complete Book of Food Counts*, 1996, Avery Publishing Group

Medical Journal Articles

(I want to be honest here, and admit that in most cases I read the abstracts of these articles, rather than the full text. Since the abstracts do include the results and conclusions, as well as the methods, of any study, one can learn a lot this way!)

Axen, K.V., Li, X., Fung, K., & Sclafani, A., "The VMH-dietary obese rat: a new model of NIDDM". Rats given a high fat, high sucrose diet showed fasting hyperinsulinism and hypertriglyceridemia within 3 weeks. Fasting hyperglycemia observed in the majority in 7 consecutive experiments. Impaired glucose tolerance was shown despite high prevailing insulin levels. Loss of insulin secretory response to glucose by week 5. Islet cells failed to suppress insulin release normally.

Beck, S.A., & Tisdale, M.J., "Effect of insulin on weight loss and tumour growth in a cachexia model". Pharmaceutical Sciences Institute, Aston University, Birmingham, UK. *Br. J. Cancer*, 1989 May, 59:5, 677-81 Showed that a ketogenic diet was superior to insulin administration for preventing cachexia (wasting) in cancer, and that the ketogenic diet had the added benefit of reducing cancer growth.

Caprio, S., Bronson, M., Sherwin, R.S., Rife, F., & Tamborlane, W.V., "Co-existence of severe insulin resistance and hyperinsulinemia in pre-adolescent obese children". Dept. Pediatrics, Yale University Medical School *Diabetologia*, 1996, Dec 39:12, 1489-97.

Chauhan, Foote, Petch, & Schofield, "Hyperinsulinemia, coronary artery disease, and syndrome X". *Journal of the American College of Cardiology.* Insulin responses to oral glucose compared in 17 patients with coronary artery disease, 17 with chest pain, positive exercise test finding, normal coronary arteries, and impaired coronary flow reserve (syndrome X), and 17 healthy volunteers. Subjects were matched for age, gender, and weight. Higher insulin levels were found in the CAD and X groups. No significant difference was found between the two groups.

Chung, Hua, Hsin, Hsueh, Kuan, Pin, & Tsa, Fujian Provincial Research Institute for Cardiovascular Disease, Fuzhov, *Chih,* 1993, Oct.; 21(5): 266-8, 314. Impaired glucose tolerance, hyperinsulinemia, and insulin resistance shown in hypertensive subjects. Also showed a relationship to coronary artery disease.

Feskens, E.J., Loeber, J.C., & Kronhout, D., "Diet and physical activity as determinants of hyperinsulinemia: the Zutphen elderly study". *American Journal of Epidemiology.* Insulin levels were shown to inversely associate with fiber and polyunsaturated fatty acid intake.

Franceschi, S., Favero, A., Decorli, A., Negri, E., La Vecchia, C., Ferraroni, M., Russo, A., Salvini, S., Amadori, D., Conti, E., et al. "Intake of macronutrients and risk of breast cancer". *Lancet,* 1996 May, 347:9012, 1351-6. A diet high in fat, especially monounsaturated fat, was shown to correlate with a reduced risk of breast cancer. A diet high in carbohydrates, especially starches, was shown to correlate with an increased risk of breast cancer.

Garg, A., Bantle, J.P., Henry, R.R., Coulston, A.M., Griver, K.A., & Roatz, S.K., "Effects of varying carbohydrate content of diet in patients w/non-insulin-dependent diabetis mellitus". *Journal of the American Medical Association,* May 11, 271(8):1421-8. High carbohydrate diet was shown to increase fasting plasma triglycerides and VLDL by 24% and 23% respectively as contrasted with a diet high in monounsaturated fatty acids, and was also shown to increase insulin levels by 10%. In NIDDM patients, high carbohydrate diets compared with high MUFA diets caused persistent deterioration of glycemic control and accentuation of hyperinsulinemia, increased triglycerides, and VLDL.

Garg, A., & Grundy, S., "High carbohydrate, low fat diet?" *Hosp. Proct. Off. Ed.*, 1992, Feb; 27 Suppl. 1:11-14, discussion on 14-16. Researchers found that triglyceride levels rise in response to increased carbohydrate intake in normal children. Moreover, carbohydrate raises blood glucose levels and insulin requirements.

Jeppesen, J., Schaaf, P., Jones, C., Zhou, M.Y., Chen, Y.D., & Reaven, G.M., "Effects of low-fat, high-carbohydrate diets on risk factors for ischemic heart disease in postmenopausal women". Dept. of Medicine, Stanford University School of Medicine *American Journal of Clinical Nutrition*. Concluded that recommending a low-fat, high carbohydrate diet for prevention of heart disease in post-menopausal women was questionable, owing to deleterious effects on blood lipid levels.

Katan, Martijn B., "Effect of low-fat diets on plasma high-density lipoprotein concentrations." Dept. Human Nutrition, Wageningen Agricultural University, Wageningen, Netherlands. *The American Journal of Clinical Nutrition,* 1998, March, 67:3. Found that low-fat, high-carbohydrate diets lead to lower HDL levels, and thus higher theoretical risk of heart disease. Weight loss on low-fat diets was found to be insufficient to offset this risk.

Martinez, F.J., Rizza, R.A., & Romero, J.C.,"High-fructose feeding elicits insulin resistance, hyperinsulinism, and hypertension in normal mongrel dogs". *Hypertension,* 1994 April 23(4): 456-63. Researchers concluded that chronic high-fructose feeding elicits hypertriglyceridemia, insulin resistance, hyperinsulinemia, hypertension, and transient sodium retention in dogs.

Nebeling, L.C., Lerner, E., "Effects of a ketogenic diet on tumor metabolism and nutritional status in pediatric ocology patients: two case reports". *Journal of the American College of Nutrition,* 1995, April, 14:2, 202-8. Two pediatric cancer patients were given a ketogenic diet high in medium-chain triglycerides. A 21.8% decrease in glucose uptake by the tumor was shown in both patients. One patient, showing a marked improvement in mood and learning on the ketogenic diet, remained on the diet for 12 months, during which time the cancer did not progress.

Nebeling, L.C., & Lerner, E.," Implementing a ketogenic diet based on medium-chain triglyceride oil in pediatric patients with cancer". *Journal of the American Dietetic Association,* 1995, June 95:6, 693-7. A ketogenic diet high in medium-chain triglycerides was fed to pediatric cancer patients to maintain weight while lowering glucose available for tumor metabolism.

Nobels, F., van Gaal, L., & de Leeuw, I., "Weight reduction with a high protein, low carbohydrate, calorie-restricted diet: effects on blood pressure, glucose, and insulin levels". *Netherlands Journal of Medicine,* 1989, Dec, 35:5-6, 295-302. Showed that high blood pressure was tied to blood glucose levels, and that a high protein, low carbohydrate weight loss diet successfully lowers blood pressure and helps to improve glucose metabolism.

Reaven, G.M., "Abnormalities of carbohydrate and lipoprotein metabolism in patients with hypertension; relationship to obesity". Stanford University Medical School *Annals of Epidemiology,* 1991, May 1:4, 304-11.

Simonson, D.C., "Hyperinsulinemia and its sequelae". Department of Internal Medicine, Joslin Diabetes Center, New England Deaconess Hospital, Boston, MA *Horm. Metab. Res. Suppl.,* 1990, 11 17-25.

Sowers, J.R., Standley, P. R., Ram J. L., Zemel, M.B., & Resnick, L.M., "Insulin resistance, carbohydrate metabolism, and hypertension". Div. Endicrinology, Wayne State University, MI *American Journal of Hypertension,* 1991, July, 4:7 Pt. 2, 4665-4725.

Tisdale, M.J., & Brennan, R.A., "A comparison of long-chain triglycerides and medium-chain triglycerides on weight loss and tumours in a cachexia model". Pharmaceutical Sciences Institute, Aston University, Birmingham, UK *British Journal of Cancer,* 1988, November, 58:5, 580-3. In animal studies, a ketogenic diet high in medium chain triglycerides reduced wasting and caused a "marked reduction in tumour size".

Williams, P.T., Krauss, R.M., Stefanick M.L., Vranizan K.M., & Wood P.D., "Effects of low-fat diet, calorie restriction and running on lipoprotein subfraction concentrations in moderately overweight men". Researchers studied the effect of exercise (primarily running), calorie restriction and low fat/high carbohydrate diet on changes in lipoprotein subfractions in moderately overweight men. After 1 year, complete data were obtained from both those simply dieting, and those combining dieting with running. Both groups reduced weight. No significant changes were found in lipoprotein mass and HDL in dieters who did not run.

Yamasaki, R., Miyoshi, T., Imaki, M., & Nakamura, T., "Evaluation of the effects of various factors on the serum triglyceride level in young adults". *Tokushima Journal of Experimental Medicine*, 1994, June; 41 (1-2):17-30. The researchers carried out surveys and laboratory studies on relationships of nutritional intake, physical activity, cigarette smoking, and alcohol consumption of young adults with serum triglyceride levels. Nutritional survey indicated significant correlation between the serum triglyceride levels and carbohydrate intake. Exercise caused a slight but not significant decrease.

————"Non-invasive management of coronary artery disease: report of a meeting at the University of Texas Medical School at Houston". *The Lancet,* Sept. 16, 1995, v346 n8977, p75(4). Study concerned one 68-year-old male with high cholesterol and a family history of heart disease. Patient was prescribed a low fat, high carbohydrate diet and medication. At the end of 1 year, testing was done, and cholesterol had increased. Medication was adjusted, and dietary fat was cut back to 10% of calories. At next testing, mild improvement was noted.

Popular Press Articles

Brody, J.E. "A new study sees no link between a low-fat diet and breast cancer. Is this the final word? Not likely." *New York Times,* February 14, 1996.

Challem, Jack. "Paleolithic Nutrition: Your Future Is in Your Dietary Past". *Nutrition Science News,* April 1997.

The Detroit News, February 8, 1996. "Link between fatty diet, breast cancer disputed".

The Herald-Times, Bloomington IN. "Study shows danger of fat in margarine". November 20, 1997.

La Voie, Angela. "Low-fat diets can have undesired effects". *Medical Tribune News Service,* March 21, 1997.

Meyer, Tara. "Diabetes reaches record levels in the U.S." *Associated Press,* May 1, 1998.

News from the Rockefeller University. "Low Fat, High Sugar Diets Prompt Production of Saturated Fats". January 23, 1998.

Richards, Mike. "'First Farmers' with no taste for grain". *British Archaeology,* March 1996, no.12. Bone analysis suggests Neolithic people preferred meat.

Ritter, Malcolm. "People are talking — Health: Diabetes becomes more prevalent as Americans age, don't exercise". *The Detroit News,* November 3, 1995.

Reuters. " Study links low cholesterol to violent death". March 14, 1998.

USA Today. "Low-fat diet may not affect women's breast cancer risk". April 27, 1998.